JOURNALISM IN THE NEW MILLENNIUM

JOURNALISM IN THE NEW MILLENNIUM

Suraj Singh

CENTRUM PRESS
NEW DELHI-110002 (INDIA)

CENTRUM PRESS
H.O.: 4360/4, Ansari Road, Daryaganj,
New Delhi-110002 (India)
Tel: 23278000, 23261597, 23255577, 23286875
B.O.: No. 1015, Ist Main Road, BSK IIIrd Stage,
IIIrd Phase, IIIrd Block, Bangalore-560085 (INDIA)
Tel: 080-41723429
Email: centrumpress@gmail.com
Visit us at: www.centrumpress.com

Journalism in the New Millennium

First Edition, 2010

ISBN 978-93-80836-18-8

PRINTED IN INDIA

Printed at Mehra Offset Press, Delhi

Contents

Preface

Attempts at a free press are occurring in virtually every country, with varying degrees of success and with varying amounts of freedom actually accorded to the media. Each country has, at some time, produced or attempted to produce, a document usually a press law designed to balance the rights and freedoms of the press with the rights of the government to govern and the rights of the citizenry to be protected from press excesses.

For the most part, those who have studied the delicate balance between these often-conflicting rights, these press laws have failed to provide the media with the freedoms so cherished, and so stridently defended. In addition, professional journalists themselves are often unable to move away from the practices ingrained in them under the old regimes where being subservient was a virtue.

Journalists who have spent their lives reading newspapers written under the Communist system of press restraints, who themselves have spent years writing in the same manner, must now remake themselves to provide direct, objective, timely, truthful news to an audience unaccustomed to such news. Gatherers and reporters of information often take back seats to columnists, essayists, and editorialists who are considered to be the "real" journalists, a view at odds with the understanding of the journalist in democratic countries. It becomes the unskilled leading the unknowing a situation that can lead to disaster.

Yet, despite everything, the desire for freedom of expression, whether as freedom of speech or as freedom of the press, burns within the hearts of both the press themselves and their audiences their fellow citizens. That desire, that longing, needs to be fulfilled. There can be no mistake, freedom of expression in its most comprehensive form is critical to the democratization of countries.

Without the right of the people and the media to speak, discuss, and report freely without fear of government censorship or pressures, democracy cannot exist and a free country cannot endure. The changes that occur first must begin within each country. Finally, the idea of a new, independent, free media must be exported to those countries in the old, and often not-so-happy alliances of the recent past.

Chapter 1

Femininity and Television News

Feminism seems to have two options to evaluate recent developments in journalism. On the one hand one might contentedly conclude that journalism is no longer a male preserve, but on the other one might also claim more cynically that the increasing access of women to the profession is part and parcel of the intimization that seems to permeate most news. I shall elaborate these two positions in the following paragraphs and conclude that both are caught in the dead end of the 'sameness-difference' dilemma of feminist theory, (too) simply put as 'should women become the same as men and thus equal, or can women be different from men but still be equal?' I then go on to argue that the 'sameness-difference' dilemma is an inextricable product of the bourgeois concept of the public sphere which dominates contemporary evaluations of journalism in western democracies.

The concept can be of no avail to a feminist perspective on journalism since it is philosophically and historically rooted in universalist concepts of gendered human nature and society, resulting in the restraints of a male public sphere and a female private sphere. In the final part of the chapter I suggest a more particularist feminist approach, which uses as a starting-point the way gendered audiences make sense of the news.

CONQUERING A MALE DOMAIN

Feminist approaches to the news have been relatively straight-forward. Criticism centres not so much on how women are presented as on how they are not present at all.

According to a global research review by Gallagher, in not one country does the number of women appearing in news coverage exceed 20 per cent. The few times women are included, they mainly appear in human interest stories, in a domestic setting or to give emotional eye-witness accounts. A more recent study carried out in the EC countries by Thoveron observes some progress in that women are being shown more often in more significant roles, but concludes that among the journalists appearing on the screen there still is a severe under-representation of women. The role of newsreader is most common for women journalists: 28 per cent of the newsreaders were found to be women.

Women's exclusion from the news is often conceived as a result of their marginal participation in the public sphere in general. In such arguments the concept of the public sphere contains all non-private and non-domestic activities people might engage in, and is not limited to spaces and occasions in which people enact their political role as citizens. Thoveron, for instance, assumes that the people running TV channels 'cannot be held responsible for women's low profile in the political, industrial and economic world. Their programmes are a mere reflection of the actual situation.'

Others, however, argue that the male dominance among reporters results in news which reflects a male view of reality, leaving little room for feminist and women's achievements, or consigning topics and approaches that traditionally belong to the realm of women to special niches in the news, like human interest and lifestyle time slots. No matter how one explains the exclusion of women from the news, there seems to be consensus about the fact that their professional and symbolic under-representation reconstructs the present division between a public male world and a private female world.

The lack of coverage of women and the placement of what coverage there is has a clear potential to affect the news audience. Beyond the obvious effect that the audience will remain uninformed about women and women's issues, the implicit symbolic messages contained in the coverage largely serve to reinforce cultural stereotypes about the insignificance of women and their 'proper place'.

Therefore feminists have argued for an increased number of female journalists as well as an increase in news items featuring women. One of the rationales behind such recommendations is the idea that 'as more women in television news succeed in positions of responsibility and high visibility, the way is paved for those who seek acceptance in traditionally male domains'. Others add that an increase in the number of women journalists would result in more balanced and less sex-stereotypical news.

Dutch television news presents an interesting test case for such beliefs. In 1965 the first woman newsreader of the 'Journaal', as the Dutch news bulletin is familiarly known, made her appearance. In the 1970s about one-third of the presentation teams consisted of women, but it wasn't until recently that anchor-women acquired a central role in the news. At the moment news bulletins are broadcast five times an evening and presented by seven alternating newsreaders. Five of them are female.

At face value this dominance of anchor-women in Dutch television news can be said to mark an uncommon and positive development. Those newsreaders provide female audiences with positive sociological role models, quite rare in other programme types: Combining the tools of a journalist with the power of the television medium the on-air newswoman knows herself to be a role model for others. Positive role models for women remain remarkably rare in television, a medium that generally creates and reinforces the classification of the female sex as secondary.

There is an equally important symbolic value to the appearance of women newsreaders. Paradoxically, the perceived objectivity of the news and its social status depend for a great deal on the perception of a presenter's personal reliability, credibility and authority. The suggestion that the presenters speak the 'objective discourse of truth' is supported by their discursive central location, materialized in their position behind the central desk in the news studio. The personality thus constructed embodies the viewers' need for a person who knows everything and who will explain the confusing and often unsafe world to them.

'This all-seeing, all-knowing, god-like person is, of course, male and white. White women, and men and women of another race ...are left to the margins of the morning and the nightly news'. In the Netherlands, however, for the greater part our guides in experiencing the threatening modern world are women.

One is tempted to conclude that the appearance of female newsreaders in the Dutch Journaal indicates that power, authority and expertise are no longer features exclusively reserved for men; it seems to indicate that 'woman' no longer automatically signifies sexuality, submissiveness, domesticity and other usual forms of televisual femininity. The high number of anchor-women in Dutch television news might tell audiences that the public sphere, of which the news is a constituent part, is no longer a male preserve, but an appropriate place for women to reside too.

The Dutch case is not that simple, however. In the context of recent changes in Dutch television news, the dominance of women newsreaders presents another scenario. The increased number of female newsreaders runs parallel with an 'intimization' of the Journaal, among other things recognizable in its modes of address. I will describe those changes below and argue that the dominance of women newsreaders can also be seen as yet another articulation of traditional femininity.

THE INTIMIZATION OF TELEVISION NEWS

Dutch television news has undergone numerous changes since it was first broadcast in 1956. The first bulletin looked more or less like the newsreels shown in movie theatres. It went on air only three times a week at 8 p.m.

Due to technical limitations and personal preferences the focus was on human interest stories and ritual functions of news, labelled as 'story journalism' by Schudson. Newsreaders appeared infrequently in that period, usually only by necessity when images to visualize events were not available. They were thought to hamper the objective character of the news.

If a newsreader were seen while giving the news, any change in his visual manner, a smile or a lift of an eyebrow might, however little this was intended, be interpreted as comment. The sacred dividing line between fact and comment would be blurred.

Although newsreaders appeared ever more frequently on the screen, the uninvolved and detached mode of reading the news remained common practice until the mid-1970s. Personal traits and peculiarities were de-emphasized. As one TV critic ironically put it:

In the first place a newsreader, be it a woman or a man, must not be too attractive, and-although this is less relevant-not too bad looking either. Of course it is strictly prohibited to read bad news in any other way than good news. Objectivity would be endangered by it.

In the mid-1970s the appointment of a new executive producer led to a shift from story journalism to 'information' journalism. Under the new regime the Journaal would be no longer guided by the availability of interesting moving pictures: 'We will not do news that is fun to watch any more', the new producer said as he took the job. Instead the focus would be on politically and socially important issues.

Although the introduction of the autocue system made a more intimate mode of address possible, enabling the semblance of face-to-face conversation between newsreader and audience, the newsreader had to remain as detached, uninvolved and blank as possible, because the aura of objectivity had to be maintained. The Journaal acquired a reputation of being serious and objective but a little dull and uninteresting to watch.

In 1985 a new editor-in-chief was appointed, a former correspondent for the Journaal in Great Britain, Peter Brusse. He wanted to change the news into a popular television programme with natural transitions; into 'more than a dull listing of events'. The news should offer audiences opportunities to identify with events and personalities.

Human interest stories therefore had to be a major ingredient of the news and newsreaders were urged to transform their serious mode of address into a more personal and intimate style:

Presenters should be more than people who merely read the news. They must inspire confidence. You must be able to trust them like you trust the neighbour next door, who is familiar to you and who keeps an eye on things while you are away. An authoritative person like Walter Cronkite, who explains which assaults are important and why.

Brusse became subject to heavy criticism from his own staff and from fellow journalists, especially from the print media. His attempt 'to make news entertaining by a light and populist appeal' was looked upon with contempt. His two-year regime was later characterized as a 'reckless period of experiments and failures'. He left the Journaal quite soon, disappointed with the possibilities of changing it. However, Brusse's efforts paved the way for his successor who managed to work out many of Brusse's ideas. Under his management the Journaal acquired its present style and format.

Three teams of reporters and presenters are responsible for five daily news bulletins. The 8 o'clock news is still the most important news bulletin in terms of allotted time, energy and audience attention. It is aimed at a family audience and is supposed to have a smooth and informal mode of address. In line with its 'family appeal' this bulletin also features sport news. The bulletin is presented by a woman and a man, alternating each week. They are both experienced newsreaders who were assigned to this bulletin because of their popularity: 'Reliable, cosy and familiar'.

The other bulletins too have their own formula and are supposed to be distinctive news *programmes* appealing to different target groups. As an internal policy paper of the Journaal states: 'Attempts to produce a more inviting and personal Journaal have to motivate audiences to watch the news, and enlarge their pleasure in watching it'. As Brusse had already argued, news-readers are now seen to be crucial in constructing a particular image for each news bulletin, and in establishing an intimate and stable relationship with the target audience. The audience must be able to identify with and relate to the anchor-person of his or her favourite news bulletin. 'We looked for journalists that can present a programme. As far as their appearance is concerned... they must look like ordinary people. They are not supposed just to read the news but to tell it from their own personal involvement'.

The intimization of Dutch television news is an example of how some values from the private sphere are transferred to the public sphere of the news. This is expressed partly by an increased attention to human interest subjects, but more telling is the way the relation between the audience and newsreader is constructed-through carefully picked personalities and intimate modes of address-as a matter of personal friendship or close family ties.

INTIMIZATION AND THE WOMAN NEWSREADER

This background sheds another light on the high presence of women newsreaders in the Dutch news. In theory, the intimization of TV news could have been achieved with an all-male anchor team. However, that would deny the gendered nature of private sphere values. It comes as no surprise then that the intimization of Dutch TV news coincides with a remarkably high number of women newsreaders. At this point a disclaimer is necessary. The women newsreaders themselves will firmly deny that the supposedly superior capacities of women to sustain intimate relationships (in this case with the audience) are the main reason for appointing them. The women newsreaders and their superiors will rightfully refer to professional standards providing criteria for recruitment policies.

Without denying their professional performance, however, women can hardly be expected to come to the public sphere playing merely a professional role, in this case as a newsreader. Again that would deny the gendered nature of subjects, the gendered nature of cultural expectations and perceptions. 'Woman' inevitably signifies a whole cultural set of feminine values. Which of these come especially to the fore varies and depends on the particular context, as comparison between the women newsreaders of BBC news and Dutch TV news shows?

Writing about BBC news, Holland wonders:

Is there some quality expected of newsreaders, which, despite the apparent contradictions, is turning this into a suitable role for women to play?... Is this role of mediation and management one that can be reconciled with the forms of femininity that have been constructed out of power relations between women and men?

She argues that newsreading might become a 'woman's job' because the newsreader's task has become that of a performer.

For women 'the invitation to speak with the voice of authority may be nothing more but an invitation, yet again, to be a decorative performer'. Holland draws her evidence from public discourse about well-known British anchor-women, in which their appearances and 'feminine' styles (often criticized as not 'feminine' at all) are continuously foregrounded. Holland concludes that the presence of women newsreaders in the BBC news expresses a common and well-known form of televisual femininity: woman as a pleasurable object for the voyeuristic (male) gaze: 'If we are not watchful we will find that once more, with the infinite flexibility of effortless power, women will have been put in their place again'.

In abstract terms her argument can be applied to Dutch television news as well. In the Dutch case too the high visibility of women marks another expression of traditional femininity, but there is a remarkable difference as to what element of femininity is exploited. As we have said, the number of women newsreaders increased when editorial policy led the Journaal to cover more 'human' aspects of the news. The former executive producer Brusse, whose arrival accelerated this trend, explicitly called this the 'women's touch' in the news. 'Men's news is to write on the front page that a fire happened, women's news is to write inside why the guy lit a fire for the third time'. During his brief period as editor, Brusse continually questioned the rationalistic underpinnings of the Journaal and emphasized the entertainment value and emotional qualities of news:

One tear on TV tells you so much more than an ever so well described tear in the newspaper. Television made us communicate and participate in world affairs with tears. A Journaal without a tear is not a real Journaal and that has to be learned.

In Brusse's ideal Journaal, newsreaders are assumed to provide the audience with a stable point of identification with the news as *a programme* among the flow of competing TV programmes. The newsreaders are assumed to establish an intimate and personal relationship with the audience of their particular bulletin. 'Audiences must be able to identify with the people who tell them the news. They must derive a sense of stability from them'. Assigning the same team of anchors to each news bulletin guarantees that audiences know who to expect and who to relate to. Consider-as a short sidestep-the common practice in most other European countries, where usually 'different individuals will read on different days so that the public does not come to associate the news with a single source'.

Thus the common conception of the anchor as the authoritative, wise and all-knowing (male) neighbour who guides you through a complex and confusing world does not seem very appropriate for the Dutch TV news. A comparison with the caring and never failing mother who tucks you in every night after a day of emotional arousal, seems more to the point. This characterization is underlined by the deliberately plain and ordinary appearances of the anchor-women. Once, one of the more popular women newsreaders was asked in a newspaper editorial:

Why do you dress in such a dull and tasteless way? Colours that don't match, blouses and jackets that often look ludicrous on you.... Throw all the old stuff away. *Although you might want to look like a 'common' woman,* common can mean charming, feminine and stylish as well.

PRIVATE SPHERE VALUES IN A PUBLIC SPHERE CONTEXT

Feminists may express different views on the developments in Dutch television news. Some feminists might value the dominance of women newsreaders in Dutch television news as evidence of women conquering the once exclusively male public domain. Other feminists will argue that women again are chained to their 'feminine' roles, since a revision of editorial policy and styles of presentation has transformed the formerly 'masculine' role of the newsreader into one that is more in line with traditional femininity.

A third group of feminists might add that the 'feminine' contributions of women newsreaders are necessary and praise-worthy adaptations of formerly detached, rationalistic and alienating news bulletins. This last argument is a customary legitimation in struggles for women's access to journalism in general. Increased access would presumably result in a reconsideration of more background information. The professional status of 'hard' and 'soft' news, less factual and All three perspectives derive their main ingredients-and take their main unresolved questions at the same time-from liberal feminist discourse.

Liberal feminism ascribes the differences between women and men to the different roles they play in society. Women's roles are primarily acted out in the private sphere of family life, men's roles in the public sphere of paid work and politics. The ultimate aim of liberal feminism is the integration of women in the public sphere. However, as women exchange their private for their public roles, they too might take on-be it gradually-the 'male' characteristics appropriate to that sphere. Although women and men would then be equal, the 'softer sides' of humanity would be lost in the process, an outcome that no liberal feminist desires. Thus, women should go public without forsaking their 'femininity'. What is argued for then is a recognition of private values as appropriate for the public sphere.

There are several problems to this argument. On a theoretical level it assumes and reconstructs the public-private division. As a consequence it reproduces traditional gender identities. I will elaborate this point later. More pragmatically, it seems a little naïve to assume that a simple transference of private sphere values to the public sphere will prove their appropriateness for it. As the professional and critical reception of the transformed Dutch television news suggests, transporting private sphere values to the public sphere is more likely to result in concerned discourses about the devaluation of the public sphere, which in the end reconstruct the gendered public-private division.

The intimization of the Journaal has met severe criticism from print journalists in particular, but from its own staff as well. The two major building blocks of the intimate news-human interest topics and an intimate mode of address-encounter most attacks. Under the headline 'Journaal on the decline' a Dutch TV critic laments 'the populist selection from possible news events with disproportionate attention for the obvious and the expected'. Nor does this critic appreciate the 'snug domesticity' created by informal chats between anchor, correspondents and the weatherman.

Critical comments of journalists are hardly ever part of a well-formulated argument referring explicitly to the norms and values the Journaal is supposed to live up to. However, the underlying discourse can be reconstructed from the work of several authors.

They express genuine concern that the 'intimacy' of television news prevents an understanding of public life that is analytical, historical and critical. The invasion of the public arena by topics, values and actions once belonging exclusively to the private sphere is said to erode the adequacy of the public sphere and to endanger effective public discourse. Sennett, for instance, talks about the 'tyranny of intimacy' that transmutes political categories into psychological ones: 'As a result, confusion has arisen between public and intimate life; people are working out in terms of personal feelings public matters which properly can be dealt with only through codes of impersonal meaning.' Kress argues that the operation of personalized language-letting the individual instead of the institution speak-assigns public events to the private sphere. 'It is to offer an account of that event which says that there is no account other than individual action and expression.' The viewer is positioned as an individual guided by common sense, while a public mode of address would position the viewer as a public citizen aware of the operation of institutional processes. Dahlgren entertains a similar argument in the assertion that although intimate modes of address can invite identification with media personalities such as politicians, they do deflect attention from the substantial issues concerned.

Such critical comments of journalists and intellectuals tend to reconstruct rigid divisions between discourse appropriate for the public sphere (analytical and detached) and discourse appropriate for the private sphere (emotional and involved). Thus the transference of private sphere values to the public world of television news hardly modifies beliefs about the legitimacy of private sphere topics, values and behaviours for the public sphere, as liberal feminists would have us believe. The opposite happens instead: it is argued that because TV news is permeated with private sphere values it has lost its traditional social and political functions. The intimacy of TV news results in its discursive expulsion from the public sphere.

BEYOND THE BOURGEOIS PUBLIC SPHERE PARADIGM

The Dutch case suggests that feminist perspectives on journalism and the public sphere are caught in a two-faced trap from which there seems to be no escape. On the one hand, women can opt for full integration in the public sphere on present conditions: they thus become the same as men and equal. Some highly esteemed private sphere values will be lost in the process. On the other hand, women can choose to maintain their private sphere values in public sphere conditions, aiming in the long run at a modification of the public sphere. They will remain different from men.

This dilemma is another expression of the 'sameness-difference' debate which emerges recurrently in the feminist movement and feminist theory. Summarized in an almost intolerably simplified manner, it pertains to the question: are women essentially the same as men but 'made' different by culture and history, in which case 'only' a reversal of culturally and historically defined roles would be necessary. Or are women essentially different from men and oppressed by masculine culture and history, in which case a total revision of the existing social set-up would be needed.

In other words, is femininity an essential or a cultural feature of women? (Note that both positions assume unambiguous and stable meanings of 'femininity', a point to which I will return later.) The question whether women are 'simply' the same, or 'obviously' different has driven much feminist theory into academically interesting but narrowly focused debates with sometimes only remote reference to acute and concrete problems. Within the feminist movement it has often led to paralysing antagonisms, with respect to media strategies for instance expressed as: is the movement best served by creating its own media or by seeking integration in existing media?

Recently feminist political philosophers have suggested ways out of the suffocating grasps of the 'sameness-difference' dilemma by pointing to its historical specificity. They claim that the dilemma is a philosophical and historical product of bourgeois society's distinction between a public sphere populated by men and a private sphere inhabited by women.

Writing about France, Landes asserts that the eighteenth century marked a turning-point for women: 'Public-private oppositions were being reinforced in ways that foreclosed women's earlier independence in the street, in the marketplace, and, for elite women, in the public spaces of the court and aristocratic households.'

She ascribes the genesis of the bourgeois public-private distinction to republican philosophies and policies rooted in a firm aversion to absolutist practices characterized among other things by stylized discourses and extreme mannerism. Elite women, through their position as *salonnières,* exercised a crucial role in shaping public speech and behaviour according to the conventions of the absolutist days. The republican complaint against the decadent and effeminate monarchy thus involved opposition to the public role of women as well: 'The metaphor of the "reign of women" signified the corruption of society at its heights'. Landes indicates convincingly that an important dimension of the bourgeois revolution pertained to the representational styles of the absolutist monarchy-the power of the *salonnières* and 'feminized' public life-by which bourgeois men felt emasculated.

She analyses the work of Montesquieu and Rousseau to argue that the central categories of bourgeois thought-universal reason, law and nature-are embedded in an ideologically sanctioned order of gender difference. 'In their preferred version of the classical universe, bourgeois men discovered a flattering reflection of themselves-one that imagined men as properly political and women as naturally domestic'. The bourgeois revolution thus banished women to the home and called men to their natural fulfilment in political life.

The 'natural' state of society-as opposed to the decadent and perverted absolutist monarchy-was restored through the revolution. Landes concludes that modern feminism is an inextricable product of the gendered structure of bourgeois society. Its prime dilemmas-sameness or difference-could only be articulated as a consequence, and within the limits of a public-private distinction rooted in the assumption of fixed gender identities. Most theorists and historians of the bourgeois public sphere, including Habermas in both his earlier and his more recent works, have failed to appreciate the gendered subtext of the concept.

Feminism has been moderately successful in crossing some of the lines of the public-private distinction. Through the slogan 'the personal is political' feminists have ensured that issues formerly considered private, such as sexual and family relations, have become legitimate subjects for political discourse. Another achievement is that supposedly private and personal experiences are now recognized as legitimate moral bases for political activism. Especially the latter feminist efforts might fundamentally alter the gendered assumptions of the bourgeois public sphere model and eventually overcome the sameness-difference dilemma.

Young asserts that the bourgeois public sphere concept presupposes a civic public consisting of impartial moral reasoners standing outside the situation discussed, adopting a detached attitude.

This civic public is not misled by particular ends and interests, but guided by universal rationality. The capacity of human beings temporarily to discard all non-rational aspects of their existence-affectivity, desire, feelings-is a necessary assumption in such deontological theory of reasoning. The ideal of universalist rationality theoretically and practically excludes women, and not as a mere accident.

'The ideal of a civic public exhibits a will to unity, and necessitates the exclusion of aspects of human existence that threaten and disperse the brotherly unity of straight and upright forms, especially the exclusion of women', Young concludes that the bourgeois concept of the public sphere is ultimately a totalitarian one for it eliminates otherness by ignoring the irreducible specificity of situations and the difference among moral subjects.

As an alternative Young proposes a contextualized evaluation of public life which would appreciate specific discourses due to e.g. the particular experiences of women and ethnic groups.

To recapitulate the argument of this section: historically and philosophically the bourgeois public sphere model assumes and prescribes a universal distinction between rational public aspects of human nature and emotional private ones. Not coincidentally this distinction is interlinked with fixed gender roles and identities.

This gendered subtext of the bourgeois public sphere model leads feminist evaluations of journalism straight into the tentacles of the 'sameness-difference' dilemma. Therefore I join feminist political philosophers who suggest replacing the universalist morality of the bourgeois public sphere model with more particularist and contextual evaluations of public life. I shall briefly address the question as to what such particularist and contextual evaluations of journalism would amount, in the final section.

Arguing for a contextual instead of a universalist evaluation of journalism raises the question as to which context should be taken into account.

The bourgeois public sphere concept is very much focused on the institutional context of journalism, e.g. the theoretical and practical autonomy of news media *vis-à-vis* the political system, the professional performance of journalists, the democratic potential of commercially produced news media.

In so far as the audiences or readers of the news ('publics') receive attention, they are often seen as mere aberrations from the ideal civic public, since much research shows that actual publics do not behave and react as ideal citizens are supposed to.

People spend less and less time reading newspapers, are not highly motivated to watch the news, have a relatively brief attention span and forget the items presented in the evening news within minutes.

Often, researchers are so concerned (sometimes even indignant) with publics *not* fulfilling their democratic duties as citizens, they forget to ask what people do with the news instead. I propose to take such concrete experiences as a starting-point for developing critical alternatives to the anachronistic bourgeois public sphere model. This would mean a shift from institutional contexts to reception contexts.

What would such a contextual and particularist feminist evaluation of the intimacy of Dutch television news amount to? I can only tentatively answer that question for Dutch audience research is minimal in this respect.

Surveys carried out in other countries usually do not reveal great differences in the numbers of women and men watching news programmes but evidence from qualitative data do show gendered ways of relating to news and current affairs programmes. 'Masculinity is primarily identified with a strong preference for factual programs (news, current affairs, documentaries) and femininity identified with a preference for fictional programs'. Several reasons are offered for such a difference.

Some authors claim that the news doesn't provide women with knowledge that enables them to make sense of their own daily experiences. Consequently they will not feel much incentive to watch.

Morley illustrates this by the observation that women do watch local news programmes very attentively. They say that they don't understand what international economic news is about and, as it has no experiential bearing on their lives, they're not interested in it. However, if there has been a crime in a local area, they feel the need to know about it, both for their own sake and their children's sake.

A related reason for gender-specific reception of TV news might be found in the relevance of another social function that TV news can fulfil for its recipients. Jensen observed that for many male viewers TV news provides 'legitimation': 'an opportunity for the recipient to...feel part of a particular social order'. Women, and other outsiders to the 'particular social order, ' might not feel part of that order and might not see the need to keep up with it at all.

These kinds of observations might suggest that the intimacy of Dutch television news would appeal to women in particular, since its subjects and mode of address seem to be in close accordance with the discourse of their life-world. However, such a conclusion again reconstructs a gendered public-private distinction.

The women that are referred to in the above-mentioned research are living (or assumed to be living) in traditional family situations. Women are more or less equated with isolated housewives, still confined to the private sphere. Aside from the theoretical problems such an analysis runs into-as discussed in the previous sections-few people still live in traditional family situations, and the 'isolated housewife' is hardly representative of 'the average woman' any more. More than half of the households in Amsterdam, for instance, consist of a single individual. The way women from different social and cultural backgrounds, with different intellectual and political predispositions and with a variety of public careers, relate to the intimacy of Dutch (TV) news and to recent trends in journalism in general, is yet to be explored, and should be an important part of the agenda for research in journalism. In many cases such explorations will result in contradictory evaluations of the feminist qualities of TV news and journalism, simply because of the increasing heterogeneity of 'woman' as a social and cultural category. But if we reject the universal and consensual bent of the bourgeois public sphere model for its exclusionary mechanisms and propose the recognition and appreciation of differences instead, we can hardly replace it with a new universal, be it feminist, norm for public life.

We need to allow for contradictions within our own feminist public discourse as well.

Chapter 2

Public Relations in the New Millennium

The communication technology revolution and the momentous political changes of the past decade are only two of the many "forces" that will reshape the public relations profession as it evolves from a strictly American concept into a globalized business and management function in the next century.

The purpose of this chapter is to examine the "forces," as explicated by Schranz Distinguished Lecturers during the past 15 years, that are converging to change the way in which public relations will be practiced in the new millennium. From a predicted revolution of "values" to the emergence of a "human climate" that fosters multicultural activism, these "forces" place public relations practitioners in the role of "community" builders responsible for helping link socially, politically, geographically and culturally diverse, and often competing, interests.

This chapter looks at the forecasts made by 15 nationally and internationally recognized senior public relations leaders and synthesizes their recommendations as to how the profession, and public relations education, should evolve to accommodate the "global village" of the 21st century. The importance of this may have been underscored by 1987 Distinguished Lecturer David Ferguson:

Public relations are in a state of transition, and in our case, rapid transition. We are forever passing from one order of practice, goals and circumstances into another. The cycles overlap. Change is constant. The implication for educators is more like uranium than gold. What is taught today will have a relatively short life and will have to be altered considerably almost on a yearly basis if education is to continue to keep pace with practice in our profession.

THE SCHRANZ LECTURE SERIES

The Vernon C. Schranz Distinguished Lectureship in Public Relations was established in 1979 by a grant from the Ball Corporation, which has its world headquarters in Muncie, Indiana. The namesake of the lecture series, Vernon C. Schranz, was Ball Corporation's first public relations practitioner. He served Ball Corporation for 25 years in that capacity, and as a corporate officer, until his retirement in 1979. Hosted each year by the Department of Journalism at Ball State University, the lecture series was intended to honour the contributions of Schranz to the field of public relations:

In his 25 years at Ball Corporation, the late Mr. Schranz developed a public relations programme based upon the principles of openness, honesty and community service....The lectureship has enabled Ball State University to recognize leaders in public relations; to provide leaders with a forum for expressing ideas and concepts; and to provide a professional development opportunity for...public relations practitioners, students, and faculty.

Each transcript was reviewed and coded to identify the themes addressed by each of the speakers. These themes were then topically clustered into categories representing each "force" suggested by the speakers. Three principal "forces" or categories emerged from the analysis: changes in the human climate and personal values, the evolving nature of the organization, and changes in the composition of the field of public relations and its practitioners.

THE HUMAN CLIMATE AND A "REVOLUTION OF VALUES"

A principal function of public relations has been, and continues to be, the building of relationships and the management of communication between organizations and individuals. To understand the global forces affecting the enterprise is to first understand how people, in the United States and around the world, are changing and how these changes affect their relationships with businesses, governments, and institutions.

In his discussion of attitudinal differences between generations, 1994 Schranz Lecturer John W. Felton, for example, argued that the key to understanding societal change, and why some public relations messages are more effective than others, is to recognize that each generation holds unique values and that those values evolve over time. Felton suggested that practitioners often fail in their efforts because they develop messages that appeal to the wrong generation's attitudes - because a message worked with one group in the past does not mean it will work in the future.

Felton, and several other Schranz lecturers, noted that the current evolution of human values may be more dramatic now than at any time in recent history. Ann H. Barkelew, who presented the 1993 lecture, explained:

There is an explosion, and some would say a celebration, of differences in this country today. We are no longer a culture of sameness. The homogeneous culture of the 1950s is gone, and it's gone forever. In its place is an increasingly diverse culture. We have greater racial and ethnic diversity, certainly, but also diversity in interests, income needs and demands for products, services and information. We are also seeing an explosion in diversity of values. Look at the families we see on television shows today - they reflect the new shape of the American household — where families are defined less by blood relationships, and more by their interests and the amount of time they spend together.

Perhaps, then, no other "force" will have greater impact on business and the public relations profession that what Philip Lesly, the 1982 Schranz lecturer, described as the "emergence of the human climate."

"The human climate," Lesly explained, "is now a determining factor in the future of every organization, institution and nation. It is determining what happens in Poland and Russia; the massive shift toward meeting expectations of Latin America; what shifts in balance will be in the Middle East and what happens in every executive office in the world...(the) emergence of the human climate as the dominant force creates both breathtaking opportunities and serious problems for the field of public relations."

Robert L. Dilenschneider, the 1991 Schranz lecturer, described the emergence of the "human climate" as a "revolution of values." And this revolution, according to Lesly, Dilenschneider and several other lecturers, has manifested itself in several forms: consumerism, global activism, the rise of single-issue groups, and a decline in personal accountability and virtue.

THE ROLE OF INFORMATION TECHNOLOGIES

According to Lesly, a number of factors have contributed to the creation of the current human climate. These include new information technologies which extend the geographical and social spheres of individual experience and influence, and which also create a growing sense of entitlement, particularly to information, and immediate gratification and need fulfillment.

He noted that communication technologies can be both "a force for bringing the world closer together and a force for segmenting people into more and more separate groups." A result of this, Lesly explained, is what he termed the "glorification of democracy," the expectation that "every individual can interfere with any process — demand, block, sue, or harass." He explained:

Many follow no leadership and respect no rules. They feel they can interfere with the working of any organization - that they can thwart government, business, education, the armed forces and law enforcement. Refusal to follow any rule is a rejection of all leadership, and without leadership there can only be disorder.

The forces I've mentioned create activist pressures to force their type of change. And even when activists attain any of their objectives, they are not likely to fade away but will then seek new and more demanding causes. The pressures for change are now a force in themselves, not to be satiated by the achievement of change.

"SINGLE-ISSUE" PUBLICS

These activist pressures, according to 1980 Schranz Lecturer Douglas G. Hearle, occur as public attitudes become factionalized around highly volatile, self-defining single issues. Hearle explained:

The growing national single issue orientation on both sides of the political aisle coupled with the continued disillusionment with political institutions has meant more independence of mind for the Voter - or fickleness of attitude, depending on your point of view. And when you add to that the growing effect of intractable economic problems inflation, unemployment as well as energy - effects which are as much psychological as they are material - we are likely to continue to have a public which is highly volatile in its attitudes as voters and as consumers.

CONFRONTATION AS A TACTIC

As single-issue publics increase and, in particular, as these publics form around sensitive, divisive and volatile topics, Dilenschneider predicted that "confrontation" would increase as a tactic of choice. "Confrontation," he explained, "is definitely back in and not just on the boarders of Croatia or in the alleys of Ulster." More than likely, he said, these confrontations will be played out in the media and in the courtroom. The emergence of "tabloid values" in the media fuels the need for "stories" in which raw emotion becomes more important than simple facts. He explained:

The information revolution is also fueling the trend. The ready availability of vast stores of details about personal lives is helping to etch the character lines of potential victims.

And in the courtroom, the opportunity to make public confrontations may be the ultimate goal of single-issue activist groups. Hearle explained:

The courtroom is increasingly where the action is and will continue to be. In that legal arena, special interest groups, like the environmentalists, do not have to "win" by getting a judgement in their favour, by convincing a judge or jury of the correctness of their point of view or by getting a damage award for their cause.

INFORMATION "CLUTTER"

Another bi-product of the information revolution, Dilenschneider explained, is "information clutter." As publics form around all-consuming single issues, their span of attention for, and ability to recall, other information, including corporate messages, becomes seriously eroded. He explained:

I think that we are just now beginning to recognize a clutter problem in recalling messages. There is just too much competition for storage space. If George Bush has trouble leaning on his war laurels within weeks of victory, imagine how hard it is for the average firm to say: Remember the good things we did back in 1989 and 1990.

ACCOUNTABILITY

Perhaps an ironic characteristic of the new "human climate," Dilenschneider argued, is the double standard in how people feel about the "value" of accountability. Americans, he suggested are ambivalent about accountability. While personal accountability is out, corporations, public institutions, and businesses should expect even closer scrutiny in the future than in the past, he said.

The implications for this, according to these Schranz lecturers, is that in the era of the new human climate, organizations will be judged less by their products and services and more by their policies and behaviour related to those values that are "hot" or "politically correct." One "value" is community involvement. Corporations, Ann H. Barkelew argued, will be judged by their involvement in local communities: Strengthening communities has been and is a part of our business strategy - as much a part as operations, distribution or human resources.

THE "NEW" ORGANIZATION

A second "force" frequently identified by the Schranz lecturers dealt with the changing nature of organizations themselves. According to these practitioners, organizations are slowly responding to what has been described as a new "social compact" between employers and their employees. Dilenschneider explained:

There are plenty of disenfranchised white-collar workers out of jobs these days and I expect that you will see more militant efforts toward job entitlement and job protection legislation — closer to what we see in Europe today — arise in the United States.

Companies, he concluded, should expect to face a growing number of accusations that they are not managing work and their employees properly or fairly. Others suggested that the role of the CEO would go through dramatic changes in response to the public's perception that corporate management has become arrogant.

The "new" CEO. "The CEO of the era beginning in the year 2000 will face a legacy unlike anything in our century," explained 1989 lecturer John Budd Jr.

By then, Europe will have faced up to its 1992 challenges; Hong Kong, its reunification with China in 1997; free enterprise will be implanted in the booming nations of East Asia; we'll see deregulation of the economies of eastern Europe and in the bastions of socialism, the Soviet Union and, I'm convinced, in China, under the pressure of its one billion restless population.

Perhaps the biggest challenge to be faced, he suggested, would be a crisis of public confidence in corporate management's competence. Dilenschneider called it the "CEO disease" - the overwhelming perception that corporate leaders have become arrogant and have lost touch with employees and customers.

According to Budd, a continuing drop in employee loyalty toward their employers, combined with the crisis of a lack of public trust, is an indication that corporate managements may have to be restructured. He predicted that the nature of the CEO's position will be the first to change. Corporations will create an "Office of the CEO," he said, in which two individuals will serve: one as the CEO for external affairs and the other as a CEO for internal affairs. Reporting to these two individuals, and working to guide their decision making, would be a "cabinet" of executive vice presidents that might include an executive vice president of ideology, an executive vice president of legal affairs, and an executive vice president of human affairs. He explained that what has been traditional public relations would, in this model, fall under the director of "ideology":

I think it's time to recognize that public relations as a term has been debased by misuse, overuse, and abuse. More importantly, in a decade's time the enhancement of - and the protection of - the credibility of a company - and its CEOs - will have outdistanced the rote, formula thinking of public relations' accepted wisdom.

It will require, as a prerequisite, people skilled in the advancement of ideas, in building broad non-political coalitions and support. It will need people comfortable in dealing with abstracts and converting them to realities. In short, it requires people with minds of originality, endowed with the intellectual resources needed to deal with subjective views, attitudes and behavioral patterns. In short, an ideologist.

Senior management, he concluded, has never been more "in need of truly creative, objective counsel, externally and internally, as now. And, never before has it been in such limited supply."

This may in fact, according to Carole Howard, facilitate the "metamorphosis" of the public relations practitioner to senior management "counselor." This change, she explained, may be so natural that the profession may not even be aware of it until it has occurred. Kerryn King, the 1985 Schranz lecturer, quoted the CEO of a major oil company, who explained:

The modern corporation is no longer perceived solely in economic terms, but as an institution which contributes to society as a whole. These changes in public expectations and in the perception of business are transforming public relations from an ancillary role in the corporation to an essential one.

Globalization. In addition, the opening of new markets in Eastern Europe and Asia have sent many firms looking for overseas opportunities, creating what Carole Howard described as "stateless corporations" with "borderless offices." This, she said, would bring challenges and opportunities:

That's certainly true in my job. With the technological advantages of FAXes, voice mail and satellite hookups at my fingertips, backed by a superb staff at our global headquarters in New York and Reader's Digest Association colleagues in more than 50 offices worldwide, I am as comfortable brainstorming magazine promotions in Sydney as I am giving a speech in Stockholm.

The "human climate," particularly consumerism and environmental movements, may be stronger abroad than in the United States now, and public relations practitioners must be aware of this, she noted.

The Changing "Face" of Public Relations: A third, significant force affecting public relations is the very composition of the field itself and the way in which public relations firms will be owned and operated in the future. Several of the Schranz lecturers intimated that recent studies which have examined the "velvet ghetto" and "glass ceilings" may have been harbingers of what may be the most serious challenge to face the profession in coming decades.

The role of women. As many as 70 per cent of the college students currently preparing for careers in public relations are women, according to Budd. These women, he explained, must be willing to take on leadership roles needed to elevate the profession's status:

If public relations is to achieve the higher destinies its leadership regularly projects for it, women are going to be the catalyst because they will increasingly represent numerically the majority of practitioners. The professional gauntlet is theirs to pick up. Women have to push determinedly upwards by the same measures of personal discipline some men adopt. Men, who currently hold the majority of seniorlevel positions must, for the good of the profession in the long run, must be willing to create opportunities for this to occur. Budd explained:

Male executives - and they hold sway in the agency management echelons - for their part have got to be less chauvinistic and give the same encouragement, the same level of mentorship and opportunity they readily provide male interns.

A return to smaller agencies? In the mergerhungry 1980s, small public relations agencies became prey for publicly owned "mega-agencies," whose own gluttony turned themselves into uncreative, non-risk taking, bottom-line-driven shops in which hundreds of clients were served, but none with the close attention that is supposed to be at the heart of what public relations is about.

Budd argued that mega-agencies cannot give personal services to hundreds of different clients at one time. This, he suggests, is a violation of the very tenets of the profession. Because of this, public relations will have to rethink its need to create these mega-agencies. He suggested that future trends will be toward small, specialized agencies looking after the needs of a handful of select clients:

In my opinion, the mega-agencies will not be a material factor then. They will have dematerialized one way or another, most likely cannibalized by new owners to extract maximum profit from the pieces.... These very special needs will become the province of small boutiques - or niches - of senior professionals who bring mature perspectives, independent judgement, front-line experience and a degree of irreverence to conventional wisdom to the assignment.

Generalists and Specialists? "The old notions," Fraser P. Seitel argued, "that people in public relations must be generalists, rather than specialists, simply won't cut it in the years ahead." While it will be important to master the "general" skills of communication, Seitel recommended that future practitioners understand they must become "generalized specialists" who are particularly conversant in and knowledgeable either of a specific aspect of public relations work investor relations or government relations or speech writing, etc. - or of a particular industry - computers or health care or sports or the arts or, as in my own case, banking and finance, or whatever.... Increasingly in the future, specific public relations jobs will be awarded to the practitioner who demonstrates specialized expertise in the particular area at issue.

Douglas Hearle suggested that many of the needed "specializations" will include history, science, law, engineering, education, political science, international affairs, and television production.

The Schranz lecturers shared the belief that public relations practitioners must be better trained to understand the dynamics of the business world and, in particular, the international marketplace. At present, public relations has "too many mechanics and too few counselors truly capable of helping management understand the complexities of today's dynamic business environment," David Ferguson explained. As a result, public relations education, he argued, must move away from its exclusive emphasis on "communication mechanics":

Public relations will never reach the status of a profession, as long as people can get into the field and prosper without having completed a fairly rigorous course of study in the field. And, until educations in public relations become sufficiently broad to include study in such subjects as economics, philosophy and law....Any attempt to expand the vision and reach of public relations education must include significant involvement in international affairs and the international business climate.

One approach to this, according to Ann H. Barkelew, would be to train future practitioners in "implications thinking." Like issues management or issues tracking, "implications thinking" requires that practitioners be able to critically evaluate the impact of external forces — business ethics, diversity, time-poor customers, health care reform, the economy - on their organizations:

We bring our thoughts to the strategy table, because that is the role of public relations at the table: to identify issues, to respond to concerns, and to position the organization effectively to meet these challenges.

In a sense, this requires practitioners to become what 1981 Schranz Lecturer Dorothy Gregg described as organizational "futurists," forecasting social trends and preparing the organization for their bottom-line impact. "Implications thinking" may be a critical skill in an era of globalization and international business. Douglas G. Hearle explained:

A generalist must have the detailed knowledge and expertise of the specialist when dealing with problems... which have far-reaching legal, social, political and economic implications. Only the specialist can know in full detail what interest groups will be aroused by a particular stand on an issue or by a particular decision. Only a specialist can know how a specific social issue is affecting a country in Europe and might, therefore, affect the United States or a country in the Pacific area.

It is this combination of "generalist managers" and "specialist counselors" that "will characterize a successful public relations profession over the next decades," Hearle concluded.

While these three principal "forces" have been identified through the observations and reflections of practitioners who represent the senior leaders of the field, it is likely that the "forces" will continue to change and evolve over time - as communication and information technologies improve, and as social and political revolutions continue to dot the globe.

Because of this, Philip Lesly suggested that public relations professionals and students should be committed to a "lifetime" education, constantly reading "the best thought in this field, on the social patterns, on the psychology of people."

David Ferguson, in his lecture, "A Practitioner Looks At Public Relations Education," argued that the only way the discipline will be able to successfully prepare current and future practitioners to respond to these changing global forces is through a partnership between professionals and educators. "It is essential," he explained, "that mutual respect be developed between those who teach and those who practice public relations."

It was recommended by several of the lecturers that public relations professionals be given the opportunity for greater involvement in the education process – through visiting lectureships, presentations, and inclusion in active advisory councils. And it was also suggested that public relations educators increase their involvement with working professionals.

Finally, a consistent theme among the lecturers was the need to move the focus of public relations education away from simply teaching "process" or mechanical skills toward greater efforts at developing critical thinking abilities through the study and application of theory, human psychology, economics, and business philosophies.

Curriculum developers in the field of gifted education raise many critical questions such as:

- What should gifted and talented students learn?,
- For what purpose?

In this chapter, these two questions will be discussed as they relate to and affect the world of gifted and talented students in the first decade of the 21st century. Most of the issues that gifted students will face in the new world landscape, such as ethnic conflict, arms escalation, overpopulation, environmental problems, poverty, and genetic engineering, cannot be solved without integrating knowledge from the natural sciences, the social sciences, and humanities.

This balance is currently not found in the teaching and learning of gifted students, since teaching what is of value, which is called "Philosophy," has less importance than teaching what is, which is called "Science."

I propose that, in order to teach our gifted students elegant problem solving in the arts and sciences (i.e., the parsimonious and e vocative description of patterns to make sense out of a confusion of detail), curriculum developers need to renew their interest in philosophical inquiry in gifted classrooms.

WHY CONSIDER PHILOSOPHICAL INQUIRY

The value of teaching and learning through philosophical inquiry is not only an intellectual adventure, but also enables learners of all ages to discover and understand elements of the human condition. It is not a new approach, nor is it necessarily unique. Vygotsky valued works of art, philosophical arguments, and anthropological data when building a theory of learning with thought and language early in the 20th century. Bruner believed a curriculum for excelling students ought to be constructed around the great issues, principles, and values that the society deemed worthy of continued concern.

Gardner has said that a culture identifies truths, beauties, and virtues it finds valuable and then gathers resources to ensure their understanding in young learners. These virtues are always being redefined and refined. Educators can not only expect students to learn about virtues such as truthfulness, goodness, and beauty, but can also help students pursue truth, beauty, and goodness in their own lives. It is essential for our gifted and talented youth to become immersed in curricula that inculcate the understanding and application of these virtues.

Especially in the new millennium, our brightest students need to discover their deepest ties to the rest of humanity and thereby help ensure that nature and culture survive for future generations.

Recently, a colleague of mine, a historian and educator, offered a historian's perspective of the value of teaching gifted students through philosophical inquiry. He said that the way we think—thought at the most reflective levels—determines what will be important in a culture. If the brightest learners have a foundation in philosophical thinking, then the nature of a nation's technology for example, will reflect that thinking. If the brightest learners know only the mechanics or the science of technology, then it is that knowledge alone that will drive its direction. Teaching through philosophy balances the personal worldview with the technical knowledge of a student as he or she becomes a stakeholder in a society.

Philosophy Within the Humanities

One may take the point of view that the legitimate study of mankind is man. The humanities comprise the study of all formal and informal acts of humankind that have resulted in creative products that portray and enhance the human condition in some form. In this light, developers of gifted curricula may view the humanities as providing a link for many disciplines interesting to gifted learners.

Important theoretical models considered for conceptualizing humanities curricula for gifted students include those of Ward and Phenix. Each of these important models incorporates philosophy as a core element in the curriculum experience. Ward's model of teaching philosophy as an integrated learning experience has sought to provide a meaningful structure to gifted curriculum, emphasizing systems of thought and great ideas as organizers. The work of Phenix is a cornerstone of the approach taken by gifted educators as a curriculum-modification procedure designed to provide more in-depth learning experiences for gifted students.

Philosophy as Curriculum

The search for meaning within the domain of philosophy and its subdisciplines is sometimes referred to as ethics, metaphysics, and epistemology. Inviting gifted students to reflect on such philosophical questions as the meaning of knowledge (epistemology), for example, can help them become receptive to all levels and types of experience. It can help prepare them to maximize their knowledge in as many subjects as possible, especially in areas of special interest to them.

Teaching ethics to gifted students expands the teaching of authentic practices in various fields. For example, making explicit to individuals their personal ethical system can help them respond to specific ethical dilemmas. This is an increasingly vital skill to possess when a talented student enters the worlds of microbiology, genetics, fiscal management, journalism, business, or education. Currently, however, teaching gifted students in the philosophical domain of metaphysics seems to be limited, and this may hinder a student from attempting to find meaning personally, as well as in the surrounding world.

The main task of the coming era is...a radical renewal of our sense of responsibility. Our conscience must catch up to our reason; otherwise we are lost.

One perplexing problem in the teaching of philosophy to gifted students is that existing curricular models, such as those discussed above, have been too abstract conceptually for easy translation and use by teachers. That can be fixed. As students from one country can easily learn the language of another by extended visits, so teachers of gifted students can allow their students regular extended visits in the realms of truth, beauty, and happiness, all the while doing the business of reading, writing, and arithmetic.

Csikszenrmihalyi has explored the possibility that the next steps in human evolution and human survival will depend on the ability to find flow in activities that nurture human community and protect the environment. In order to do this, schools could promote the activities that bring about flow, including those that could inculcate in students a kind of love for the Cosmos, a cosmic conscientiousness. You don't want to only teach book learning or skills, but also a kind of feeling that the universe is a wonderful place to inhabit and that somehow you love every part of it.

Gifted and talented students, their teachers, and their teachers' teachers should be thinking about, talking about, and doing something about these philosophical ideas as they learn in school. Students need to know that teachers are seekers, too.

As educators of the gifted, we must question what to teach our students and to what end. The answers become important as we look beyond the year 2000 and realise the problems facing the next generations of students. Developing curricula for the gifted that incorporate teaching through philosophy is my answer to the first question. Establishing the teaching of philosophy as a cornerstone of the integration of knowledge from the natural sciences, social sciences, and humanities so that gifted students may be able to solve the problems of the new millennium is my answer to the second question.

Once a commitment is made to the teaching of philosophy to gifted students, theoretical models can be developed that are easily understood and used by teachers who then become active partners with students, joining together to build meaningful paths to the future.

Chapter 3

Reflections on Oral History in the New Millennium

It is a rather daunting task that we have been assigned, particularly since the very word "millennium" carries so much weight for those who inhabit the Western, Christian-influenced world. And with the proliferation of scholarly output on oral history, it is overwhelming to think, even fleetingly, about trying to synthesize these materials into a coherent statement that reflects our past, present and future and that is international in scope.

Nevertheless, what is so amazing and rewarding about the Oral History Association is the incredible mix that is to be found in our membership and in the papers delivered at our conferences—offering everyone something to which they can relate, yet at the same time providing an arena for dialogue among the generations of practitioners. And while "live and let live" has come to characterize some of the relationships between the generations—as can be seen in the predictable differences in the composition of the audience at different sessions at OHA conferences—there is also remarkable agreement on some issues of long-standing concern.

For instance, despite the greater fascination and ease with which the later generations approach the application of new technologies, we still seem to share some common ethical concerns across the generations, as revealed in the recent discussions at the Buffalo OHA Annual Meeting on revising the standards, principles, and guidelines of the profession.

Each of the generations has very different origins, and the state of the field was not the same at our various entry points. I can remember, for instance, when I set out with my tape recorder in October 1972 to interview 104 year old suffragist Sylvia Thygeson, there were no guidelines for "doing" women's oral history.

And although gender did not enter into their considerations, the two page mimeographed set of Goals and Guidelines of the OHA, along with Baum's pamphlet on Oral History for the Local Historical Society, helped me to set my course.

Of course, as someone trained originally in sociology by professors who came out of the "Chicago school," I was familiar with the life history method.

In any event, the guidelines issued by various practitioners in this early period, only five years after the OHA was founded, reflected a kind of prescriptive certainty.

What perhaps distinguished our recommendations for women's oral history from others was the attention paid to women's everyday life.

This meant not only interviewing "non-elite"—in contrast to the first generation's heavy emphasis on the elite—but it meant exploring "the personal."

For feminists anchored in community projects and academia alike, this reflected our belief captured in the mantra of the period: "the personal is political." As a result, it was not only who we interviewed, but the questions we asked that set us apart.

Furthermore, we viewed the oral history interview as an empowering process for interviewer and narrator alike. Because we were so busy developing our own "women's oral history movement," I don't think we realized at the time that we were very much like other second generation historians who were not only carrying the banner of the "new social history" and changing historical practice, but were creating an "oral history movement." And although most of us still might testify to how our interviews validated life experiences of the "everywomen" we were interviewing, our naive faith in its empowering potential eventually gave way to a more critical analysis of the power dynamics inherent in the process.

Indeed, this critical stance, inspired and reinforced by the post-modernist spell under which many of us fell, as well as the focus on reflexivity encouraged by "the new anthropology," led to more theorizing both about the interview process and the resultant product. And although oral narratives still were being presented as transparent by some practitioners, increasingly the later generations treated them as representations, or cultural constructions, that were influenced by a host of factors.

This meant, among other things, taking the final step away from whatever semblance remained of the "myth of objectivity." Instead, the focus shifted to subjectivity, to how memory was constructed, to the implications of our narrators' and our various and shifting positionalities, to an appreciation of the interview as a linguistic and performative event, and finally, to the treatment of the oral history (narrative) as a text.

Although it sounds as if these shifts represent a linear development, as historians we know how artificial and misleading periodization is. While certain tendencies differentiate one generation of practitioners from another, drawing these with such broad strokes overstates the initial emphasis on objectivity, on the one hand, and the lack of earlier theorizing, on the other. Indeed, at the same time that some practitioners were attempting to justify the "objectivity" of the oral history process by applying conventional social science standards of reliability and validity, there were others who were urging more highly nuanced approaches for evaluating interviews.

Nevertheless, even as some members of the second generation called for more theorizing, most of us in the 1970s, and even into the early 1980s—at least among most feminist pratitioners—were still caught up in a more uncritical celebratory mode. It was not until well into the 1980s, and largely as a result of the writings of U.S. women of colour and of the post-colonial theorists that we began to problematize the feminist mantle of "sisterhood" that earlier had promoted false universalisms.

Groundbreaking works that should have prompted more U.S. oral history practitioners of all stripes to pay closer attention to questions about memory and representation were largely ignored until more fertile ground enabled them to take root in the 1980s and 1990s. The growing interdisciplinarity of oral history, as well as the increased exposure to European writings contributed to considerably more theorizing. Unfortunately, some of this theorizing resulted in the oral history becoming viewed and treated as merely a disembodied text.

On the other hand, even if we resisted embracing this tendency whole-heartedly, it did help us to introduce much more complexity into our work and into the practical advice we gave others. As a result, the recent manual, Don Ritchie's Doing Oral History, stands in sharp contrast to the earlier highly prescriptive ones. His responses to a series of very down-to-earth questions lay out the range of thinking and options about the issues, reflecting much more interaction between the generations and a great deal of flexibility and change.

Before conjecturing on where we seem to be heading in the new millennium, and perhaps as an introduction to that topic—we have to acknowledge the major turnaround in the acceptance of oral history in the historical profession. It is ironic that this acceptance has come just as we have forsaken the need to defend "objectivity" and have moved further away from positivism. Much credit for the increased acceptance goes to the hard work of the several past OHA presidents, but the process has been a dialectical one.

A new generation has been using oral history in their doctoral research. In my own department, for instance, our three last hires—ranging in fields from Latin American history to U.S. Western history—all utilized oral history, as did a large proportion of the candidates for our recent positions. Another indicator of the fact that we have "arrived" is the understanding of why oral history does not fit the usual requirements of the Institutional Review Boards on Human Subjects.

It is not surprising that an increasing number of doctoral students are engaged in oral history, particularly since it has been incorporated into so much of the undergraduate curriculum, if nothing else as optional assignments or as historical literature.

Nor should we be surprised that they are using it and theorizing about it in ways that sometimes seem quite foreign to the earlier generations of practitioners. What is more surprising is the growing popularity at the other end of the age spectrum, young school children, especially among populations with heavy minority enrollment. For many years the OHA has encouraged using oral history in secondary, and even middle schools, but we have not emphasized its utility and value for the earlier grades.

Yet, teachers are becoming enthralled by this prospect. For instance, a third grade teacher in one of our Long Beach schools is using oral history to help his second generation Cambodian students who have been classified "limited English proficiency" access the core curriculum. In this context, oral history is a means of learning social studies, being introduced to literature, and of gaining communication skills. Other teachers in the district are being encouraged to follow suit through a collaborative project between the university and the school district.

While these developments seem far removed from the intellectual debates among oral historians in academia, their implications for the new millennium may very well be more significant when it comes to thinking about future audiences and uses, including the application of new technologies. This generation of nascent oral historians, as well as those who Dunaway referred to as the fourth generation, are much more media oriented.

As any of us who teach them can attest, they seem to respond, absorb, and be challenged more by visual images and sound than by the written word. As a result, the aurality of oral history will become increasingly important returning the "voice" of the interviewees, narrators, and oral biographers to centre stage. Ironically, and as yet one more indication of just how flexible the boundary between generations of oral historians is, as early as 1977 Louis Starr rather presciently predicted just this aural orientation.

Not only will oral/aural histories and accompanying visual imagery in CD-ROM programs like those produced by the American Social History project become more widely used, but the new technology will enable scholars to access original interview recordings with considerably greater ease. Even if many of us have grave reservations right now about putting entire oral history recordings on the internet, I think we could agree to transfer them to CD-ROMs that could be loaned or even sold to users, with all the appropriate restrictions that we presently place on the use of transcripts.

Oral history interviews on CD-ROM, accompanied by key word indexing, and coupled with the ability to download and then transcribe appropriate portions through voice recognition programs will make thumbing through and xeroxing transcripts seem quite tedious. While these developments probably are only the tip of the iceberg of the new technologies that can make oral histories more widely accessible, they represent a quantum leap from the New York Times 1976 microfilming project.

Significantly, these technological breakthroughs point to recentering of the narrator's voice, perhaps providing a corrective to some of the more disembodied theoretical and literary treatments of oral history narratives. At the same time, they offer an opportunity for more complex exploration of how people construct their narratives. "Hearing" the silences and listening to intonation, pitch, and style of delivery adds an entirely new dimension to the sense we make of people's stories—a possibility until now explored mainly by those who, following Dennis Tedlock, have attempted to transform the spoken word into a free verse "score."

Furthermore, in hearing the interviewer as well as the narrator, their dynamics can also be grasped, including how each of their agendas and subjectivities interface, and their shifting power relations. Lacking a crystal ball, I cannot predict what new turns theory will take, how our thinking about memory and language and narrative might change; but the fourth generation and the one to follow—like those Cambodian-American third graders—undoubtedly will think about and use oral history quite differently than their predecessors.

Already, we are seeing serious efforts to integrate some of the valuable critical insights from postmodernism with the earlier political focus of writing more complex and richly layered histories.

Insights from poststructuralist theorists may have helped us to understand the complexity of the power dynamic between interviewer and narrator and may have pointed us towards more complex analysis of oral history narratives (texts), but I believe that they also undermined some of the democratic impulses that marked oral history. As Gail Stearns suggests in the latest of the four women's oral history issues of Frontiers, even as we engage in reflexive analysis and comparison of the power relations between "ethnic, classed and gendered positions of researcher and subject," we must recognize the moral agency of both participants.

I would expect that in the next millennium, as in the past thirty some years since the founding of the OHA, the dialectical relationship between theorists and empiricists, between practitioners in the academy and in the community (not necessarily different people), between "techno-buffs" and "Luddites," between long time oral historians and newer generations will continue to push the practice of oral history in exciting new directions.

And although I might not have admitted this twenty-seven years ago when I first began my work in women's oral history—a time when many of us of the second generation were busy distancing ourselves from the first—if we go back and re-read some of the early classics, we might very well find hints that the first generation of oral historians in the U.S. would have welcomed these new directions.

"Are you ready?" people ask repeatedly in a recent series

of television commercials. This apocalyptic-sounding refrain turns out to advertise the leading manufacturer of network routers for the Internet. Ready or not, the ad implies, the future lies in digital electronic communications. If that is tree, are oral historians ready?

It's a fair question considering the steady procession of technology that made oral history possible. During this past century, sound recordings evolved from wax cylinders, aluminum disks, vinyl records, wire recorders, belt recorders, reel-to-reel tape recorders, and cassette recorders to digital audio tape recorders and camcorders. Each wave of technology produced less expensive, more portable means of recording, which in turn launched more projects and enabled more interviews to be conducted with a wider cross-section of people. Personal computers similarly facilitated the transcription and preservation of interviews. Now the Internet offers innovative opportunities for the mass distribution of oral history output.

To this succession of technological breakthroughs, oral historians have reacted with a mixture of eagerness and trepidation. New technology opens new possibilities and can reduce costs, unless a project has invested heavily in older equipment that it is reluctant to abandon. Learning how to operate and make maximum use of new apparatus can disrupt comfortable routines. Nor does new technology always represent progress. None of the successors to reel-to-reel magnetic tape recorders have performed as satisfactorily in terms of long-term audio archival preservation. It is safe to say that the needs of oral historians do not rank high among manufacturers' priorities.

Technological innovations have also required adjustment to the standards and principles by which oral historians operate. A decade ago when the Oral History Association sponsored a thorough overhaul of its Evaluation Guidelines, the process took two years and involved an array of committees reviewing every perceived aspect of the methodology. Despite intense scrutiny, few anticipated the suddenness of the digital electronic communications revolution, which has now spurred another revision of the guidelines.

In setting standards, oral historians always run the risk of elevating practice into principle. Some projects that initially could not afford costly transcription argued passionately for the preservation of high-quality sound recordings and extolled the "aural" nature of oral history. These worthwhile issues enriched the dialogue between practitioners but they also prevented some from admitting the value of transcription as it became more affordable.

Other oral historians found that transcription greatly facilitated both research use and archival preservation, yet some pioneering projects so embraced transcription that they overlooked the value of the sound recording, arguing that corrections to the transcripts invalidated the tapes, and that allowing researchers to listen to them would violate the confidences of the interviewees.

Back when tapes were pricey, they rerecorded over them once they had finished transcribing, and were slow to change even after it became affordable to preserve both the tape and transcript. Similar debates have raged between those who videotaped to capture the expressions of the speakers and to expand the documentary and exhibit uses of the interviews and those who feared that videotaping would interfere with the rapport necessary to conduct meaningful interviews.

The assertion that the future of oral history is digital will undoubtedly cheers some practitioners and distresses others. Beyond its enormous potentials, the digital revolution will threaten financial and intellectual investments in technologies that are moving toward obsolescence.

Just as some oral history archives possess recordings made on wire and belt recordings they can no longer play, magnetic tape recorders someday will no longer be manufactured, regardless of archival concerns about the potential shelf life of digital tape and CD-ROM recordings. The preservation of electronic data will be further complicated by fast-changing technology that will confront archives with periodic choices of convening older electronic records into new formats or preserving the relics on which they were originally recorded.

Most oral historians first approached personal computers as glorified typewriters. The benefits became obvious as transcribers discovered that they could work faster on computer, edit more easily, and no longer had to retype a second "clean" copy of the transcript after the editing. They could preserve transcripts on disk and reproduced them on demand. But a few visionaries grasped that the computer offered ways to bridge the gulf between the tape and the transcript.

They could preserve spoken words, pictures, maps, and other illustrations on the same disk along with the printed transcript. In Alaska, "Project Jukebox" recorded oral histories with native Americans and other Alaskans on CD-ROM, combining interviews in native languages with English translations and appropriate illustrations. Books began to appear in electronic format, such as Who Built America? which blended the voices of interviewees together with music, pictures and text on CD-ROM.

Then the addition of a modem made the personal computer a link to the world. An "information superhighway" carried vast amounts of digitized information across fibre-optic telecommunication circuits at rapid speed. The Cold War spawned the original computer network in 1969 when ARPANET first linked the Pentagon with contractors and universities working on defence projects.

By the 1990s, the Internet had gone civilian and commercial, linking government, corporations, and universities, together with millions of individuals in their own homes. The World Wide Web offered easy access to information on a global scale. Users could browse library catalogs, purchase an airline ticket, locate a restaurant review, or chat electronically with others of similar interests. Newspapers, magazines, radio, and television networks established Web sites on which they posted up-to-the-minute news, feature articles, and entire programs.

If radio and television interviews are available online,

what about oral history? A search on the Internet quickly locates oral history transcripts at various Web sites, among them several presidential libraries and the Washington Press Club Foundation's Women in Journalism Oral History Project. Generally, these sites list all of the oral histories in the collection and include full texts of some, with biographical information about the interviewers and descriptions of the project's objectives.

The Centre for Legislative Archives at the National Archives has posted an interview that I conducted for the Senate Historical Office with the veteran Washington news photographer George Tames. One can also read the interviews that high school students in Kingstown, Rhode Island conducted about the tumultuous events of 1968: "The Whole World Was Watching: An Oral History." Nearby Brown University's Scholarly Technology Group helped the students post their interview transcripts and audio recordings.

Students have also shown creative research use of the Internet. As a judge at the National History Day finals, I reviewed a project on "Rosie the Riveter" of World War II fame. Since scholarly books and documentary films have dealt with the subject, I expected the students' work to be largely derivative.

Instead, they offered a fresh and lively approach that drew from interviews with women war workers from across the country. How had they found so many Rosies? They had posted inquiries on the Internet for information from other students whose grandmothers might have worked in a factory during the Second World War. Responses from the Internet gave them a national selection of candidates for telephone interviews.

That students tend to be more adventurous with new technology should come as no surprise. Many of them grew up in households where the computer was as much a part of daily life as the television. Their elementary and secondary schools provided computer education and their textbooks came equipped with CD-ROM supplements. Undergraduate and graduate students increasingly conduct their studies and do their research electronically. University archivists report that use of manuscript collections and other materials whose finding aids are available online far exceeds that of collections whose catalogs exist only on paper. A large proportion of younger adults now get their daily news more frequently from Internet sites than from newspapers or television. Even political candidates have started campaigning online to attract the next generation of voters.

Not everyone has exhibited as much enthusiasm for the Internet. At the Oral History Association's annual meeting in Buffalo, New York, in 1998, a number of archivists raised reservations about putting interviews online, ranging from the need to protect interviewees' privacy to the danger of misuse and manipulation of sound recordings and transcripts, and the "unmonitored access" of the Internet which would result in a loss of archival control over the interviews. They questioned whether deeds of gift that had not anticipated electronic reproduction and distribution would permit the posting of interviews on the Internet without the express permission of the interviewees or their next of kin. Ethical questions of this nature have caused some oral history projects to hesitate going on the Web for fear of stepping into a minefield.

It is imperative that oral historians grapple with the ethical issue of the Internet and avoid exploitation of their interviewees. Projects may need to revise their deeds of gift and to notify living interviewees before placing their interviews on the Internet (although it seems excessive to track down the next of kin, whose intentions may conflict with those of the interviewee).

At the same time there is a danger of falling into the mode of thinking that Sinclair Lewis satirized in Main Street, when his idealistic heroine suggested to the town librarian that "the chief task of a librarian is to get people to read," only to rebuffed with the argument that "the first duty of the conscientious librarian is to preserve the books." Having talked earnestly about returning interviews to the community, we need to ask: what constitutes the boundaries of that community? How broadly or narrowly do we want to define our audience? Did interviewees expect their life stories to remain relatively unused except by the occasional scholar, or did they hope to leave something of themselves for posterity, where their memories might be published, exhibited, and otherwise not forgotten?

Given the democratic impulses of the oral history movement, it seems contradictory for oral historians not to avail themselves of the most universal and cost-effective means of mass communication and dissemination of information ever devised.

Some oral historians have equated downloading an oral history with publishing it, and have decried the lack of explanatory context for the interview. But the Internet is a distributor rather than a publisher (Congress specifically defined it that way to protect it from libel suits), and oral history transcripts are raw data rather than books. In practice, the Internet has not proved conducive for reading book-length manuscripts, although publishers have begun advertising new books by posting first chapters on their Web sites.

The Internet does best with screen-sized chunks of information. Exclusively online magazines like Slate and Salon feature short essays with eye-catching graphics. The ideal text for easy reading on a computer screen runs about the length of a newspaper column.

Longer texts are available online—one can find the full version of the Start Report and of entire books, from the Bible to Moby Dick. They are easy to scan by word and key phrase for ready reference, but awkward to read at length. The probability is that most interviews will attract researchers seeking to locate specific information instead of casual readers who will peruse the entire document.

Researchers who consult interview transcripts online will want the product to resemble as much as possible the original document. Some of the early attempts at downloading oral histories did not include the original pagination. Although researchers can scan the text by word on the screen, they will need page numbers for their citations as well as to make use of the prepared indexes if they print out a copy of the interview.

Oral historians themselves will use the Internet when doing the research needed to prepare for their interviews. The Internet can provide genealogical data, newspaper clippings, alumni news, and background material on the organizations and communities with which interviewees were associated, and even maps and driving directions to their homes.

Newer projects should build the Internet into the operating plans, fully informing participants of the project's intentions and of the interviewees' options, drafting deeds of gift that specifically permit digital electronic reproduction of the interviews, and preparing transcripts in formats convenient for downloading. For long-established oral history archives the task of digitizing a large collection might appear so daunting as to paralyze.

A reasonable strategy would be to start by making finding aids available on the Internet. That will alert researchers as to what exists where. Since many interview transcripts are already available on microfilm or through interlibrary loan, researchers can obtain copies without traveling to distant collections. Projects can next turn to interviews already transcribed on disk, or scan older transcripts, and post a sample of their interviews to display the richness of the collection. Researchers will pay virtual visits to archives, searching the finding aides, reading transcripts, listening to some of the recordings, and consulting with the archivists electronically.

Looking ahead, computers will eventually transcribe our tapes, which will help to get older interviews online. Voice recognition and deciphering technology is already available, although difficult to use accurately with multiple speakers. The Internet will facilitate large data bases of oral history, with intricate cross-referencing and word searching capabilities along with linkage to specific archives and interview transcripts. Improved telecommunications may also boost distance interviewing. In the past telephone interviews have been less than satisfying because of the difficulty in building rapport when one is not present and maintaining eye contact. The merger of phone and computer systems and more prevalent use of video phones may well prompt experiments in long-distance interviewing.

Keep in mind that digital electronic communication is ephemeral. Web sites keep permutating. Material that a researcher previously consulted may be reported "Not Found" on the next visit. So far, the Internet has shown little interest in archiving its vast store of material. During an encounter with an Internet producer for a television network doing some imaginative educational work connected with its news programs, the producer admitted that he had no idea whether his network was saving any of the material he was creating weekly, nor did he seem to care. Much will vanish through neglect. Some of the Web addresses listed here may have changed before this chapter appears in print. Only change is constant on the Internet.

The World Wide Web will not replace oral history archives, which will continue to house the original records and preservation copies of tapes and transcripts. Instead it can extend archives' user services from their immediate locations to the furthest reaches of the globe, and perhaps beyond. It can make the next generation of researchers far more aware of the panoramic scope of oral history conducted during the twentieth century, and keep them better apprised of the interviewing that continues in the twenty-first. Wider scrutiny could lead to increased peer review of interviews, with greater attention to issues of evidence and content, and even more rigorous methodological standards. The Internet is the new millennium for oral history. Are you ready?

ORAL HISTORY AND THE NEW CENTURY

Oral history has always been formed by interaction and change. Oral memoirs pivot upon a unique interaction between historian and historymaker. Changing or redefining the subject of history—integrating the actions, experiences, and ideas of "ordinary" women and men—is crucial to the attraction of oral history. And the promise of oral history goes further, seeking to transform the relationship between historian and audience, looking for ways to make study of history more accessible, more engaging, and ultimately more participatory. For inherent to oral history are the democratic notions that everyone can be a historian; that memory is in itself a meaningful form of historical interpretation; and that, through oral history projects, students and others can make a meaningful contribution to our understanding of the past.

As the twentieth century ends, new technology is emerging that may significantly enhance our ability to realise these aspects of oral history's promise. Our growing ability to digitize—and thereby control and transmit—information will affect many aspects of oral history in the century to come.

Already, surveying the World Wide Web, we can see indicators of significant change that will greatly improve the accessibility, usability, and transparency of oral history collections; transform the use of oral history in teaching and learning processes; and spur our return to orality, to the fundamental core of oral history as process that involves speaking and listening. New technology is no panacea for oral historians (or anyone else). Many challenges will remain and new ones will emerge, some directly related to technology itself. But digital media is providing us with new tools that will affect the ways we do—and think about—our work.

LET A THOUSAND FLOWERS BLOOM

The first signs of the changes taking place in oral history are already visible on the World Wide Web. An examination of web sites related to oral history reveals some interesting ways we are utilizing new digital technology. There is no consensus on the best way for oral historians to use the Web. As a field, we are still figuring this out. But important trends are already visible.

Most oral history-related web sites are created by established archives and provide lists of the memoirs archived by the institution. There are literally thousands of such sites, ranging from Hogan Jazz Archive of Tulane University to the U.S. Naval Institute Oral History Project. One elaborate site, the Chicago Architects Oral History Project site, constructed by the Art Institute of Chicago, offers for each respondent a photograph, a biographical summary, lists of interview highlights and related interviews, and a one-paragraph transcript excerpt. A master index can be searched and transcripts can be ordered online. While limited in scope, such sites make it much easier for users, working from home or school, to quickly assess the quality and relevance of the collection.

Other web sites go further to provide larger transcript excerpts. Probably the richest transcript site is the American Memory Collection, created by the Library of Congress, which presents tens of thousands of items, from George Washington's papers to historic baseball cards. Among its most used collections are the transcripts and notes from more than 2,900 oral narratives created by the Federal Writers' Project of the 1930s, addressing work and family, memories of slavery and immigration, and stories about local history.

Though constrained in various ways, these narratives provide abundant opportunities to examine the nation's collective memories; on-line presentation opens the collection to teachers, students, and the public, as well as to scholars. The size of the collection is exciting and daunting. Fortunately, the collection's search engine allows Boulean searches across all the transcripts. For example, if you are researching sharecropping, a search can quickly find (and take you to) every mention of sharecropping in every transcript. The computer's ability to quickly analyse digitized text can significantly speed the research process, allowing users to deal more effectively with the collection's massive size.

Few archives can match the Library of Congress, but some have started the process of digitizing and web-publishing. The University of Florida Oral History Programme web site offers excerpts from transcripts focusing on the Seminole Indians and the Florida activities of the Civilian Conservation Corps. Out of 200 interviews conducted on the Seminoles, the site provides seven page transcript excerpts for each of five interviews. The Oral History Office of the Sacramento Air Logistics Centre provides complete transcripts of half a dozen interviews. As archives add electronic avenues to traditional routes, access to oral memoirs will expand, encouraging the growth of the field.

Other sites use the Web differently. The Women's Centre at Virginia Technological University has created a small but fascinating site on the Black Women at Virginia Tech History Project, tracing the 1960s experiences of the university's first African American female students.

For each interview, the Centre has published yearbook photographs, family snapshots, period newspaper articles, and papers and letters written by the women at the time. A timeline places the narratives in a chronological framework. Similarly, the Hoover Dam Visitor Centre site contextualizes its transcript excerpts from interviews with workers who built the dam by providing photographs of the workers and the dam, background on the construction process, and a virtual tour of the dam today. Given the particular nature of oral memoirs, the ability to link transcripts to contextual information can be vital in helping users situate and analyse the interviews.

Both the American Memory Collection and the Black Women at Virginia Tech site help us see how technology can do more than provide increased access to oral memoirs. Using the search engine provided by American Memory—or even the "Find" function provided by Netscape or Internet Explorer—not only helps researchers to find what they are looking for; it also allows researchers to examine patterns of word usage and language formation within and across interviews.

Enabling scholars to more easily consider who uses certain words and in what situations and in what ways, the supple search tools provided by digital technology can clarify the extent to which oral memoirs are not merely data (or evidence) but also databases. And while technology can be used in this way to get inside an oral memoir—what could be called a "micro" usage—it can also be used to draw "macro" connections to broader issues and other relevant sources. The promise of the electronic environment, in this case, is that it can facilitate both the "micro" and the "macro," without threatening the integrity of the oral history archive itself.

YOU MUST BE MADE TO WEAR EARPHONES

As we move from web-published finding aids to transcripts, search engines, and contextual information, the amount of labour and the degree of technical difficulty required goes up; and, not surprisingly, the number of Web sites goes down. The next category—offering interviews in audio form over the Web—is significantly more demanding and more rare.

One Web site for audio presentation of oral memoirs is History Matters, constructed by my organization, the American Social History Project of City University of New York. History Matters offers approximately sixty audio excerpts (and related transcripts), most of them five to ten minutes in length. Unlike most sites, which are created by archives and present only their own collections, History Matters assembles material contributed by scholars nationwide and organizes it for classroom use. In addition to oral histories, the site includes other primary documents, classroom lesson plans, links to related sites, and on-line discussions of topics in history teaching. The material is organized to fit with the chronological framework of the U.S. History survey, and is searchable by theme and document type.

(History Matters is closely tied to ASHP's Who Built America? CD-ROM, which presented oral histories, archival songs and speeches, photographs, and other primary documents. CD-ROMs offer a more contained but reliable way to present digitized audio material, and some oral history archives are exploring ways to use this medium as well as the Web. A new audio CD, Stories from the Collection, created by the Columbia Oral History Research Office, provides excerpts from sixteen interviews.)

Other Web sites offering digitized audio include the

Archives of the Billy Graham Centre of Wheaton College, which documents the lives of evangelical Protestant missionaries, providing fifty full interview transcripts and ten audio excerpts.

The website of Voice & Visions: Holocaust Survivors Oral Histories provides audio excerpts of interviews with a dozen concentration camp survivors. The Journal of MultiMedia History Web site demonstrates another approach, in which audio excerpts of oral memoirs are integrated into a scholarly article. In the first issue, an article by Thomas Kriger traces the story of a 1939 strike by dairy workers of New York State and features a dozen audio excerpts, which function both as supporting footnotes and as audio illustrations.

Listening to audio excerpts on the Web or CD-ROM has its problems. On the Web, audio is often slow to download. And various sites use different software, requiring users to invest additional time downloading the software itself. Downloading the audio excerpts can be frustrating; if the software is not working right, you wind up at a screen that says "Sound File Invalid." Audio publishing on the Web is new, and there is work to be done to smooth the process. CD-ROMs tend to be easier to use, but problems are not uncommon.

That said, when the software works right, the results can be transformative. One oral memoir on History Matters is the narrative of William Brown, who recalls what it was like growing up black in the South at the turn of the century. Interviewed by Charles Hardy, he tells the story of a lynching of a local man that took place when he was five years old, and recalls how the smell of burning flesh spread for miles. His printed words are powerful.

But hearing his voice, listening to him struggle for the right words, hearing him move in his chair and slap the table in anger as he recalls his feelings of that day, adds layers of meaning to the story. The same is true for listening to the lilt and the relief of Shad Weiss' voice (on Voices and Visions) as she recalls her first sight of the American soldiers, the "beautiful, beautiful young men in uniform, on tanks," who liberated her from Auschwitz. And true as well for heating the mix of strength and pain in the voice of Mary Thomas as she recalls her efforts to fill the rifles of the striking miners fighting for their lives at Ludlow, Colorado in 1914.

The oral quality of oral memoirs is, in many ways, essential to their meaning. In conversations and in interviews, we convey meaning with pitch and tone of voice, giving cues both subtle and obvious to our listeners. Pacing and pauses, volume and inflection, pronunciation of words and sounds that are not even words—coughs, sighs, exhalations, and moans—all give nuance and depth to the choice of words themselves. Some speakers are almost singers, playing their voices as instruments. Transcription, no matter how skillful, inevitably flattens the spoken quality of oral memoirs. Reading a transcript and listening to the interview are vastly different experiences. While not the same as witnessing the original interview, listening to a recording connects us to the speaker both affectively and cognitively, facilitating empathy and deepening our understanding.

Oral historians have, of course, long discussed the relationship of audio and text, and the difficulty of providing broad access to audio recordings. For the most part, the audio record has been confined to archives, or to brief excerpts available through radio and film documentaries. Now, through the Web and CD-ROM, it is increasingly feasible to offer the audio record to millions of people, to anyone with even modest access to computer technology. Ironically, in this case technology, instead of distancing us, can help us get closer to the real human interaction at the heart of oral history.

The Web and CD-ROM not only make longer audio recordings more widely available. These media also make it easier to connect audio with text, including transcripts, scholarly commentary, and related primary documents. Comparing the written and audio versions of an oral memoir is a rich exercise in understanding the process of transcription, the kinds of choices made by transcribers and editors, and the complex relationship between written and spoken language. Juxtaposing the print and audio formats encourages deeper understanding of the memoir than utilizing either format by itself. Examining such juxtapositions has been largely limited to special sessions at scholarly events. The Journal of MultiMedia History suggests the possibility of making that experience integral to scholarly presentation. And sites such as History Matters open the experience to students and the public, offering the possibility of making it a common step in developing a clearer understanding of the nature of oral memoirs.

Everyone A Historian

Over the past three decades, oral history has lent itself to thousands of classroom projects, where students conduct interviews and develop their understandings of the historians' craft. Digital technology opens new possibilities in this area. In the past two years the software for creating Web sites has grown easier to use, and this trend will continue. It is increasingly feasible for students to construct their own oral history Web sites and share their projects with the world.

One of the most impressive student-constructed oral history sites is "1968: The Whole World Was Watching," produced by the students of South Kingston High School, with help from the Brown University Scholarly Technology Group. In the spring of 1998, guided by librarian Linda Wood and English teacher Sharon Schmid, students asked thirty local residents for their memories of the 1960s in general and 1968 in particular.

Their well-organized Web site presents these interviews in their entirety, both in transcript and audio format. The site also offers a detailed index of each interview, hotlinked to the relevant sections of the transcript. The user can easily compare the audio and textual versions of the interview and trace the process of transcription, editing, and selection. Finally, students wrote "stories" based on the interviews, summaries which assemble selected interview excerpts into cohesive and well-framed narratives.

The "1968" site also offers other valuable hypertext features. At the end of each transcript is a list of vocabulary words, such as "sit-in," or "teach-in" or "Woodstock." Clicking on the word takes the user to a glossary where the reference is explained. A timeline provides a chronological framework; some items are hotlinked to other sites.

For example, clicking on the timeline item of Lyndon Johnson's January 17, 1968 State of the Union speech takes the reader to the text of that speech, on the Web site of the LBJ Presidential Library. Together, the timeline and the glossary provide a contextual framework for understanding the memoirs.

Presenting the interviews in different formats, with contextual information, makes them more accessible and useful; it also makes the process more transparent to outside readers. And the hypertext quality of the Web makes navigation between different elements quicker and easier.

Web publishing also makes the project accessible to the whole field—and to other students. When South Kingston students discussed this project at this year's OHA convention, they highlighted the excitement of publishing their work on the Web, and the ways that having a global audience made their work feel particularly meaningful.

The number of student-created oral history archives available on the Web is slowly growing. The South Kingston site is exceptional, but other sites are interesting as well.

The Miami Valley Cultural Heritage Project, created by Miami University of Ohio professor Marjorie McClellan, offers student-generated interviews on women's history, the steel industry, and local history topics. The Behind the Veil site, created by the Centre for Documentary Studies at Duke University, offers interview transcripts generated in student projects on African American history.

Interviews at all student sites are uneven, as one would expect. But they are impressive in many ways, and point towards future possibilities for training students and sharing their research with a broader audience. If such projects flourish, they will significantly increase students' ability to contribute to the on-going construction of a new, more multivocal narrative of American history.

Many Rivers to Cross

These Web-based projects suggest ways that our use of digital technology may change our field. Utilizing the Web to publish transcripts could feed growing interest in oral memoirs and attract new users. Drawing on the multimedia capacities of the new technology to provide audio access to digitized interviews can help bring oral history back to its roots in spoken language. The constructive aspect of the Web should facilitate the visibility and value of student oral history projects, allowing oral history to better realise its democratic promise. At the same time, however, oral historians will face many challenges in the coming century, including some generated by new technology.

One limitation of oral history has been its labour-intensive quality. Generating and recording quality interviews is, in some ways, the easiest step in an oral history project. Transcribing, checking, and indexing are incredibly time-consuming and/or expensive. Many oral history projects have foundered on this rock. And the process of publishing interviews on the Web or on CD-ROM can multiply the amount of time and energy involved.

Moreover, the new technology itself can be expensive. Impressive school-based projects such as the "1968" site usually require the involvement of an outside university or cultural institution, providing funds and expertise. Voice-recognition and audio-indexing software now becoming available may soon facilitate or greatly reduce the need for transcription, and further the trend towards audio presentation. But the issues of time and expense are likely to remain, if not grow in size.

Another major challenge is the question of appropriate access. Archivists are struggling with what transcripts they should publish on the Web. Permissions for most existing collections do not address the issue of Web publishing. And archivists are justifiably concerned about losing control of their collections; once an interview is published online, the archive loses any ability to control its use. The spread of digital technology is forcing archives to rethink their role and function, and to confront difficult questions of security, protection, and accessibility.

The closely related issue of reliability confronts those who use the Web to study oral memoirs. The increasing ease of Web publishing is a double-edged sword. It encourages a free flow of information, always valuable to a democratic society. But it also highlights questions about accuracy.

Scholars have traditionally relied on archivists and publishers to serve as gatekeepers; now the gates they control are less vital.

While most oral history sites are still posted by archives, the possibility for flawed or even counterfeit sites is undeniable.

Those who use oral memoirs from the Web must carefully evaluate who created the site and their point of view. Developing critical thinking skills is important for any use of the Web.

Happily, oral historians are no stranger to the issues of subjectivity, critical thinking, and the evaluation of sources. In this sense, the challenges long confronted by oral historians may be particularly relevant for the emerging issues of the coming decades.

This highlights another problem for the field: the ongoing need for sophisticated training. Since the 1980s, American oral historians have become increasingly aware of the theoretical questions and approaches modeled by European scholars.

Raising questions about narrative, identity, and historical memory, Ronald Grele, Michael Frisch and others have deepened our thinking about the nature of oral memoirs. But many practitioners have had limited exposure to this sophisticated discussion.

The "how to do oral history" guides now published on the Web, while valuable, are in themselves not sufficient. There is a great need for training in oral history theory and methodology; and if technology spurs the growth of the field, the need will only increase.

This last point reminds us of an obvious but fundamental

troth that may be reassuring or troubling, depending on your point of view. No matter how the technology evolves, the human element will remain crucial to the future of our field. Digital technology may provide us with tools that can help us build our field, transform our representational craft, and move toward our vision of a democratic practice. Ultimately, however, the impact of the technology—and the vitality and direction of our field in the twenty-first century—will depend on us.

Chapter 4

Diversity Advances

Based on microeconomic theory, McManus states that competition and exchange in four distinct markets drive news production. Those markets are investors, advertisers, sources and consumers. Investors are part of the corporate structure, theoretically giving them the most influence. Advertisers are the next most powerful influence because they are the largest revenue producers, compelling media to act prudently so as not to antagonize advertisers with adverse editorial copy. Sources and news departments enjoy a directly reciprocal relationship, with sources depending on the media to carry their information to the public and the media depending on sources for information. In the fourth competitive market, consumers' attention is traded for information. In turn, the media seek consumer attention to sell it to advertisers.

Newsmakers operate not only within the confines of these four market exchanges but also within the constraints of organizational culture, which is governed by two sets of norms: journalism (editorial) and business.

McManus describes news as "an elaborate compromise" between the two ideals governing news production and among the four market forces acting on media corporations.

This compromise yields "the least expensive mix of content that protects the interest of sponsors and investors while garnering the largest audience advertisers will pay to reach.

"Although McManus claims the business and journalistic models are not necessarily mutually exclusive, during the frequent instances in which they do diverge, their influence is unequal: "Where investor direction is for maximum profit, market norms will dominate journalism norms when the two conflict."

In McManus' terms, economic rationalism is replacing social responsibility as the reasoning underlying media routines. Empirical tests of the model are few. An earlier survey of newspaper staffers, found that staff at chain-owned papers believed their papers stressed business principles, whereas staff at family-owned papers believed their papers stressed editorial.

A slight majority of staffers at all papers thought that when business principles were given more emphasis, the overall quality of the paper was better. The authors concluded:

Journalism purists may be dismayed that market-oriented principles have so deeply permeated the newsroom.... Newspapers are catering to the marketplace with their greater emphasis on customer-oriented journalism. But they appear to be doing this while trying to preserve the traditional journalistic values of editorial autonomy and community service so prized by news workers.

Clearly the issue of market-driven journalism remains a divisive one in the profession. The literature suggests that ownership structure and variables are not strong predictors of a market-driven orientation, whereas internal uncertainty over readership concerns and steady sources of advertising revenues are strong predictors. One source of that uncertainty may be due to the increasing fragmentation of markets as well as the need to address increasingly diverse audiences. Both sources are evident in the market area of the newspaper that forms the basis of this study.

DIVERSITY

Along with the increased emphasis on readership research to increase circulation has come the realization that certain populations have been traditionally underserved by newspapers, especially in urban areas. Circulation efforts have concentrated on wealthy readers who provide an attractive demographic to advertisers. Covering poor, inner city peoples and issues was deemed counterproductive because they were neither the paper's readers nor the advertisers' target market. Even today, the publishers of papers facing declining penetration, among them The New York Times, talk instead in terms of "market effectiveness" — providing advertisers with upscale readers. New professional programs demonstrate how papers can use minority consumer research to develop editorial and business opportunities through special sections and new outlooks.

Despite the lack of formal evidence for such a claim, observers of the Unity '94 conference noted, "A favourite line from executives was some variation of 'We want diversity not just because it's the right thing to do — but because it's the smart thing for business too.'" Pease takes the economic import of diversity even further: "Diversity is an... economic [issue]; what's at risk is nothing less than survival of newspapers as a mass medium."

To create diverse content, newspapers have sought to hire more minority journalists. A 1996 APME survey found that more than three-fourths of journalists believed the racial composition of news staffs should reflect that of society and even more (86 per cent) believed a diverse news staff resulted in better and more credible news coverage. As of 1994, 46 per cent of daily newspapers had no minority employees, and those who did were experiencing only an 80 per cent retention rate.

While the situation has improved, it has resulted in new criticism. Some in the newsroom have complained of "knee-jerk diversity" or "affirmative angst," resulting in a loss of talent in the face of political correctness. Many industry analysts believe that if the focus is on hiring rather than on content, the result is newsroom polarization rather than unity. A 1996 APME study found that 40 per cent of white journalists believed minorities were held to a lower standard, whereas 66 per cent of blacks thought minorities were held to higher standards.

In a telephone survey of minority newsroom managers, one complained that minorities are "held to a higher standard of proof." Many respondents spoke of the pressures and isolation inherent in being a "token" or "panic" hire.

It is also not clear whether increasing the number of minorities in the newsroom results in improved coverage of minorities. Hiring more minorities may not be the answer, as one critic noted: By some mysterious alchemy, the whole task of providing better coverage of minority issues seems to have become tied to the effort to bring more minority individuals into journalism. The idea seems to be that if we can just get more minority reporters into our newsrooms, they will make sure that we provide more accurate and representative coverage of minorities in society.

The few empirical studies of the issue suggest such skepticism is warranted: a review of ASNE proceedings found that editors believed increased numbers of minority hires have not resulted in improved minority coverage, and a survey of members of the National Association of Hispanic Journalists notes that the increasing diversity of communities may have one cause: "The more integrated a community, the less important a role ethnicity plays in newsgathering." The literature on diversity mirrors that of market-driven journalism: these issues remain sharply divisive in the field.

Content audits have been praised for ensuring minority representation and damned for providing meaningless quotas that ignore the real issues. For some, market-driven journalism and commitment to diversity represent savvy and informed industry moves to renew public faith in newspapers and to reconnect with alienated readers. For others, they represent the loss of all that journalism in a free speech environment has traditionally stood for: supplying the public with what it needs to know, serving as the watchdog of government, demonstrating independence from special interests, and exercising complete autonomy over news matters.

THE LOS ANGELES TIMES AND ITS CONSTITUENCY

This study was conducted at the Los Angeles Times by researchers from the Missouri School of Journalism. The Times serves a region that is among the most economically, culturally and ethnically diverse metropolitan areas in the United States. Its market area is roughly the size of the state of Ohio. The region is home to several million residents, well over 100 language communities and scores of incorporated cities. Hispanics are the most rapidly growing, non-white ethnic group, making up 31 per cent of the population in the newspaper's circulation area in 1991. That proportion could soon double.

In 1995, then-publisher Mark Willes decided to take a more aggressive marketing approach to help pull the newspaper out of the severe advertising recession it had been experiencing.

Along with this more market-driven approach, new consideration was given to enhancing diversity. This diversity was encouraged both in the newsroom in the form of hiring, in the newspaper itself in the form of attention to the diversity of content and in the publication's overall product philosophy, resulting in ethnically targeted offshoots. A new advertising campaign accompanied these internal changes. The publisher's approach was to seek to be successful on the business side in order to nourish the health of the newspaper's editorial side.

To demonstrate its concern about the issue of diversity, the newspaper appointed a diversity commission whose task it was to encourage newsroom dialogue that began in response to internal concern that certain communities were not being adequately covered by the newspaper.

The newspaper made a commitment to minority hiring, nearly doubling its minority editorial staffers. The newspaper experimented with editions and special products targeted at communities not well represented among its readership. These included a weekly tabloid, a Monday forum for community columns and letters and even a bilingual edition. Not everyone greeted these changes with approval.

Critics contended that these changes resulted in formulaic content that panders to advertisers, not readers. Controversy erupted when it was suggested that the paper was setting hiring quotas for the numbers of minorities and women. The changes have much support in an industry not known for its business acumen.

Marilyn Lee, vice president of employee relations for the newspaper, says change just makes good business sense: "If newspapers don't reflect and serve their communities, readers and-advertisers won't support them." Do such programs amount to reverse discrimination, intimating that talented white males need not apply?

Scholarship in this area is negligible. Therefore, the 35 hours of in-depth interviewing analysed for this study offer a rich understanding.

The attempt to understand attitudes newspaper editorial staffers hold toward their publisher's drive to promote diversity while increasing profits is both a rare and important glimpse at the face of the future of journalism and its practitioners.

SAMPLE AND INTERVIEW PROCEDURE

The convenience sample examined for this study consisted of 76 subjects who worked in editorial positions at the Times. The subjects were reporters, editors or photographers whose experience with the company ranged from a few years to decades.

In drawing the editorial employee sample, only employees with an active role in creating daily newspaper content were selected.

Journalists were invited to make appointments with interviewers to talk about diversity matters. Interviews averaged about one-half hour each and took place during two separate visits to the newsroom, with each visit lasting two days. Interviews were conducted fall 1998 through winter 1999.

Missouri researchers designed an interview guide. Five senior researchers from the school conducted the interviews: one African-American, one Latino, and three Caucasians. The guide was used to assure continuity during interviews conducted by the five researchers. The guide contained a set of general questions and probes relevant to the larger study's primary research objective of assessing diversity issues in the newsroom and diversity in the newspaper's content.

Respondents were asked, "What do you believe is the company's motivation in its concern about diversity issues?" The question sought to elicit responses ascribing the publisher's concern about diversity to either editorial content or market-driven issues or both.

Responses were open-ended. Respondents were candid and deliberate in their assessment, taking their time to consider and respond.

All newsroom staffers participated voluntarily in the study. The Times company encouraged participation through a series of memos that emphasized the importance of the study and the need for candid input from staffers. There was no evidence that those who volunteered felt compelled to participate.

The respondents' candor during interviews suggests that the independence of an academic team and the disclosure statement from the team's Human Subjects Review Board offered adequate assurance of confidentiality. Subsequent assessment of the interviews suggested strongly that the candid views expressed were truly those of the respondents.

The interviews were conducted at the Los Angeles Times over a three-day period. All interviews were recorded with the permission of the participants. This allowed the researchers to pay careful attention to each participant's responses while taking minimal notes. Following the interview guide, each session moved from general to specific questions.

DATA ANALYSIS PLAN

In analyzing the interview data, the researchers employed the analytic induction strategy described in Wimmer and Dominick as adapted by Stainback and Stainback. One of the researchers for this study reviewed transcripts of the taped interview data, as well as the notes of the interviewers. The researcher used this information to select themes and formulate the research questions. Cases were examined to determine the viability of the themes and research questions.

A second researcher then independently examined the interview data and interviewers' notes focusing exclusively on the market-driven versus quality journalism issues.

To ensure that all interview comments regarding the market-driven motives of diversity initiatives at the publishing company had been gathered, this second researcher listened to each of the 76 interviews without benefit of seeing the first set of transcriptions. This was done to provide fresh perspective in challenging, modifying and adding to the analysis.

The two researchers then compared their separate findings to ensure thoroughness, accuracy in transcription and validity of the theme statements.

FINDINGS AND DISCUSSION

What is the motive for the publisher's emphasis on diversity? This is the fundamental question the researchers sought to answer. The first respondent set the tone for virtually all respondents who addressed the issue, saying:

- Because they (the publishers) are not stupid.
- Bottom line.

The city is changing demographically. The Latino community is growing and growing fast. The Asian American community is growing fast. It's the future of this city and I think the paper is smart enough to realise that financially.

If the first respondent appeared to offer a seemingly one-sided, market-driven point of view toward the publisher's impetus for diversity coverage, one suggesting as does McManus that economic considerations were supplanting journalistic ones, subsequent respondents clarified the issue.

One (Respondent) said: I think there is a genuine desire to improve the coverage of our community. (The city) is changing and we have to keep up with that change. So, I think it's partly journalistic. It's also financial in that we have to bring in readers and one way to do it is to make the paper accessible to them.

Added another (Respondent): (The reason) is twofold. There is a feeling among the top editors and managers that it is the right thing to do. Diversify the workforce. I also think it's a business thing: to have a diverse workforce makes the product better at covering diverse communities.

To some extent most respondents seemed to accept both journalistic improvements and financial necessity as the twin motives for their newspaper publisher's push to enhance diversity in the newsroom and in the newspaper. None of the 21 respondents who addressed both journalistic and market-driven pressures directly mentioned anything negative about financial considerations.

This is not to say the responses were completely absent of any concern. Rather, like Respondent, the participants seemed genuinely reflective and desirous that their newspaper change to reflect the changes that were ongoing in their community:

I think (the effort to enhance diversity coverage) is market-driven, but I don't mean that in the typical, pejorative sort of way... the quick response of jadedness.

I think it's market-driven in the sense that... if you say you want to serve the community better, to do that they have to purchase the paper. I think it's just sort of a pragmatic thing.

Population is growing and changing. You have to respond somehow. So, I guess I would say it's market-driven, but I don't mean market-driven necessarily as a strictly commercial decision.

The emphasis of most respondents focused on market-driven forces as a necessary consideration in a city that is changing. Some respondents, among them Respondent, noted that the immediacy of the drive to enhance diversity was a function of the newspaper publisher's concerns that the paper reflect the community:

This is not the kind of city it once was. If we are going to grow as a newspaper, we have to reflect the differences that are out there in the world. This has proceeded with fits and starts throughout the years. I don't think it's a new concern, but now, it's coming from the top. All respondents cited both journalistic and market-driven considerations as twin reasons for the Times' executives' emphasis on diversity.

The researchers found that virtually all respondents who commented on the positive or negative nature of the philosophical changes had positive attitudes toward its effect on the Times, both as a journalistic product and as a healthy business entity.

Indeed, they seem to reflect the attitude that business health was good for journalistic health. Said Respondent #34: You know, every paper has a market they want to reach. I don't think there's anything wrong per se in picking out a group of people that you want to reach.

Respondent responded in a similar vein, saying, "Someone has to worry about increasing circulation. Reporters and editors don't really know about that." Respondent tied the ongoing changes in the circulation region with the more competitive business atmosphere in which the newspaper now operates:

Numbers attract advertisers. The city has seen a dramatic change in the major advertisers. We have lost supermarkets. We have lost department stores. We have lost all those big, full-page ads that made us a fat, rich newspaper. We have to fight for those ads now that used to just float in before. To do that, we have to have numbers. We have to have the demographics.

The journalists who responded to these issues seem to have the attitude that the change to a more market-driven philosophy on the part of the Times publisher was motivated by both journalistic and business concerns. The diversity effort was also regarded as being largely positive in terms of its effect on the newspaper, making it representative of its readership.

The journalists had concerns about becoming too focused on market-driven motivations. Most, like Respondent, drew the line at altering the editorial content for solely market-driven reasons, saying, "If you start monkeying with the content, that's where most of us are having a problem."

However, the same respondent quickly added: I've never had that happen. I've never been told 'write this story differently' (because of financial concerns)... and I don't know anyone who has (been told to do that).

Many subjects experienced difficulty with the term "market-driven journalism" because it has taken on a pejorative meaning among many journalists. Respondents were hesitant to use it, particularly in reference to the paper for which they worked.

Yet respondents believed that their paper should be more responsive to present and prospective readers. In this sense, they embraced the use of the term "market-driven journalism" and believe it reflects a commitment to serve the changing and diverse community of readers in their market area. What emerges from the data, then, may be recognition that in today's marketplace, one increasingly competitive for audience attention, both traditional journalistic norms and business norms form a necessary baseline.

Unlike McManus, who often places these two in competition, the respondents in this study viewed the inherent tension between these two sets of norms as a healthy relationship, provided the tension remained within bounds. These results confirm those of Underwood and Stamm who found that reporters believed an emphasis on market principles provided a healthy environment for focusing on the content of the newspaper, provided those market principles did not override journalistic ones.

Other studies have found that editors welcome more interaction between the editorial and business sides of newspapers.

The comment by one respondent that reporters and editors do not know about issues such as increasing circulation may be something of an anachronism. Reporters and editors want to know more about their audience members and how best to serve them not as a "selling out" of the traditional norms of journalism, but as an expansion of their traditional role to include market considerations and demographic changes as well.

Certainly the field-based observations from this study confirm the quantitative ones of Beam, namely that newspapers respond more to uncertainty in the journalism environment and the resulting internal uncertainty than they do to deterministic microeconomic market forces, such as McManus suggests.

This study is part of a growing body of literature that suggests McManus' model may not be sufficient to explain the dynamics that take place when the need for the paper to thrive as a business is co-mingled with the traditional public watchdog and social conscience roles of journalism.

Economic pressures in the broadcast industry, which served as the basis for McManus' work, are more severe and may be more determinative of the pressures and conflict experienced in broadcast news.

All of the journalists who commented on the journalistic versus market-driven concerns of their publisher's goal of enhancing diversity in coverage and representation at the newspaper agreed that both motives were in effect and that diversity would encourage circulation growth and financial health of the newspaper.

These expressed opinions can be seen either as the genuine beliefs of a generation of journalists unencumbered by the need to hold a traditional ideology or the guarded statements of employees concerned about holding their jobs. There is evidence to support both possibilities.

By embracing both social and economic goals as being attainable through the adoption of a diversity strategy, the respondents may be manifesting one of two cognitive strategies first identified by John E.

Bowes and Keith R. Stamm in the growing literature of public relations. Bowes and Stamm referred to these cognitive strategies as hedging and wedging. People are said to hedge when they simultaneously hold two seemingly conflicting beliefs; they wedge when they choose to hold one belief and reject the other.

One way of explaining our respondents' belief that both traditional journalistic goals and market realities argue for a policy of diversity is to say that the respondents were hedging. Fueling this possibility is the fact that the newspaper in question recently suffered permanent personnel cutbacks numbering in the hundreds in the wake of a persistent decline in advertising revenue. Threats of losing one's job can be strong motivation to embrace acceptable attitudes about a policy change when one has little choice anyway.

There is a more positive way of interpreting the respondents' expressed attitudes. Their region is indeed changing, as is the nation as a whole. As several respondents stated outright or inferred, Hispanic and Asian minority groups would soon combine to form, along with African Americans, the region's majority population. Respondents believe that if the newspaper's publisher overlooked this fact, the paper's journalistic mission and credibility would suffer and its circulation would decline.

Whereas the publisher may be marketing the newspaper as a business, the respondents may see this as an opportunity to market the newspaper as a journalistic product. The respondents are either hedging well, or they do not believe that journalistic considerations have been sacrificed to those of business. Rather, they perceive a healthy tension and an expansion of roles have followed in the wake of the publisher's enhanced diversity effort.

Will a more market-driven orientation on the part of journalists affect the integrity of their work? Is it possible that journalists are so imbued with the ethos of their chosen profession that even attempts to co-mingle "church and state" will fail? Can the newspaper thrive as a business and simultaneously fulfill its mission to provide a fresher sense of social responsibility to its newly targeted market? Gans noted that, journalists' beliefs notwithstanding, he believed journalists hold "enduring values," a cluster of eight attributes he said are "... sometimes unfairly belittled as `motherhood values.'"

These "enduring values" include, among others, responsible capitalism, a belief that business people will fairly compete for both profits and social well-being. It is exactly this kind of approach to market incentives the authors see reflected in the responses of the journalists surveyed. One journalist-respondent summarized the issue as seen by the authors in the following manner. The response is worthy of quoting in full:

The history of journalism is a tension between the idealism of the profession and the people who have worked in it... and the fact that we are a moneymaking operation. That's always driven what the newspaper is. For example, even the whole idea of objectivity was not commonly seen in American journalism at the turn of the century. The idea that a newspaper could be an objective source of information that citizens could rely on was itself a marketing tool used to build up circulation after years of Yellow Journalism and all that. So, I think there's a dialectic going on here.

On the one hand, here there's a huge market that the newspaper has a potential (to reach). The newspaper knows that it has to respond to that for its own survival. Miami realized long ago that it was becoming a Cuban town. (We) are realizing that, too. At the same time, there are a lot of people here who realise that it is the right thing to do anyway. That it's more fair, more open... because those are values with which Americans were brought up. That was what makes us a good country, that's why we should be proud to be American. We open our arms to everybody. It is both a moral and an economic issue here.

Finally, it is premature to assert that promoting diversity in the editorial offices and pages of a newspaper necessarily has a positive impact on circulation. Using the experience of the Los Angeles Times, however, there is reason to believe increased diversity among newspapers generally may result in a rise in circulation. The Los Angeles Times suffered circulation declines from 1990 to 1995 that left the daily edition with a circulation of 1,013,000. By April 2000, daily circulation had risen to 1,098,350, an increase of 85,350.

There is no certainty that this 8.5 per cent increase was not influenced by other factors, such as an increase in circulation-area population or the economic boom of the past several years. Still, that this increase occurs in tandem with the institution of the Times' diversity effort offers reason for optimism as well as an avenue for additional investigation. The researchers involved in this study are presently expanding their efforts to study the impact of diversity on the LA Times. These efforts will entail new surveys in the newsroom and among the newspaper's readership. As demographic changes sweep over society and economic changes ripple through the newspaper industry, additional study will be of value at newspapers nationwide.

Chapter 5

Management and Journalist Perceptions

Less than a decade ago, there was a growing concern among corporate executives, scholars, and even many editors about the future of the newspaper industry. Newspapers faced stiff challenges on every horizon: circulation was stagnant, and a smaller percentage of the public was reading newspapers than at any time in the past half-century; the Internet was competing for the populace's time and advertisers' money; the costs of doing business were rising and unpredictable; and, for public companies, profit pressures were increasing as corporate managers sought to maintain control over their companies amidst waves of hostile buyouts and takeovers. The message to those leading the industry was clear: change or fall victim to the forces redefining your environment.

There were also rumblings within the industry for change. Some influential editors and journalists became outspoken critics of how newspapers had lost sight of their public service mission and lost touch with their communities. These critiques often focused on the insular nature of journalism, emphasizing that journalists are "insider-oriented" elitists. This inner directedness could be understood in at least two ways: first, journalists tended to assess the value of their work in relation to how it is viewed by other journalists, not the public; second, working close to politicians and other powerful sources resulted in reporting more focused on power struggles and personal political battles than the issues that affect the daily lives of average citizens. Some editors - buoyed by support from scholars, a small body of research, and philanthropic organizations - became convinced that if journalists were able to get closer to readers, reconnect with their democratic mission, and begin framing stories from the centre of their communities, then newspapers would reclaim their relevance.

It is within this framework that newspaper executives - addressing both internal and external issues - re-evaluated the goals and practices of the industry and set out to put it back on course. In 1994, the American Society of Newspaper Editors created a Change Committee, a group of editors given a 5-year period to develop and experiment with initiatives that would ensure the long-term viability of the industry. Founded on the heels of a recession that had lingered since the late 1980s and resulted in smaller newsroom staffs and budgets, the committee focused its attention on exploring ways to:

- Reorganize newsrooms for better efficiency
- Realign journalists' values more closely with those of readers and citizens.

Change initiatives emerged that attempted to transform the culture of the newsroom, making it more externally focused on markets and readers, while internally changing the nature of work by abandoning the century-old beat system of news coverage and replacing it with collaborative teams. "Change" became the mantra of many leading editors and executives, and the new, restructured approach to producing newspapers was labeled "strategic," "reader-driven," or "market-driven" journalism. Newsroom managers, recognizing that they lacked the organizational background to plan, execute, and monitor fundamental change, increasingly looked to outside consultants to guide their efforts and alleviate employee resistance. The process of change, seldom easy in any organization, became a target of skepticism for journalists, who worried that initiatives jeopardized core journalism values and credibility.

Organizational development (OD) is the study of how

organizations evolve, learn, and adapt. This lino of inquiry is well suited, although it lias been rarely used, to explore and understand the process of change in the newspaper industry. The research reported in this monograph uses OD theory as a framework for assessing the perceptions and attitudes that top newsroom managers and rank-and-file journalists have about initiatives aimed at changing the newsroom culture. This study also explores the impact of two newer, largely unstudied variables that have been a part of change initiatives - newsroom restucturing and the reader-oriented redefinition of news values - to better understand how journalists perceive change and its impact.

Organizational development scholarship is rooted in social psychology and management. OD scholars concede that because organizations vary in size and resources and have different goals, OD research has generally focused on one organization at a time. Argyris acknowledges that this situation-by-situation approach, which relies on on-site observations, in-depth interviews, and situation-specific variables, makes the task of generalizing results and theory building more difficult.

This study takes a different approach than most OD research and attempts to advance OD theory building and the practical understanding of ongoing newspaper change by surveying a relatively large probability sample of rank-and-file journalists and a census of top newsroom managers from 17 newspapers most experienced in ASNE-sanctioned change initiatives. The logic of the approach is that journalists working at newspapers that have experimented with similar change initiatives create a population of cohorts who have clear perceptions regarding change based on their common experiences. This commonality should permit valid research that extends beyond single organizations and site-specific variables, producing results that can benefit newsrooms embarking on change initiatives. Accordingly, this study extends newspaper change research by addressing the problem differently, both in terms of its theoretical framework and methodological design.

The extent to which change initiatives can be tied to economics is uncertain. By 2001, a recessionary national economy led the nation's largest public newspaper companies to downsize their workforces between 5 and 10% to maintain profit levels attractive to investors. However, the late 1990s, a period of a strong economy and fast and furious change, saw the same high profits that had characterized the industry a decade earlier. Publicly owned companies, which account for nearly half the nation's daily circulation, returned an average profit of 20.7% in 1998 and 22.2% in 1999. Advertising revenue was also at record levels, reaching $46.3 billion in 1999, the eighth consecutive year of record highs, casting doubt on prognosticators who only a half-decade earlier had predicted the Internet would spell doom for newspapers.

Following the lead of the Change Committee and continuing today under the rubric of change, newsrooms are being reorganized, news values are being redefined, and the nature of newspaper journalism work is changing. The seriousness of prominent editors leading this effort can be understood by their numerous references to the need to "blow up" the newsroom and its associated routines and values; another editor, using a less violent metaphor, claims his goal for change is "cultural transformation". However, a large body of organizational development scholarship indicates that changing an organization's culture (its values and beliefs and form and function of work that supports them) is not easily accomplished, and understanding the need for change is not often enough to convince employees, and even members of management, to accept change.

CHANGING ORGANIZATIONAL STRUCTURES

Following a national manufacturing trend, by the mid-1990s, newspaper managers began disassembling the assembly line, creating instead self-contained work teams. The team-based structure flattened the traditional top-down manufacturing hierarchy, grouping editors and reporters into 6- to 10-member teams responsible for reporting, writing, editing, and packaging news in their coverage areas.

The most controversial changes have come in those newsrooms using cross-departmental teams section development teams at The Los Angeles Times include people from advertising, classified, editorial, marketing, and research. Former Times Publisher Mark Willes said these teams are necessary to create a stronger marketing consciousness at the newspaper. Journalists and scholars have questioned whether cross-departmental teams compromise the traditional "wall" between the news and business sides of news organizations.

This controversy was fueled in October 1999 whon the Times created a special Sunday magazine promoting the new downtown Staples Centre. Written by journalists, the section garnered nearly $2 million in advertising, which the paper split with the Staples Centre. Perhaps more indicative of the direction the industry is heading is that 63% of the editors responding to a 1999 Editor & Publisher survey agreed that there should be more cooperation between news departments and business/marketing departments, while 29% disagreed. Clearly, editors are becoming more active in marketing. A 1998 study found that 57% of the 192 newspapers surveyed have marketing teams that include editorial members.

A less controversial change that none the less has had an impact on the nature of newspaper work has been the reorganization from a beat system to a team system of news coverage. Some of the reorganization plans of newspapers in this study are described briefly. After a year of planning, the Si. Louis Post-Dispatch scrapped the beat system in 1999 for topic-driven teams. Staff had to reapply for jobs, 19 general assignment positions were redefined in the team structure, and editors became team leaders. Each team created a mission statement and set its goals. At The State, the news and features desks were abolished to facilitate a team structure. The paper also created an "office of the managing editor," which at any given time could be staffed by one of five different people. At many newspapers, changes in newsroom structure have brought with them new job titles that many news veterans would not recognize, including duty officer, maestro, circle editor, news manager of public life, and change facilitator.

At the Grand Forks (N.D.) Herald, editor Mike Jacobs said the change to reporting teams was initially resisted. He learned that change requires people in leadership positions who believe in change and are committed to executing it. To help staffers work through their problems with change initiatives, Jacobs brought in a marriage counselor to serve as "a listening post" between staff and upper management.

The Dayton (Ohio) Daily News adopted a "newsroom without walls" concept. Conceived by an architect, the reorganization eliminated departments and placed newsroom staff in gathering and producing teams. Managing editor Steven Sidlo said the model is "a system that breaches our walls of tradition, encouraging a more effective, fluid use of our resources".

In Portland, The Oregonian's "warp-speed nine" initiative prompted managing editor Peter Bhatia to joke "Reorganization 'R' Us." More than 80 jobs were posted in the newsroom as open assignments. Nearly every writer, regardless of experience or seniority, had to reapply. The final result was 10 teams, with a flattened newsroom hierarchy that saw former editors become team leaders. Bhatia, aware that the flattened hierarchy offers fewer career advancement opportunities, said, "The satisfaction that people will get from this system is in the quality of their work and what they put in the paper as compared to a traditional careerpath".

Flattened newsroom hierarchies have resulted in some editors returning to the reporting ranks. In Tacoma, Wash., editor David Zeeck's reorganization of The News Tribune resulted in 34% of his staff changing jobs, and 23% of the editors becoming reporters. At the Wichita (Kan.) Eagle, the copy desk was eliminated in 1995 and copy editors were assigned to reporting teams. Former managing editor Janet Weaver said "blowing up the copy desk" resulted in eight more staff reporters. Weaver said the reorganization took the Eagle from a six-tiered hierarchy to just three tiers: editor, managing editor, and three equal teams - content, organization, and presentation. Stepp writes the goal behind eliminating the editors at many papers was not only to cut payroll, but to simplify chains of command and reduce the number of news managers resistant to change.

CHANGING NEWS VALUES

Aware that their readership is stagnant and influence declining, newspaper managers and journalists have been reexamining their news values. This introspection has manifested itself in several ways: an increased marketing consciousness, a desire for more credibility, the involvement of readers in deciding news and how it should be reported, and a sense the media are failing to live up to their historic democratic role of informing people of issues important to successful governance.

American Journalism Review, in a 2000 cover story titled "Reader Friendly, "reported that the emerging culture of restructured newsrooms around the country is characterized by:

- Enthroning readers as the "invisible giants," elevating them to near equal partners in decision making;
- Erring on the side of caution rather than aggressiveness, rejecting stories that might offend readers as lacking compassion or sensitivity;
- Promoting cooperation with everyone, from City Hall to the paper's advertising departments.

The long-time taboo of "pandering" to readers has been swept away by an attempt to reverse what some editors have called a "disconnection" between newspapers and the public. Following a series of meetings called the Journalism Values Institute in which 30 editors from around the country debated the problems of the industry, Peck wrote, "The essence of these evaluations comes down to this: American journalists continue to say they practice good journalism in the public's interest - but the public doesn't believe we deliver". Editors left the meetings agreeing that newspaper content includes too much gossip, not enough substance, bias but no balance, and a preoccupation with conflict and few solutions. The Oregonian's Bhatia summed up the problems: "Our comfort zones are painting the world in black and white. And our comfort zones are seeing the traditional good side and evil side of whatever issue it might bo. We've got to blow that up".

Many of the editors most active in the ASNE Change Committee borrowed ideas from and adopted the language of civic (or public) journalism. Civic journalism broadens the concept of journalistic social responsibility into a more active role, with the goal of journalism becoming a catalyst for the revival of civic life by promoting citizen engagement and dialogue. Merritt insists the practice of civic journalism requires journalists to abandon several common and traditional practices, including: valuing conflict as the primary narrative device, framing issues at extremes, maintaining an adversarial role with institutions, treating the readers as audiences rather than participants, and insisting that journalism credibility arises from detachment.

Stopp (2000) wrote that a cross-country tour of newsrooms left him impressed by how many newsrooms were using the language and techniques of civic journalism. he notes that when he raised this issue many editors and journalists dismissed it, suggesting civic journalism is a project-driven formula that they don't understand. Stepp, however, concluded: "Perhaps the resistance to the civic journalism label simply underlines how much some of the techniques have seeped into the newsroom groundwater".

CHANGING THE NEWSROOM CULTURE

Nearly all editors who have involved their newsrooms in change initiatives have suggested the key to making change work is to create a new culture. Weaver said changing the newsroom culture requires "getting the staff to think of the whole paper, as opposed to their own story or small piece they contributed." She said that reporters need to be trained to work in a new system, as many lack the editing, headline writing, and design skills required in the team structure. Managers, too, have more pressure, as the staff is often competing for the attention of fewer bosses. And, because of the changing nature of journalism work, job performance evaluations need revision to reflect the standards and goals of a new system. She admits that "newsroom stars" under the old system often fool stifled by the team structure. Teams require a "new breed" of journalist with different personality traits and skills than the "lone wolf" who worked well alone and often produced breakthrough stories.

Sue Deans, editor of The Sun News, said for change initiatives to work staff members need to understand that change is a constant; it will not go away after a short time or a few experiments. The two "core issues" of change are continuous product improvement, and keeping aware of what readers want and the market demands. She said changing the newsroom culture requires emphasizing "passion" for the newspaper business and:

- Impressing on people who do not want change that they must change or leave;
- Eliminating "silo" thinking by creating cross-departmental approaches to work and evaluating work quality;
- Staying focused on strategy and on the market.

Campbell, who resigned in April 2000 as Si. Louis Post-Dispatch editor after a stormy 3 1/2 years, had embarked on an ambitious attempt at "cultural transformation" at the paper. he claims the existing newsroom "judgmental culture" is part of the problem with American journalism, and he attempted to change the Post-Dispatch's culture from one based on "judgmentalism" to one based on "collaboration."

By the millennium, the ideas for change that began in a couple dozen newsrooms in the mid-1990s were becoming the industry norm. Stepp wrote:

"From civic journalism to New Directions for News, from credibility reforms to the Committee of Concerned Journalists, a host of foundations, trade groups and other forces have been pouring millions of dollars into attempts to remodel how journalists think and act".

IMPACT OF CHANGE ON MORALE

Change initiatives have required journalists to rethink

some fundamental principles of their work: their sense of news, audience, organization, and even the purpose of journalism. Signs of eroding morale were present before change began in the mid-1990s, and morale problems in relation to change initiatives have been reported in trade journals.

Columbia Journalism Review, in a 2001 cover story, reported that its national survey found 84% of the responding journalists indicate that low morale is widespread in their newsrooms.

This finding is supported by a 2001 ASNE study that found 54% of the respondents saying they weren't sure if they would remain in the newspaper business. Among the reasons for low morale: ineffective leadership, management and editors who don't listen, not enough opportunity to be creative, and increasing budget pressures that arise from the drive to maintain high profits.

Underwood wrote that the mid-1990s layoffs and a widespread belief that management used downsizing as a way of getting rid of unhappy journalists - many of whom were aggressive, good journalists in a traditional sense - have left "a deep and growing cultural divide between newsroom managers and their reporters". Many veteran reporters think that change initiatives - and associated reader-driven, marketing consciousness - made newspapers look needlessly desperate in the late 1990s when newspaper companies were posting record profits.

Stepp wrote that changes in management goals may mark a historic period of journalism. Journalists always considered themselves bestowed by the First Amendment with special status, feeling they were public servants who value social responsibility; however, he writes, "You feel it in virtually every newsroom, the sag, the deflation, the suspicion that a special way of life is teetering".

The frustration is not limited to rank-and-file, but includes editors who face the challenge of leading changes they may not understand or support. Stepp (2000) wrote that editors are no longer seen by their staffs as in control of the newsroom, as publishers look for top editors who understand "a different approach" based on what the market needs and the reader wants.

This leaves editors less time to focus on journalism and interact with their staffs, further widening the gulf between managers leading change and rank-and-file.

The Newspaper Association of America surveyed more than 2,600 newspaper journalists who left their jobs in the mid-1990s, trying to find the factors that caused journalists to leave the profession.

The NAA found, beyond the expected reasons of stress and long hours, that people left newspapers because of low morale, lack of advancement, and perceived inequities in pay and promotions. The authors conclude all of these reasons are issues that management can control.

ORGANIZATIONAL NEWSPAPER RESEARCH

In the past half-decade, a line of organizational newspaper research has looked at the impact of public ownership (companies that publicly trade stocks) on corporate goals and identifying the level of newspapers' market orientation.

This section reviews three areas of research that were relevant to the conception of this study: early organizational studies, the recent profit and market-orientation research, and the few attempts in recent years to study the process of managing change in the nation's newsrooms.

Breed and Argyris were pioneers in newspaper industry organizational research. Breed, a sociologist, suggested that role theory provides a model that explains the organizational relationships in newsrooms he asserted that all newspapers, whether management and journalists admit it or not, operate under the influence of a publisher policy.

The publisher, as a representative of ownership, has the authority to set and enforce the policy. Journalists learn the policy, which is often covert because it betrays journalistic values, through experience and observation. The social norms and conventions of the newsroom teach journalists how and when to conform or deviate from the policy. Breed concluded: Thus the cultural patterns of the newsroom produce results insufficient for wider democratic needs. Any important change toward a more 'free and responsible press' must stem from the various pressures on the publisher, who epitomizes the policy making and coordinating role.

Argyris, an organizational development scholar, studied one of the nation's largest newspapers for 3 1/2 years, exploring the paper's internal dynamics and how they related to problems of press credibility. He also provided the paper an organizational development programme and advised during its implementation.

In his book, Behind the Front Page, he concluded the internal system at the paper helped create policy clashes, one-upmanship among reporters, and fear of authoritarian bosses. he found the greatest resistance to new ideas came from mid-level editors and managers, who, despite acknowledging the need to change, would not participate in organizational efforts at change.

Discussing his frustration about why the problems his systems analysis identified were not addressed, he wrote:

The reason is not (italics Argyris) a lack of motivation to solve them on the part of top management. The problems will not be solved because the individuals and groups behave in ways that create a living system which teaches them (they become acculturated) to be hard of hearing, to be unable and unwilling to take action on threatening issues.

Gassaway used observation and survey to study the social construction of a journalist's reality. He found news judgment decisions were most often the result of "preordained news," determined by coverage beats and how editors decide to use their resources.

Editors and reporters struggle for control of information because they often disagree on what should be communicated to the public. Editors' authority is derived from organizational hierarchies, but reporters can deny editors' authority by controlling information obtained in iiewsgathoriiig. Gassaway concluded editors 'and reporters negotiate for control to prevent confrontations and reduce resorting to power. Jeffers and Lewis studied organizational communication at a midsized newspaper and found rank-and-file journalists perceived their communication with their immediate supervisor and publisher as poor.

They suggested the organizational climate could be improved by increasing the amount and frequency of communication at all levels. The authors concluded their study supported the findings of Pincuss, Knipp, and Rayfield, who found rank-and-file employees' communication relationship with their immediate supervisor is a predictor of job satisfaction; however, employees' sense of having meaningful communication with top-level managers was as strong a predictor of satisfaction as immediate-supervisor communication.

In the mid-1990s, several scholars began to assess organizational structure and goals, often considering profit motive and its impact on normative journalism values. Deniers integrated organizational and economic theory in his book, The Menace of the Corporate Newspaper: Fact or Fiction?, to define the corporate newspaper, its characteristics, and organizational dynamics. Demers asserted that corporate newspapers are complex bureaucracies controlled by trained managers, not owners.

These managers are best understood as innovative professionals or "technocrats" who are morn interested in professional, organizational, and technical goals than profit goals. Demers juxtaposed the roles of managers to those of owners, defining the latter as "capitalists" most interested in returns on their investments.

In the 20th century, managers replaced owners as the driving force; in corporations because llie organizations had become complex bureaucracies that required professional management. Further aiding the transition was the death of the original owners, whose influence was dispersed over time and divided among heirs.

Deniers wrote the result is that corporate newspapers are efficiently managed and structured to maximize profits, but they place less emphasis on profit than non-corporate newspapers, which tend to be family-owned, less bureaucratic organizations.

In two studies, his results indicate that newspapers become more rigorous editorially as they become larger, more complex organizations.

In studies that both support and refute Deniers' work, Beam studied the conditions that influence newspapers' market orientation and whether market orientation affects content. To define and measure market orientation, Beam explored the extent that newspapers:

- Have one or more departments active in understanding customer needs and the factors affecting the needs,
- Share this information across departments,
- Have various departments engaged in meeting select customer needs.

He found that ownership by a large group is the most important predictor of a newspaper's market orientation, suggesting the corporate parent may not be involved in specific content decisions but is more likely to require certain general processes be followed in making content decisions. He concluded that traditional journalistic values are important at market-oriented papers, and while more market-oriented newsrooms are more committed to special interest and visual content, they are not less committed to traditional content, including public affairs.

Beam (2000) has also found that newspapers that are part of privately owned companies are more market oriented than those of public companies. Using his survey data, Beam (2001) then chose 10 newspapers for a content analysis - 5 papers with strong market orientation and 5 papers with weak market orientation.

He found the majority of items on page one of both orientations was "public sphere" content, which includes government affairs; however, the percentage of public sphere items on page one for weak market orientation newspapers was significantly higher (65.6%) than for strong market orientation papers (54.9%). Overall, Beam analysed the display pages (section front or topic lead page) and found papers with strong market orientation have proportionately more items devoted to private life, coping, and sports, while proportionately fewer items about government and public life.

Martin compared profits earned by 15 public newspaper companies to profits of publishing companies and yields from corporate and government bonds over an 11-year period. For the entire period, newspaper profits averaged 90% higher than publishing companies, 78% higher than government bond yields, and 54% higher than interest payments from corporate bonds.

Using a scale created by an economist that labels profits 50% above those of comparable measures as "excessive," Martin found that in 23 of 33 annual comparative indices (70%) the newspaper companies in the sample earned excessive profits.

In some cases, these excessive comparative profits occurred in the early 1990s during what an analyst called "the biggest advertising recession since World War II".

After newspapers embarked on broad, and in some cases bold, change initiatives in the 1990s, a few researchers began to study these initiatives through the lens of organizational development. Gentry observed while a small California daily embarked on several change initiatives aimed at better aligning its content with community interests. The year-long efforts, orchestrated by New Directions for News, led Gentry to conclude the following elements were essential for successful newspaper organizational change:

- Strong leadership;
- Management communication about: why change is needed, management's vision, and new performance standards;
- Staff involvement in the change process;
- Management rewarding correct behaviour and extinguishing improper behaviour;
- Anticipating problems of acceptance and implementation.

Working a few years later with the American Press Institute, Gentry (1996) developed a model he calls "A Roadmap for Change" that added several variables, including:

- Prechange analysis of the current culture to determine the extent and types of changes needed;
- Use of mission statements to clarify core values for employees;
- Flexible management strategies and putting people in the proper roles to execute them;
- Enabling structures, such as job training;
- Creating visible symbols of the new culture.

Testing the model, Gentry surveyed management and rank-and-file at six newspapers and found management thought it was doing a better job than the staff thought it was doing on all 10 elements of change the study addressed.

In a longitudinal case study, Gade and Perry measured newsroom employees' perceptions of change initiatives. Over 4 years, Campbell, known as an industry innovator, had some success making news values more reader driven, but the 1999 reorganization of newsroom coverage from beats to teams left much of the staff confused about their roles and job responsibilities. Campbell's embrace of public journalism did not resonate with a majority of the staff. Morale declined and was lowest among respondents with management duties. Respondents consistently indicated they wern open minded toward change until after reorganization, which apparently was the last straw in a series of changes that underscored Campbell's tenure as editor. Over the course of the study, respondents consistently indicated that they failed to see how change initiatives contributed to better journalism.

At a time when cross-departmental teams were still new to the industry, Sylvie studied how department heads of news, advertising, and circulation perceived their identity and ability to cooperate with each other. News managers named advertising as the most difficult department, while the advertising directors named the news editors as least cooperative. Newsroom managers woro the only dupurlmimt heads nol Io rank lhcir respective department's concerns as most important, ranking circulation success the most important. News editors showed a significantly greater tendency to say more cooperation between departments is needed. Sylvie concluded the news managers exhibit a "surprising sensitivity" to market-oriented concepts, which gives credibility to journalists' anecdotal claims that the newspaper industry is moving toward a greater market orientation.

A meager amount of research exists on newspaper team performance. Russial studied changes in health and science content at The Oregonian after that paper created a Health and Science team. he found that the team produced more coverage that received better play (Al or Metro section front) than before the team was created. Russial suggested that although his study did not measure coverage quality, the creation of a team-based system represents a realignment in the use of newsroom resources that may have important consequences on news content.

Neuzil, Hansen, and Ward surveyed Minneapolis Star Tribune and St. Paul Pioneer Press journalists working in teams and found most thought they had less authority and less success getting story ideas in the paper than before teams were created. Those who thought they had less authority also said they were unsure of the chain of command, worked on larger teams, and wore reporters more than editors. The researchers concluded if agoal ofteam work was to "empower" journalists by granting them more autonomy to be innovative, this goal was not being met.

In sum, trade journals and a developing body of research provide evidence that newspapers are changing in some fundamental ways: flattening organizational structures, replacing traditional beats with teams, revising job descriptions and required skills, rethinking organizational values, and redefining news judgment.

USING ORGANIZATIONAL THEORY TO MAKE SENSE OF CHANGE

The study of "organizations" is a relatively new

discipline. Drucker wrote that "no one in the United States - or anyplace else - talked of Organizations' until after World War?" Drucker said that the modern idea of an organization - as a purposely designed and specialized entity that is defined by its task and is distinct from society's other institutions - emerged in the second half of the 20th century with what he calls the "management revolution." Initial theoretical assumptions of this revolution were largely shaped by turn-of-the-century scholars:

Taylor's views on "scientific management" and Weber's ideas on the rational and specialized bureaucracy. This organizational model is characterized by a hierarchical division of labour where managers are the "thinkers" and laborers are the "doers". Employees develop highly specialized skills that increase performance and productivity, while management's job is to ensure the conditions exist for the organizational "machine" to run smoothly.

Recognizing that organizations must evolve and adapt to survive in changing environments, Lewin suggested a "natural" (as opposed to mechanical) metaphor to explain organizational dynamics; change, he wrote, can be best understood and managed through a process of "unfreeze, change, refreeze." These early attempts to understand organizations and their dynamics prepared the intellectual soil for the growth of organizational development, which attracted the interest of U.S. scholars and corporate managers in the last quarter of the 20th century as the changing global marketplace threatened U.S. dominance.

Although Taylor's and Weber's (and to a lesser extent Lewin's) ideas are considered outdated, they have proven resilient and modest adaptations of them are still very much alive in both theory and practice. Bergquist wrote that most organizational theorists have conceived organizations as pendulum-like mechanisms, which value "simplicity in motion" and homeostasis. When organizations experience turbulent times, they tend to seek equilibrium by returning to their previous form and function. However, the structured and predictable environment in which U.S. companies once thrived no longer exists, and Bergquist contends a more accurate metaphor in the postmodern world is that of the organization as a liquid, "poised on the edge of order and chaos".

The liquid system, he wrote, contains at the same time both elements of stability and change, especially along the edges, or shifting boundaries. In an organizational sense, it is the shifting boundaries that offer potential for understanding the change process. It is these places on the "edge" where innovation occurs and where organizational traits such as mission, communication, and leadership become integral to success.

In perhaps the seminal book on organizational change and development, Kanter wrote American companies that value "innovation" are better placed to use their employees' creative capacities and stay ahead in changing environments. Interviews with 65 corporate executives led Kanter to conclude the innovative companies are integrated (my italics); they grant power to individuals to encourage fresh thinking and create opportunities for new ideas to cross organizational boundaries.

She juxtaposed integrated companies with "segmented" companies, which are characterized by an "ovorspecification" of resources and consider themselves successful when every segment works well independently, without much need for communication. Segmented companies, Kanter wrote, seek stasis, because they are constantly looking to the past to define the future; accordingly, habits and routines that maintain the course are valued.

Kanter identified five major building blocks in change initiatives that increase the company's capacity to meet new challenges:

- Departures from tradition: activities or ideas that require the organization to think and behave in new ways.
- Crisis or galvanizing event: a critical event that cannot be solved by traditional means. This allows a non-traditional idea to be pushed forward.

- Strategic decisions: the opportunity for management to create a vision by articulating a deliberate and conscious direction.
- Individual "prime movers": people who push the innovative strategy through the organization by communicating strategic decisions and manipulating the symbols of the organizational culture toward the direction of change.
- Action vehicles: mechanisms that allow new action. These include training programs, successful results for people using new practices, new organizational rewards that support new practices, and ongoing messages of the benefits experienced by individuals using the now practices.

Kanter wrote that managers need three new sets of skills to operate effectively in integrated, innovative environments: "power skills" used to persuade others to invest in new initiatives; ability to manage problems associated with teams and greater employee participation; and understanding of how organizational change is designed and constructed. She concluded that "the art and architecture of change" requires managers to abandon their reliance on traditional analytical tools, which measure what already exists or has occurred.

"Change efforts have to mobilize people around what is not yet known, not yet experienced... they require a leap of faith that cannot be eliminated by presentation of all the forecasts, figures, and advance guarantees that can be accumulated". Accordingly, the paradox of managing changes, she wrote, is "there needs to be a plan, and the plan has to acknowledge that it will be departed from".

Most attempts at organizational development involve efforts to transform an organization's culture. Schneider, Brief, and Guzzo wrote that the values and beliefs that are the foundation of an organization's culture can be changed by focusing on the tangible things - such as practices, policies, and procedures - that define daily life in the organization. It is these tangible phenomena that comprise an organization's climate, and for real cultural change to occur, management must change the climate in which the employees exist. The authors contend that many efforts at cultural change are focused on "macro" issues such as values and beliefs, while overlooking the more tangible issues that create the organizational climate in which employees experience everyday life. They wrote: "Sustainable organizational change is most assured when both the climate - what the organization's members experience - and the culture - what the members believe the organization values - change".

Successful companies have increasingly educated workforces, and they are creating cultures that are more innovative and flexible. The new, desired culture is one in which power and accountability are shared between managers and employees in a manner that allows companies to respond quickly to challenges and opportunities.

The goal of these efforts is to unleash and channel the power of employees' knowledge in an organizational "culture of contribution." Fisher acknowledges that this is a major cultural shift for most U.S. companies because - unlike the Japanese, whose collective society adapted easily to a team-building, egalitarian corporate model - "America's professional workers value their individualism and often express it in counterproductive ways".

Corporate America also clings to some values that work against creating a culture of contribution; most prominent among these, Fisher wrote, is the corporate view on job attachment. Workers are expected to accept such surprises as downsizing, job reclassification, or relocation with quiet stoicism, which contradicts companies' claims they are striving to empower employees as co-partners with management.

Fisher contends that U.S. managers need to be aware that there is no single ideal corporate culture; rather, corporate culture is better understood as a combination of macro and micro cultures. Many senior managers claim to embrace a culture of contribution, but Fisher contends that few have ideas about how to put a programme or process in place to let the transformation occur. On the other hand, the changing nature of professional work, driven by new technology, has organizations acting as though they are horizontally constructed even though most corporate organizational charts still reflect a vertical hierarchy.

If management is to be successful creating the culture of contribution, it must cede some of its "span of control" and forge a "span of relationships," with workers and managers acting more as "learners than knowers, listeners than tellers, partners than adversaries". Fisher cautions that management should not be too optimistic that a reorganization into teams will solve the ills of the company; rather, a culture of contribution is more likely to develop in a climate where workers are trusted and have the freedom to think and act like owners.

At the core of many organizational development efforts over the past two decades has been the restructuring of organizations from vertical hierarchies into more horizontal, "flattened" designs where most of the work is done by self-directed teams.

In theory, teams "empower" employees by giving team members more decision-making authority and eliminating vertical chains of command. However, empowerment efforts not only require management to share power, they also demand that individual team members think differently about the nature of work.

Labianca, Gray, and Brass found that empowerment efforts require a change in "schemas" - cognitive frameworks that give meaning to experience - for both management and lower level employees. The authors analysed a 2-year organizational development project involving team building and increased participation of lower level employees in decision making.

Before the project, the "schema-in-use" for organizational decision making was that management should maintain control of events and decision making, and this schema was understood by both management and employees. The expected new schema for management included: making the organization more team oriented and collaborative, empowering lower level employees, aligning organizational structure effectively, and keeping current workers. For the ruiik-aiid-filu, the expected new schema was characterized by working on team building, creating more avenues of communication, and encouraging employees to air their "beefs."

The authors found: a great amount of employee skepticism at the outset about the likelihood of real change; despite a series of organization-wide meetings, interviews revealed both managers and nonmanagers were unclear about the project's goals; resistance was heightened when managerial behaviour failed to conform with its stated expectations; and management incorrectly assumed that employees would postpone judgment of the reorganization plan until after it was implemented. The authors concluded that employees' resistance to the empowerment plan was motivated less by intentional self-interest than by constraints of well-established, ingrained schema.

Randolph (2000) wrote that few managers or employees fully understand how empowerment affects traditional patterns of corporate hierarchy and behaviour. Management confuses empowerment as "giving people the power to make decisions," and this perception misses the essential notion of empowerment, that a great amount of power already exists in employees' knowledge, experience, and motivation. Rank-and-file perceive empowerment to mean they will be given the freedom to make all major decisions about their jobs. Randolph wrote that empowerment efforts do require a cultural shift; however, the shift is from one person making decisions to team-based shared decision making. he asserts that empowerment makes employees more accountable than the older, hierarchical culture, and it is best understood as a strange combination of opportunity and risk. An organization moves toward team-based empowered culture through three stages:

- Starting and orienting the process of change,
- Making changes and dealing with discouragement,
- Adopting and refining empowerment to fit the organization.

Each stage utilizes three "interlocking tools" - sharing information, creating autonomy through boundaries, and replacing the hierarchy with self-directed teams.

Hirschhorn, a management scholar whose work focuses on team-based organizations, wrote that the entire philosophy of management is changing as corporations flatten hierarchies and adopt new team environments. Successful managers develop roles for team members and "manage the boundary," communicating the company's needs to the team and the team's needs to the company.

Managers lead by creating a structure in which the team can be successful and by positioning themselves to defend the team's efforts. Managers must realise they are both cause of and solution to many team problems. To be successful, managers must show their vulnerability (a traditional management faux pas) and willingness to learn from team members. Exhibiting these traits shows that managers are open to new ways to solve problems and encourages team members to respond to challenges that can enhance team performance.

Although development efforts are characterized by dispersing power throughout an organization, management's ability to provide leadership remains a key to organizational success. Kets de Vries (1993), a psychologist who focuses on the "psychodynamics of organizations," wrote that organizational culture depends on the psychological contract that exists between its leaders and followers.

Effective leaders need to: articulate a vision of the future; create symbolic impressions to communicate the vision; build networks; empower followers; make choices (often painful ones); and keep perspectives of the followers based in reality. he wrote that the leader/follower relationship a process of social comparison that involves power, authority, hero worship, flattery, ambition, and attention seeking - provides tremendous opportunities for distorted management reasoning.

The key is for managers to "preserve their hold on reality." Trust is essential for a healthy organization, and trust is dependent upon communication, support, respect, fairness, competence, and consistency on the part of the leaders. he concluded, "In order for the leader to understand the meaning of these words, it is important that he or she realise what it means to be a follower, how it feels to be in that position".

The importance of communication in organizations, especially during times of change, has spawned its own discipline of study. Lewis wrote that a growing body of empirical research indicates that the communication process and organizational change efforts are "inextricably linked processes".

Communication plays an important role in several aspects of the change process, including: creating and articulating a vision; soliciting input and channeling feedback to and from all levels of the organizational hierarchy; and propelling and altering the paths of change. The organizational communication literature reveals that communication has been shown to reduce uncertainty associated with change efforts, increase accuracy in perceptions about the reasons and goals of change, and increase willingness to participate in planned change.

Studying the methods and channels organizations use to communicate change, Lewis found change agents consider themselves to be the primary sources of change-related information, and they solicit input much less frequently than they disseminate information. She suggests that management's lack of use of channels of communication, especially upward channels, limits feedback from lower level employees who do the work of the organization.

This approach can affect the success of change efforts, as "changes in status, reward structures, job descriptions, roles, work methods, work relationships, and procedures bring significant organizational issues to the surface" that increase rank-and-file employees' need to communicate with their supervisors.

There is a small body of literature; on organizational attempts to initiate market-oriented cultural change. Narver and Slater described a market-oriented culture as one that most effectively and efficiently creates superior customer value. Harris defined a market-oriented culture as "the dominant, dynamic segment of an organization whoso orientation, attitudes and actions are geared towards the market".

Harris contends that most reseachers err when they assume an organization has a single, unitary culture. This approach ignores the dynamic interaction of many aspects of an organization's culture and denies the possibility of the existence of multiple cultures. Generally, developing a market-oriented culture can be understood as a means to improve organizational efficiency and effectiveness.

However, Piercy maintains the success of developing such a culture is largely dependent on internal power relationships and organizational politics, which - at least in the short term - do not necessarily lead to high levels of organization-wide motivation, commitment, or satisfaction. When understood in this context, developing a market-oriented culture can be seen as one of many ways that an organization can impose cultural control over the attitudes, actions, and behaviors of its members.

Overall, Harris and Ogbonna wrote that the literature on the effects of developing market-oriented cultures is inconsistent, with some studies suggesting that the new culture improves employee satisfaction and commitment and others indicating this is not the case. However, researchers tend to agree that the success of any attempt at creating a market-oriented culture is contingent on employees who have to implement it.

In nearly all cases, this is the front-line employees who are the primary link between an organization and its customers. The authors also contend that developing a market-oriented culture should be concerned with the long-term generation of values, attitudes, and behaviors, but the underlying assumption of the market culture is continuing responsiveness to customer needs. The dilemma for organizations is how they can craft short-term responses to "increasingly fickle" customer needs in a manner that does not conflict with long-term organizational objectives. Harris and Ogbonna concluded that this condition is "a contradiction yet to be resolved or fully understood".

Change, because it requires giving up what is known and routine for something new that may not be understood, is often met with resistance. De Jager wrote that many managers perceive employees who resist change as a problem. he contends this a short-sighted view that fundamentally misunderstands the causes of resistance and the potential benefits resistance can exert on an organization. De Jager wrote that businesses today acknowledge the need to change, but there is so much change that employees become confused and see themselves pushed in conflicting directions.

Management is wise to understand that resistance to change is a tool that can be used to guide an organization. "Another way of looking at resistance is as a gateway or filter. Resistance to change helps us select from all possible changes the one that is most appropriate to the current situation". Because change involves replacing old organizational routines and values with new ones, managers must be able to provide answers for employees to some fundamental questions:

- Why is the old status quo no longer sufficient?
- What will it cost to make the transition from the old to new ways of doing things? De Jager identified several likely costs: disruption of routines, training, temporary low morale, new hires, people leaving, and the emotional cost of destroying what was.
- Is the cost of change justified by the incremental benefits of the change proposed?
- Does the proposed change support and reinforce existing core values?

As the millennium approached, the newspaper industry faced imposing, concurrent challenges on several fronts: stagnant circulation and a slowly dwindling base of readers; a fragmenting mass modin market; new electronic media that are changing the way people access and use information; threats to traditional sources of advertising; and unpredictable but rising costs of production. In the wake of a mid-1990s recession that saw significant cutbacks, layoffs, and downsizings, newsrooms were restructured and reorganized. Hierarchical newsroom designs were flattened, and the beat system of coverage centered on social institutions was replaced by a team system that defined coverage areas by topics believed of greater interest to readers and consumers. What becomes apparent from the industry trade journals is that "change" became the guiding light of the industry in the late 1990s.

Feeling out of step with the social patterns and interests of the public, the industry questioned its news values and management has focused on changing the culture of the newsroom to include greater marketing awareness and knowledge.

Editors are increasingly taking on marketing duties, working in cross-departmental teams with advertising, circulation, and marketing directors to create strategies to attract readers, often in specific demographic groups that advertisers are willing to pay to reach. Rank-and-file journalists are expected to accept restructuring, redefined news values, and a greater sensitivity to marketing as part of a larger cultural change process that is redefining their jobs and norms as journalists.

Organizational theory suggests that integrated organizations are more innovative and flexible and respond more quickly to opportunities and challenges. The basis of power and decision making in integrated organizations shifts from being solely in the hands of management to a shared arrangement that empowers employees to use their knowledge and skills in team-based systems. Teams, and their individual members, respond to more decision-making power and autonomy by taking more responsibility for the quality of their work and becoming more productive.

Organizational change and development is understood as a process with several stages, including planning, executing, and monitoring the progress and results. Because organizations have different values and goals, the study of OD has usually focused on one organization at a time, identifying the impact of site-specific variables on organizational development. This approach, while making theory building more difficult, has, however, led to researchers identifying several variables that impact the success of OD efforts.

These variables include an organization having a clear mission, employees who understand the mission and organization's core values, effective organizational communication, employee participation in Grafting and implementing change initiatives, strong leadership, trust, flexibility, and mechanisms that monitor the progress of change initiatives and reward desired behaviour. The effect of successful OD efforts should be empowered employees who, in self-directed work teams, are more motivated, productive, and responsible for their work. In theory, at least, successful OD efforts should in the long term improve employee morale.

However, change is also understood as a difficult and risky process. It requires employees (both management and rank-and-file) to embrace new values, to alter routines, and to think differently about their organizational roles and the nature of their work. It requires greater accountability from empowered rank-and-file and a new, less autocratic style from management. Accordingly, resistance to change should be expected, and in some cases is rational. For management, successful OD includes understanding the reasons for resistance and having the flexibility to find ways of working through resistance.

In short, the challenge of conceiving and leading change falls on management, while rank-and-file are expected to enact and embrace change initiatives that affect many of their conventions and values. Management perceives it is initiating change in the best interests of the organization and industry, while rank-and-file ponder the reasons for change and are sensitive to how it is implemented. Organizational theory and change models provide conceptual guidelines that should help predict effective organizational development (OD) initiatives.

Given the vast amount of change in the newspaper industry and the relative dearth of research studying these OD initiatives, this study of top newsroom managers and rank-and-file journalists at newspapers leading industry change explores the following research questions and tests three hypotheses.

*RQ*l: What are the attitudes and opinions of management and rank-and-file journalists toward organizational change?

*RQ*2: How do management and rank-and-file perceive the change process in relation to organizational development theory?

*RQ*3: How do management and rank-and-file perceive organizational change in relation to the normative values of journalism and marketing?

*RQ*4: Have change efforts affected rank-and-file perceptions of news values and organizational structure?

*RQ*5: Have change efforts affected rank-and-file morale?

*RQ*6: Does organization size (measured by circulation) affect how rank-and-file perceive change?

*H*1: Management will perceive it has done significantly better at organizational development than rank-and-file.

*H*2: Morale among rank-and-file will be low.

*H*3: Rank-and-file perceptions of organizational development will predict morale.

METHODS

This study used two survey instruments: a 62-statement survey sent to a sample of rank-and-file at 17 newspapers that have been engaged in change initiatives and a 20-statement survey sent to a census of top newsroom managers at the same papers.

The rank-and-file survey was designed to explore respondents' attitudes toward concepts important to all newspapers experimenting with change: news values, organizational structure, and morale. The survey included statements that allowed measuring the degree to which the newsroom change process has adhered to organizational development theory.

There were also statements asking rank-and-file to assess the relationship of change with journalistic and marketing goals.

The 20-statement management survey focused primarily on issues of organizational development, asking managers to assess the change process and their leadership of it. These 20 statements also appeared on the rank-and-file survey, allowing for a comparison between managers and rank-and-file on issues important to successful organization development.

On both surveys, respondents were asked to record their level of agreement or disagreement to stimulus statements along a 5-point Likert-like intensity scale.

CHOOSING THE NEWSPAPERS

The intent was to generate a large enough number of respondents from abroad enough sample of newspapers (in terms of size, geographic location, types of ownership, and experience with change) to have results that are generalizable to newspapers implementing change. To ensure the newspapers in the sample were among those most experienced in change initiatives, the 1997 ASNE Change Committee annual report was used to draw a purposive sample.

These newspapers had top managers who were members of the 1997 Change Committee, or the newspapers' experiments with change were discussed in the committee's annual report.

The publisher or a top news executive of all 17 U.S. newspapers active on the committee was contacted by telephone.

Three newspapers were added to the study: Si. Louis Post-Dispatch; Kansas City Star; and The Los Angeles Times. The Post-Dispatch was chosen because its editor at the time, Cole Campbell, instituted sweeping changes focused on issues relevant to this study.

The Kansas City Star was chosen because that paper was sold and restructured in the years immediately preceding the study, and its publisher, Arthur Brisbane, was the chair of the 1998 Change Committee.

The Los Angeles Times was chosen because of its self-proclaimed desire to set an industry example of how to restructure a news organization into cross-departmental teams that are more marketing conscious.

The additions created a sample of 18 newspapers with a circulation range from about 5,000 (Columbia Missourian) to more than 1 million (The Los Angeles Times). The papers come from 14 states, representing every major geographic region of the nation.

At the time of the survey, newspapers from 11 companies were in the sample, including 9 newspaper groups or chains and 2 family-owned papers. Thirteen of tho papers were owned by public companies (those that offer public stock), and 4 were private.

CREATING THE SAMPLE

Sixteen of the papers supplied the researcher with a list of newsroom employees. At the remaining paper, the San Jose Mercury News, a contact person worked with the researcher to identify top newsroom managers and draw a random sample of rank-and-file.

To ensure a response from managers that would be large enough to allow for statistical comparison with rank-and-file data, a census of the top newsroom managers at each paper was included in the overall sample.

Each paper was asked to identify its top newsroom managers or those people at the rank of department head, section editor, or team leader and above. These managers were chosen because they are responsible for creating or implementing and overseeing newsroom policies and procedures.

At several papers, there were as few as a half-dozen people at these ranks or higher, and at some of the larger papers, there were more than a dozen managers in these positions.

The rank-and-file sample was determined by newspaper

size. The first consideration was to have enough responses from the smaller papers for statistical analysis by organizational size.

Accordingly, all rank-and-file at the four smaller papers (less than 50,000 circulation) were included in the sample (n=137). Overall, a sample was sought that would enable an approximate proportional representation of journalists for all three circulation strata.

From the seven papers between 50,000 and 250,000 (the actual range is 71,000 to 156,000), a random sample of 1 of 3 newsroom employees was drawn from each newspaper (n=259); from the six papers with more than 250,000 circulation, 1 of 5 newsroom employees was randomly selected (n=313), except for The Los Angeles Times, where 1 of 10 employees was randomly selected (n=98).

A total of 989 surveys - 182 to top managers and 807 to rank-and-file - was mailed in May 1998. Following closely Dillman's Total Design Method, a postcard was sent as a reminder to nonrespondents about 10 days after the first mailing; a complete survey packet was sent to nonrespondents about 3 weeks after the first mailing.

RESULTS

Of 807 surveys sent to rank-and-file, 457 were completed and returned, a response rate of 56.6%. The 182 surveys sent to top managers yielded 68 responses, or 3 7.3%. The instrument sent to management had 20 statements, mostly about organizational development, that were also on the rank-and-file survey.

This approach allowed for a comparison of management and rank-and-file responses. The lower response rate for management can be partially explained by the instrument; beyond the 20-statement survey, management was asked to complete a Q study (not reported in this monograph). Comparative results are reported first, followed by rank-and-file data.

Management respondents' demographics:

- 26 women, 42 men;

- 1 African-American, 2 Asian-Americans, 2 Hispanics, 62 whites, and 1 indicated othor;
- Ages ranged from 26 to 59, with a mean of 44.5;
- Experience ranged from 3 to 38 years, with the mean 22.0 years.

Rank-and-filo respondents' demographics:

- 177 females, 274 males, and 6 did not respond;
- 25 African-Americans, 19 Asian-Americans, 9 Hispanics, 2 Native Americans, 382 whites, and 20 indicated other or did not respond;
- Ages ranged from 22 to 77, with the mean 41.98;
- Experience ranged from 1 to 60 years, with the mean 17.72 years;
- 272 indicated they had "no managerial duties," 181 said they had "some managerial duties," and 4 did not respond.

Variable Measures. Most of the 62 rank-and-file survey statements were written to probe change initiatives in relation to news values, organizational structure, organizational development, and morale.

The statements exploring news values incorporate ideas from trade journals about the changing nature of news, but also reflect norms articulated in the Libertarian and Social Responsibility theories of the press. The statements that construct the organizational structure variable were taken from trade journal and organizational development literature. The statements in the organizational development construct were all derived from the OD literature.

Morale statements were written to explore both individual respondents' attitudes about their own morale and their perceptions of morale in the newsroom. Factor analysis of the rank-and-file data assisted construction of the four concepts: 14 statements measure news values; 12 statements measure organizational structure; 14 statements measure organizational development; 6 statements measure morale.

Statement responses - on a 5-point scale with 1 strongly agree, 5 strongly disagree, and 3 neutral - were coded so that a positive response indicated support for the concept (i.e., positive response indicated high morale). Conceptual quotients were created by calculating the mean response to the set of statements measuring the concepts. Accordingly, a quotient significantly below 3.0 (the assumed population mean on the 5-point scale) indicates positive agreement with the concept, and a quotient significantly above 3.0 indicates that respondents disagree with the concept (i.e., disagree with statements suggesting high morale).

COMPARISONS BETWEEN MANAGEMENT AND RANK-AND-FILE

ORGANIZATIONAL DEVELOPMENT

The literature indicates that cultural change is difficult, requiring management and rank-and-file to adapt to new values, structures, routines, and goals. However, management and rank-and-file have different roles in the change process. Management is responsible for conceiving, guiding, and monitoring change, while rank-and-file must execute management's vision and live with the new roles and values associated with change.

Management is expected to perceive OD initiatives more broadly, in concert with strategic organizational goals, and guide and assess the change process from a position of leadership and accountability. It is expected that management will perceive that its OD initiatives are rooted in sound strategies and practices, while rank-and-file will question the reasons for change and be sensitive to how it is implemented. This logic is the basis of the following hypothesis:

Hl: Management will perceive it has done significantly better at OD than rank-and-file.

At test of independent samples was used to compare the OD quotients (mean value of the 14 statements in the construct) of management and rank-and-file. This hypothesis is supported. The data indicate that management believes OD initiatives have generally followed theoretical guidelines, as the OD quotient for management shows modest overall agreement with the statements (quotient is less than 3.0).

Conversely, the rank-and-file OD quotient shows general disagreement that change initiatives are in accordance with the parameters defined by OD theory.

Thus, there is not only a significant difference between the OD quotients, there is also a clear difference of attitudes: management perceives it has generally implemented change in accordance with OD, while rank-and-file think the process of change has not adhered to ideas and practices consistent with successful OD. This finding is further reinforced by looking at the pattern of responses to the variable statements. Of the 14 OD statements, management agrees with 9 and rank-and-file agree with only 3.

T tests wore also used to compare individual statement means, and there are significant differences on 11 of the 14 statements. Because the OD variable is a broad measure of change, with survey statements addressing planning, training, commitment, leadership, communication, participation, and a system of rewards, the significant differences on so many OD aspects reflect both the intensity and broad-based nature of the differences between the groups.

Six of the statistically significant OD statements show a clear difference of attitudes, with management agreeing with the statement and rank-and-file disagreeing. The two groups have differing opinions on some of the most basic aspects of change (means noted parenthetically). Management believes the newspaper's mission and core values are understood by newsroom employees, while rank-and-file are apparently unsure about their paper's mission and values.

Management believes the staff has participated in drafting change, while rank-and-file disagree; and management says that it has asked for staff feedback about change, while rank-and-file apparently think management is not interested in feedback, or at least not interested enough to ask.

The importance of communication in the change process is also shown, as management agrees that change initiatives and the reasons for change have been continually communicated (2.88), while rank-and-file disagree.

Most telling about communication is the large difference of opinion concerning honesty. Management shows quite strong agreement that it has been open and honest with staff about the reasons for change, but rank-and-file exhibit equally strong disagreement. This mean difference on honesty (on a 5-point scale) is the largest gap between the groups' responses to any of the 14 statements in the OD variable.

Even on the eight statements where the groups tend to agree, there are significant differences in their intensity of agreement on five statements. Although rank-and-file credit management for its strong leadership role and unified commitment to change, management assesses its leadership role and commitment in significantly more optimistic terms. In those areas where management is relatively self-critical, rank-and-file tend to be more critical.

Management concedes it has not thought through the long-term implications of change, but rank-and-file take a harsher view; the scenario is similar concerning a system of rewards for work that meets the goals of change, with management disagreeing that such a system is in place, but rank-and-file disagreeing significantly more.

This trend might be best shown with management's relatively strong disagreement to the statement that change initiatives have helped build stronger trust between management and rank-and-file. Management's response is a candid assessment of an unpleasant reality and a subtle admission of a failure of change; yet, rank-and-file are significantly harsher in their assessment, with their strongest level of disagreement to any of the 14 statements. These differences underscore that even when management and rank-and-file find areas of common ground, they still tend to disagree.

Of the 14 OD statements, management has a stronger level of disagreement to only 2, and these 2 statements are among the 3 statements that do not have significant mean differences. Management disagrees that it has overestimated resistance to change, while rank-and-file are neutral; and managers disagree that the staff is open-minded toward change marginally more than rank-and-file. Although not significant, taken together, the ideas that management perceives more resistance and less open-mindedness suggest that management believes their staffs are generally resistant to change initiatives.

This perception is likely to influence how managers approach leading change. Managers would be likely to view with more optimism the task of managing a staff that is open to new ideas and practices. Conversely, managers who perceive a resistant and inflexible staff are more likely to judge the task of leading change as more difficult.

Comparisons of Statements Not in the OD Variable. There were six statements appearing on both surveys that were not part of the OD variable. T tests were performed on the responses, and significant differences were found on four of the statements. Two of the significant statements show a clear difference of attitudes. Management, consistent with other responses that show more optimism about change than rank-and-file, agrees that there has been a noticeable change in the newsroom culture that has improved the organization (2.76), while rank-and-file disagree quite strongly.

This large difference of opinion (.82 on a 5-point scale) underscores the different experiences and perceptions the two groups have about the impact of change on the newsroom culture.

But the pattern of management optimism is reversed when the groups are asked about an indicator of journalism quality. In this case, rank-and-file agree that newspapers arc doing a boiler job portraying a representative picture of society than in the past, while management is significantly more pessimistic, disagreeing with the statement. This finding could help explain why management sees a need to get closer to readers and redefine news to be more aligned with the lives of people in a changing and diverse marketplace.

Management and rank-and-file show similar attitudes toward two of the statements, and one of the responses is quite surprising.

The two groups both slightly disagree that "I look

forward to when change is no longer a large part of work." Given the difficulty of change, especially rank-and-file's general frustration with the process, it seems logical that rank-and-file have had enough change, but this is not the case. Rank-and-file actually disagree slightly more to the statement than management. This finding supports an issue discussed earlier: management tends to perceive a culture of resistance to change; however, rank-and-file respond that they have accepted change as a part of work.

The increased profit pressure is acknowledged by the groups, with both agreeing strongly with the statement that there is more emphasis on profits than there used to be. Considering the extent of differences between the groups on most of the measures, it is quite revealing that the groups believe with approximate equal strength that there is an increasing emphasis on profit. For both groups, their level of agreement was stronger with this statement than any of the 20 statements that appeared on both instruments.

Exploring the relationship between change and morale, both groups disagreed with the statement: "Morale in our newsroom appears to be getting better." However, consistent with statements that indicate management does not perceive the newsroom climate to be as bad as rank-and-file, there was a significant difference in the groups' level of disagreement. Management disagreed with the statement, but its disagreement was not nearly as strong as rank-and-file's.

Rank-and-File Results

Morale: Low morale among newspaper journalists has been an industry issue for more than a decade. OD research indicates that change initiatives tied to creating a different organizational culture can be threatening for employees because embodied in the new culture are new organizational values, work routines, job skills, and rewards. Based on this evidence, it was hypothesized:

H2: Morale among rank-and-file will be low (morale quotient significantly higher than 3.0).

The morale quotient is 3.32. A one-sample t test indicates

the quotient mean is significantly higher than the assumed population mean (t value = 9.26; $p < .001$). This hypothesis is supported.

Six statements comprise morale. T tests on each statement and the assumed population mean found that 5 of the 6 statements were statistically significant. Respondents agreed with only one statement indicating high morale: "I am committed to this newspaper's plans for change". Respondents were neutral to the notion that changes have given them more job skills, and they disagreed that changes have created more job autonomy.

The remaining three statements constituting this concept make more general (non-first person) references to morale, and these had higher levels of disagreement.

Rank-and-file's relatively strong disagreement that changes have been implemented smoothly supports theory that suggests change affecting jobs, skills, and values is difficult. This difficulty of embracing change draws more support from respondents' disagreement that there has been a positive change in the newsroom culture. However, most telling is the statement that is probably the purest measure of morale. Journalists show their highest level of disagreement to the idea that morale in our newsroom appears to be getting better.

NEWS VALUES

The 14 statements that construct this study's measure of news values probe how rank-and-file journalists perceive newsroom changes have impacted their news judgment and news content.

The news values quotient is 3.23. A one-sample t test indicates the quotient mean is significantly higher than the assumed population mean. Accordingly, rank-and-file have a negative attitude about changes in news values. In general, respondents think they are doing what they can to preserve some traditional journalism values in an era when newspapers are more market driven.

Responses to the individual statements shed some light

on specific news value issues that shape respondents' attitudes (statement means noted parenthetically). Journalists agree that newspapers are doing a better job portraying a representative picture of society than in tho past, but they are neutral about whether papers are doing better at providing a truthful account of the day's events in a meaningful context than in the past.

The rank-and-file journalists do not believe that content decisions are based solely on journalism criteria, as they agree strongly that more gossip, trivia, and non-news features are used to fill the paper and recent changes in design stress style over substance to the point that look and feel of the paper are more important to editors than the depth of the news.

They have slight agreement that their newspaper has less breaking news than before change initiatives, and significant disagreement that changes in the industry have made papers more thoughtful and provocative. Journalists feel the impact of new methods and structures on their news values. They agree focus groups, surveys, and community meetings are good methods to generate ideas for news coverage, but they acknowledge an impact of organizational integration, showing strong agreement that journalists working at papers that have eliminated divisions between news and business are more likely to engage in self-censorship when writing about issues important to advertisers.

And they disagree that change has increased resources for practicing journalism and led to more investigative reporting. This point is underscored by journalists' agreement that an important issue is less likely to become news if it takes a great deal of time to uncover and report. The respondents see journalism independence, a traditional benchmark of news values and credibility, as on the road to obsolescence. Journalists agree that the opportunity for independent-minded publishers or editors to run their own newsrooms is coming to an end and are neutral when asked whether the role models for today's managers are those editors and publishers who in the past told the truth when it was not popular or profitable to do so.

ORGANIZATIONAL STRUCTURE

The quotient for the 12 statements that construct this variable is 3.55, which a one-sample t test shows is significant to the assumed population mean.

This finding suggests that journalists generally responded negatively to the impact of changing newsroom structures. When viewed individually, the statement means indicate that journalists recognize that changes in structure (the most common being from beats to teams) have impacted their work, but seldom in ways theory would predict nor management would desire.

Journalists indicate modest (but significant) agreement that they work more closely with their colleagues than in the past, but they agree much more strongly that newsroom changes have too often meant attending meetings that cut into time spent on journalism. Contrary to theory, rank-and-file don't see that restructuring the newsroom has flattened the hierarchy, disagreeing strongly that the number of layers of management has decreased. This finding is reinforced by nearly equally strong agreement that newsroom restructuring seems to require more editors who send out memos about the new goals of restructuring.

The journalists in this sample are still wary of the impact of cross-departmental teams, indicating strong disagreement that directors of advertising, circulation, and marketing should participate in news planning. Also, they do not see a connection between the team structure and better journalism, disagreeing that reorganization has helped the staff better understand readers and that work teams have improved product quality.

Moreover, the rank-and-file see media executives as having different values than they do, with executives more focused on market and strategy than on the experiences of their employees; respondents also disagree strongly that structural changes place more emphasis on nonprofit goals (organizational efficiency, the latest technology, product quality, and worker autonomy and creativity) than profit goals.

VARIABLES AFFECTING MORALE

Considering the vast amount of change being implemented at newspapers in the sample and the difficulties associated with OD in general, a particular interest of this research project was to measure the impact of change initiatives on morale. Toward this end, the variables constructed to measure the three concepts common to change efforts at newspapers - OD, news values, and organizational structure - were used as independent variables in a regression model to assess their relative impact on morale.

Because OD is a broad measure of change and OD initiatives impact an organization's structure and values, it was expected that the 4 variables (OD, news values, structure, and morale) would be highly correlated. This was indeed what occurred, as the correlations were all significant at the $p < .001$ level. A colinearity test for tolerance showed these correlations did not violate the assumptions of multiple regression. A multiple regression model was then built to test:

*H*3: Rank-and-file perceptions of organizational development will predict morale.

To control for the demographic variables of age, ethnicity, gender, experience, and duties, these variables were entered as a block into the regression model before the three independent variables. Experience, duties ("some managerial duties" or "no managerial duties"), and age were significant predictors in the block. Together, the demographic variables accounted for 5.77% of the variance.

H3 is supported. Organizational development, entered as the second block in the model, explained 45.8% of the variance after controlling for demographies. OD is clearly the strongest predictor of morale among all the independent variables. Accordingly, the data indicate that as rank-and-file's attitudes toward OD become more positive their morale increases; or, as rank-and-file's attitudes toward OD become more negative their morale decreases.

After all the independent variables were entered in the regression model, OD, structure, and news values are significant predictors of morale. However, after controlling for demographics, the explained variance each variable adds differs notably. OD explains 45.8% of the variance, organizational structure accounts for 7.8% of the variance and news values accounts for 2.0%. What is interesting is that news values, so basic to journalists' jobs and how they perceive their roles, explains a relatively small amount of the variance.

Perhaps this is because in the midst of organizational changes that affect the most basic elements of work - schedules and routines - journalists continue to see the basic elements of news as information gathering, interviewing, writing, and editing. It is logical that news values impact morale, but change initiatives that require training and re-ordering of work priorities, as well as newsroom restructuring, are tangible symbols of a new culture. Because they are the most easily identified signs of change, they are the most likely targets for acceptance or resistance. Thus, it appears that changes most affecting morale are those OD and restructuring initiatives that management believes will eventually reconstitute news. News values are changing, but the results suggest that among the types of change, rank-and-file see changing news values as having a smaller impact on their morale.

After all the variables were entered in the model, duties was also shown to be a significant predictor of morale. A dichotomous variable (0 = no managerial duties, 1 = some managerial duties), the negative beta weight indicates an inverse relationship. In other words, journalists who have some managerial duties have significantly lower morale than those who have no managerial duties; or, those with no managerial duties have higher morale than those with some managerial duties. This result supports anecdotal evidence that change has been most difficult for low- and mid-level managers. These managers tend to get "squeezed" by change, expected to execute the change initiatives of top management while working most closely with non-managers.

Statements Not Part of Variables. The statements not part of variables also provide some useful insights. One of the research questions in this study was whether newsroom employees think the direction of change better fits the goals of journalism or marketing. As noted in the comparative results, of the 62 statements in the survey, rank-and-file's strongest agreement was with the statement: "There is more emphasis on maintaining or increasing the paper's profits than there used to be".

There was also strong agreement that newsroom managers have become increasingly aware of the concerns of stockholders and capital investors. Respondents think this increased awareness or pressure created by financial performance does not need to be expanded, as there is significant disagreement to the statement that the newspaper industry needs a culture that requires greater marketing intelligence in the newsroom. Taken together, these statements indicate rank-and-file journalists believe newspapers are becoming more sensitive to marketing and this movement has gone far enough.

There is also a concern about the ethical issues and threats to journalism independence that removing the wall between the news and business may initiate. There is strong agreement that ethical committees are needed to draft guidelines for editorial staff participation in promotional events and significant agreement that journalistic independence has helped establish newspapers as credible. The journalists in this sample still use journalism excellence as the standard for quality, and they like competition. Even in the era of increased profit pressures, there is significant disagreement that most newspaper companies would trade Pulitzer Prizes for consistently high profits, and, in an apparent longing for days past, respondents show strong agreement that journalism has suffered in the era of one-newspaper towns.

There is additional evidence that rank-and-file do not perceive OD as progressing in accordance with theory. Rank-and-file disagree that management has done a good job preparing employees for change, and they disagree that management has done a good job measuring the results of change. Respondents have even stronger beliefs that management is ego driven and inflexible.

Rank-and-file agree that some managers have embraced formulas of change because they have invested so much money, time, and ego in them that they can't admit their lack of success. And there is a similar strong agreement to the idea that managers who have found resistance to change have responded by saying in effect, "The train is leaving the station, you can get on or get off".

Furthermore, journalists don't see change meeting its stated objectives, as they show strong agreement there is little evidence that common changes (i.e., redefining of news, newsroom restructuring, and use of emerging technologies) are attracting more readers and advertisers.

The data also lend support to the idea that news managers and the growing number of consultants employed in newsrooms misunderstand journalists' resistance to change. The journalists in this study do not see themselves as opposed to change; in fact, they show significant disagreement to the statement that they look forward to when change is no longer such a large part of work. But journalists tend to like to be left alono to do their jobs which runs counter to theory that predicts workers are happier when they collaborate and more productive in teams. The more than 450 rank-and-file in this sample significantly agree with the statement: "I am happier when I can work alone".

ANALYSIS BY CIRCULATION

Because organizational resources are determined in part by an organization's size and group dynamics can be impacted by group size, this study explored whether newspaper size (measured by circulation) impacted respondents' attitudes toward change. To test for differences by circulation, means for each variable were calculated by circulation size (4 small papers with circulations less than 50,000; 7 mid-size papers with circulations between 50,000 and 250,000 [actual range is 71,000 to 156,000]; and 6 large papers with circulations more than 250,000).

The data show that small newspapers are having more difficulty with change as it relates to two variables: OD and morale. A one-way analysis-of-variance test indicates that morale is significantly lower at small papers; also, small paper respondents indicate significantly higher disagreement that OD initiatives have been in accordance with theory. It is worth noting that the means for all four variables are higher for small papers.

These results also reveal no significant differences between mid-size and large papers. But perhaps more telling about this analysis is that there is not a positive attitude toward any of the variables at any size paper. In other words, even though some aspects of change are more difficult at small papers, these strata show that respondents do not believe change has gone well (or in accordance with theory) on any of the measures, regardless of newspaper size.

DISCUSSION

The challenge of change from the standpoint of management is getting rank-and-file to accept the core values that embody management's vision for a transformed newsroom culture. The data provide strong evidence that management's OD initiatives are failing to win rank-and-file support - regardless of whether the initiatives are in concert with theory. What is surprising in these findings is the extent to which management and rank-and-file disagree and how often.

Of the 20 statements that appeared on both surveys, there are significant differences on 15 of them. Of these 15, the responses to 9 statements indicate clear differences of attitudes, with one group agreeing and the other disagreeing. Of the 14 statements that construct the OD variable, there are significant differences on responses to 11 statements. Taken as a whole, the responses show that many important divisions exist between management and rank-and-file, and even when the groups can agree, they often disagree on their level of agreement. In many instances the gap between responses is so large that it is hard to understand the two groups are sharing the same experiences, and perhaps they are not.

The groups' roles in the change process differ. The sample

of newsroom managers in this study is comprised of many of the nation's leading editors. Their involvement in the ASNE Change Committee reflects their interests beyond the walls of their newsrooms, and suggests they positioned themselves as leaders in an industry-wide effort to respond to the forces mandating change.

The rank-and-file in this sample must adapt to management's vision by executing their jobs in accordance with the new procedures and goals of change. Despite these different roles, however, as part of the same organizations, management and rank-and-file should share similar values. Both groups are journalists.

Management's self-assessment may be a bit optimistic, but it is grounded in reality and is at times unflatteringly candid. Managers have a great deal invested in change initiatives, both in terms of organizational resources and their individual careers.

A role of management is to "see the big picture," which suggests that management should be able to assess the process and progress of change within its overall strategic goals better than rank-and-file. Thus, management's general optimism regarding change may be a reflection that the broader process is proceeding in the right direction, even if certain aspects tend to get off course.

The data support this. Management gives itself high marks for leadership and generally following the prescriptions for change articulated in OD models and theory. Management views itself as trying to do what should be done to enable change to succeed.

Yet, as Kanter suggests, change requires a "leap of faith" to get people to embrace an organizational reality that is not yet known. And on this issue, the data show management to be quite honest, admitting the entire change formula has not been worked out. Even more candid, however, is management's admission that certain parts of the process that it can control have not been well-managed.

Management concedes that it has not adequately thought through the long-term implications of change, and it acknowledges there is not a system of rewards for work that meets the goals of change initiatives.

Accordingly, it is not surprising that management recognizes that its short-comings have contributed to a breakdown of trust with rank-and-file, while at the same time perceiving a cultural change that has improved the organization.

This apparent contradiction must be perplexing and difficult for newsroom managers. There is some evidence in the data that managers are a bit frustrated, placing the "blame" for a lack of success on rank-and-file, who are perceived as close minded and resistant to change.

However, the results from the rank-and-file survey suggest it is not accurate to simply dismiss journalists as resistant to change.

Rank-and-file indicate they accept change as a part of work and are personally committed to their paper's change efforts. They credit their managers for taking leadership roles and being committed to change.

However, they question the factors motivating change and are able to distinguish between intentions and results. In brief, while management says it has articulated a vision, included employees in creating changes, been flexible, and sought feedback about the change process, rank-and-file respond that they are confused about the vision, fool loft out of the process, and perceive their managers as inflexible.

Rank-and-file also sense management's vulnerability and frustration in leading change, showing strong agreement that change is ego driven by inflexible managers who, refusing to recognize its lack of success, resort to authoritarian measures to counter pockets of resistance.

Rank-and-file's perception that management has failed at nearly every step of the process, combined with their sense that profit is increasingly important to newsroom managers, further explains the low level of trust rank-and-file express toward their managers. Numerous scholars cite trust as a prerequisite condition for successful OD initiatives.

Thus, despite management's general optimism about an

improving newsroom culture, the breakdown of trust that both management and rank-and-file acknowledge does not bode well for continuing efforts at change, as theory suggests and common sense reveals that people do not readily accept the ideas of those whom they do not trust.

Beyond the organizational development issues associated with change, rank-and-file's skepticism about change can be understood by an apparent lack of producing successful results. Change initiatives are not only failing to create more efficient, productive, and happier newsrooms, they are also falling short on their stated goals. Journalists don't perceive changes as attracting more readers and advertisers, or helping to produce better newspapers. Instead, rank-and-file connect change initiatives with fewer resources for journalism in a more market-driven culture and industry.

Kanter, Drucker, Bergquist, and many organizational scholars would suggest that "breaking down the wall" between the newsroom and other departments in the news organization is an important step toward creating the "integrated" and "innovative" organizational culture required to meet challenges swiftly and capitalize on opportunities in the postmodern business world. The data in this study suggest that rank-and-file perceive the new, integrated culture as a threat to their values, most of which are rooted in journalism.

Much of rank-and-file's resistance to change is related to a sense that the "journalism-based" culture of their newsrooms is being replaced with a culture that places less value on journalism norms. In this way, there is a cultural "battle" unfolding in news organizations as they become more integrated. Harris, writing about the clash that occurs when an organization attempts to create a market-oriented culture, asserts that the market-oriented values that define the culture must come to dominate the existing cultures for the transformation to succeed.

This study indicates that this type of cultural struggle is being waged in newsrooms experimenting with change. When viewed in this regard, resistance to change can be understood as both rational and part of a cultural conflict. However, if cultural change is achieved through a combination of macro (values and beliefs) and micro forces (the tangible things such as practices, policies, and procedures that define daily life in the organization), then management's attempt to change the newsroom culture by changing the organization's structure and work routines appears to be well-advised and well under way.

This study also opens for re-examination several theoretical assumptions. The idea that modern newspaper organizations are characterized by complex, hierarchical bureaucracies and specialized labour appears to be less accurate today than it was before "change" became an industry buzzword and organizational goal. Media corporations, no doubt large bureaucracies, can however be understood to be "disassembling the assembly line." The goals of OD and change most often focus on creating flatter corporate flowcharts with the expectation that employees need to be more versatile and multiskilled. Clearly, this is the opposite of labour specialization.

Furthermore, the empowerment assumptions of restructuring hierarchical organizations into flatter, team-based units have not materialized for the rank-and-file journalists in this sample. Rank-and-file understand restructuring as a mechanism that affords them fewer resources to practice journalism, and, contrary to theory, rank-and-file perceive restructuring has created more layers of managers and a more "managed" newsroom. The journalists in this sample say that the team-based structure has not brought them more autonomy, nor has it provided more decision-making authority.

It is possible that the empowerment expected to result from restructured newsrooms is misconceived. A primary rationale for less hierarchical organizations is the team-based structure unleashes the knowledge and creativity of lower level employees. This view presupposes that management, under the hierarchical structure, has not previously afforded employees the power to effectively utilize these assets. However, this assumption seems to neglect the nature of newspaper work, which has traditionally afforded rank-and-file a great deal of latitude, encouraging journalists to apply their knowledge and be creative.

Long before empowerment became a management cliche, Gassaway's 1984 social construction work found that rank-and-file journalists and newspaper managers negotiate for power, with rank-and-file having considerable leverage, because as newsgatherers they control the initial flow of information. Furthermore, journalism is one of the few occupations where employees at the bottom of the corporate ladder consider themselves professionals.

Valuable newsroom employees have long been those who could work well on their own, digging for stories and building relationships with sources. Interviewing is a craft, writing and design are forms of self-expression, and editing is a skill built on an individual's grasp of language and professional values. To require journalists to give up the individual nature of their work asks them to sacrifice some of the skills that have become a part of their professional identities. There is strong evidence in this study that journalists have not accepted the idea that team-based newsrooms empower them or better utilize their skills. This finding supports previous research and reinforces the idea that the organizational theory that managers are using to empower their employees and restructure their newsrooms could be misapplied, as it misunderstands the nature of newspaper journalism work.

The assumptions about the organizational role of management are changing, too. This study finds little support that newsroom managers are "technocrats" who value organizational and technical development more than the profit goals of their "capitalist" owners. The data indicate it is more accurate, as Kanter and others suggest, to understand change as a process of integration, where the marketing goals of the traditional "business side" of the news organization have become more apparent to journalists and more valued by management throughout the organization (my italics).

Galbraith's "approved contradiction" concept - that innovative managers will focus on professional and organizational goals while returning just enough profit to keep their capitalist owners satisfied - is a core assumption of Demers'research on the corporate newspaper. This study found little support for the existence of an approved contradiction; rather, managers and rank-and-file perceive change as both market and profit driven at the expense of organizational issues thought to be of prime concern to professional managers (product quality, technology, and employee development).

These findings suggest that modern news executives are no longer "technocrats" in the sense Galbraith defined them, but are closer to the "capitalists" who sought maximum financial return on their investments. The practice of offering newsroom managers incentives (salary bonuses or stock options) tied to the financial performance of the company is one way corporations subtly "disapprove" of the approved contradiction.

Limitations of the study. An obvious shortcoming of this survey method is that it can only provide a "snapshot" of attitudes at the time of the study. Change is an ongoing process, and the instruments used can only provide a one-time glimpso of the process. As the change process unfolds in newsrooms across the country, it would be wise to continue to monitor change initiatives and journalists' attitudes toward them. Also, this study did not attempt to measure the amount of change orthe phases of the change process. Thus, while all the respondents have a commonality of change experiences, it is not clear if attitudes toward change differ based on the amount of change or stages in the change process.

There is also a chance to refine the instruments and measures of change used in this study. Organizational development research has generally focused on one organization at a time, using site-specific variables. By taking a different approach, there were very few established measures. Accordingly, the attempt here was to create "tools" from which scholars can begin to empirically assess change.

Suggestions for future research. The findings in this study point to several theoretical areas that should prove fertile ground for exploration. This study adds to the small amount ol research thai suggests restructuring newsrooms into team-based systems does not "empower" journalists in the manner theory predicts. If team-based newsrooms are the future of the industry, then changing organizational relationships spawned by restructuring offer interesting opportunities for study.

Among some of the questions these changes suggest: Do team-based structures impact the ways journalists work with one another? Do teams impact the ways journalists develop relationships and interact with their sources? Do teams require and reward different personality traits? How does the resourceful journalist, the "gumshoe" who worked well alone, often producing front page stories in the beat system, perform in the team structure? Do team-based newsrooms produce different content than the beat system does? And possibly most important to understanding the values that will drive the industry in the future are the questions of management influence and power.

Do newsroom managers and editors see themselves as the innovative "technocrats" that theory presupposes? How much influence do newsroom managers have when it comes to setting the vision for change? To what extent do newsroom managers embrace the changes they are expected to lead? These questions, along with the need to develop better change-related measures over time (throughout the process of change], provide an abundance of directions for research.

This study surveyed a purposive sample of the nation's newspaper managers most experienced in industry-wide change initiatives; it also surveyed a much larger sample of rank-and-file from those same papers. The managers in this study have, in effect, used their newsrooms as laboratories to experiment with new and far-reaching change initiatives. These changes have become - depending on whom you ask - new standards of excellence or points of controversy and resistance.

Although the results from this purposive sample cannot be generalized to the entire industry, the relatively large sample gives a good indication of what change has meant to journalists at newspapers on the cutting edge of industry-wide change. These findings should prove useful for the many news managers and editors who find their newsrooms embarking on or considering similar change initiatives. This study has also tested the key concepts of organizational development, making it one of only a few attempts to understand the complexities of newspaper industry change through the lens of organizational theory.

Given the size of the sample and the scope of the newspapers (circulations ranging from 5,000 to more than 1,000,000, including public, private, and family-owned papers that are located in every major geographic region of the country), this study represents one of the largest scale attempts to date to assess journalists' perceptions about change initiatives that are sweeping through newsrooms nationwide.

Management, despite some res- ervations about the market-driven nature of change, thinks it is doing reasonably well following the guidelines of organizational development in a manner consistent with creating a more outer-directed and reader-driven newsroom culture. In short, management believes it has "managed" the change process in general accordance with theory. Rank-and-file, on the other hand, feel more victims of change than participants in it. The gulf between management and rank-and-file experiences with change has facilitated a breakdown in trust that could seriously hamper ongoing change initiatives. Morale among rank-and-file is low, and data suggest it is getting worse.

The newspaper industry finds itself in the throes of a cultural revolution precipitated by internal and external forces. Yet, the industry remains highly profitable and has shown resiliency in the information age, remaining a respected and widely utilized source of news and information. The predictions of doom are far from materializing, but many of the challenges that served as catalysts for cultural change remain. The findings of this study suggest there is a struggle unfolding between the core values of two cultures - marketing and journalism - and rank-and-file perceive organizational development efforts are focused on creating a more dominant marketing culture, often at the expense of journalistic norms.

This study has extended previous change research by approaching the problem differently. Organizational research has seldom been conducted on more than one organization at a time, and its methods are usually qualitative. The constructs in this study held up quite well to tests of reliability and statistical analysis, showing the depth of common experiences of journalists at newspapers implementing change. An important methodological finding of this study is that change can be studied at more than one newspaper at a time. Studies that go beyond site-specific variables are possible, which should encourage more research using larger, representative samples with the goal of testing and building theory.

Chapter 6

User Agreements and Implications for Readers

The contracting of news on the Web represents a fundamental shift in the way consumers receive their news. Rather than engaging in a traditional sale of information-in which the publisher receives payment for a printed newspaper-today's online news publishers often provide free content in exchange for tacit agreement to an online user agreement. Under such agreements, news consumers often agree not to redistribute content, expect reliability, or submit offensive material. In return, users are given permission to access news content, provided they abide by the terms.

Online user agreements have evolved as an accepted business practice on the Web, and at first glance, the newspaper industry's adoption of these agreements would seem only natural. But the news industry's commitment to maintaining a vibrant marketplace of ideas and its role in contributing to and using the public domain3 may be at risk under a system that promotes licensing and access to news to readers over the sale and ownership of one or more personal copies of that news.

This study of online news user agreements at the Top 50 circulation daily newspapers attempts to explain why. It suggests that some online news user agreements are adhesion contracts that place the publisher in the role of controlling the use of information that might otherwise flow freely in the public domain. It also argues that some provisions may expand the scope of the law, particularly copyright law.

Finally, it reveals efforts by publishers to limit speech in online news forums and limit liability for unlawful and objectionable content. While these latter provisions may be well within the rights of online news publishers, the content and effect of such agreements pose new questions about fundamental First Amendment and journalistic values online.

Background: User Agreements, Contract Theory, and the Issue of Assent. The enforcement of online user agreements-particularly without the negotiated consent of the user-is an evolving area of law. In a traditional contract, each party formally agrees to something. User agreements are adhesion contracts, often standard form contracts "prepared by one party, to be (accepted) by the party in a weaker position, usually a consumer who has little choice about the terms." Adhesion contracts may or may not be enforceable depending upon the actions of the weaker party in showing his acceptance.

Contracts today are interpreted based on the parties' actions as much as on outward signs of assent. "This approach in its purest form holds that a party's actual, provable intent or meaning is irrelevant. Its standard-bearer, the figurative reasonable person, has the duty to inquire into the meaning of the words and acts implored by the parties." In terms of online user agreements, then, it is conceivable that a user, by simply accessing a Web site, agrees to its terms.

But some scholars maintain there is a growing body of case law against the support of adhesion contracts. Simply posting fine print without a formal negotiation may render portions of a user agreement unenforceable. These scholars argue that it is dangerous to "...define contract as a series of consequences the law attaches to the outward conduct of the parties if one cannot explain why the law attaches some consequences rather than others.

There is widespread agreement that any viable theory of contract will have to take the fairness of a contract into account, yet there is no agreement as how to do so." Thus, the nature of contract law and what it requires of both parties is still debated. This debate is influenced by these larger theoretical questions and by at least one major court decision and Uniform Commercial Code (UCC) legislation known as the Uniform Computer Information Transactions Act or UCITA.

UCITA, ProCD, and the Public Domain. In a controversial 1996 Seventh Circuit Court of Appeals case, ProCD, Inc. v. Zeidenberg, the Seventh Circuit Court of Appeals upheld the use of a shrinkwrap license and ruled that such contracts do not preempt federal copyright law. Preemption is a "doctrine adopted by the U.S. Supreme Court holding that certain matters are of such a national, as opposed to local, character that federal laws preempt or take precedence over state laws. As such, a state may not pass a law inconsistent with the federal law." Copyright law has its own preemption section, which prohibits any "legal or equitable rights (under state law) that are equivalent to any of the exclusive rights within the general scope of copyright... and that come within the subject matter of copyright."

ProCD sued Zeidenberg for copyright infringement and breach of its shrinkwrap license agreement. Zeidenberg argued the terms of the license were not enforceable because he did not agree to them and was unable to review them before using the product. The district court ruled in Zeidenberg's favour, stating that the purchaser "did not have the opportunity to bargain or object to the proposed user agreement or even review it before purchase." The district court also ruled that the contract was a violation of copyright law under the preemption clause.

But the Seventh Circuit court reversed, holding that the shrinkwrap license was enforceable and withstood preemption. The court said that even though Zeidenberg was unaware of the terms of the agreement until after the sale was made, the contract was valid because he had agreed to the terms of the license by his conduct. In essence, his purchase of the software constituted his consent to the agreement. Cases since ProCD have upheld various user agreement provisions, including limitations on damages, forum selection clauses, and prohibitions on spam.

In a response that may further strengthen the ProCD decision and the enforcement of shrinkwrap and user agreements, the drafters of the Uniform Commercial Code have proposed the Uniform Computer Information Transactions Act (UCITA). UCITA, which has been adopted by Maryland and Virginia, specifies the standards for user agreements and mass market computer licenses, among other provisions.

Although UCITA calls for an opportunity for users to review contract terms, it does not require a formal acknowledgement of the terms. It only calls for "the opportunity to review a record or term only if it is made available in a manner that ought to call it to the attention of a reasonable person and permit review."

Critics of ProCD and UCITA, and the user agreements and mass market licenses they support, argue that such contracts often expand the scope of copyright and in effect, "privatize copyright." Scholars also argue such agreements restrict information that might otherwise be in the public domain.

The concept of the public domain has received renewed attention by scholars in the wake of UCITA and an upsurge in congressional legislation awarding new and expanded rights to intellectual property owners. Although definitions of it vary, the public domain is widely thought of as that mass of freely available material such as facts, data, systems, methods, ideas, theories, and other uncopyrightable material from which new intellectual creations, such as news stories, are born.

Lessig described the public domain as a "commons" which is "a part of our world, here and now, that we all get to enjoy without the permission of any." Benkler said it is an institutional device "that entails government abstention from designating anyone as having primary decisionmaking power over use of a resource."

Litman wrote that "the term describes a true commons comprising elements of intellectual property that are ineligible for private ownership. The contents of the public domain may be mined by any member of the public." In essence, the public domain's purpose is to "safeguard the raw material that makes authorship possible." Boyle wrote that the U.S. Supreme Court acknowledged as much in Graham v. John Deere Co. of Kansas City and gave the public domain "a constitutional dimension." The Court wrote:

The Congress in the exercise of the patent power may not overreach the restraints imposed by the stated constitutional purpose. Nor may it enlarge the patent monopoly without regard to the innovation, advancement or social benefit gained thereby. Moreover, Congress may not authorize the issuance of patents whose effects are to remove existent knowledge from the public domain, or to restrict free access to materials already available.

Thus, because the public domain is comprised of freely available and accessible material from which new expressions and creations are composed, it contributes in large measure to our free speech protections under the First Amendment. It is something that the news industry both contributes to and benefits from.

Protecting Publisher Liability. In the last several years, Congress has offered internet service providers (ISPs) protection from liability for republishing potentially libelous or infringing content on the theory that providers should not be held responsible for what their users write and transmit. Section 230 of the Communications Decency Act provides that "no provider or user of an interactive service shall be treated as the publisher or speaker of any information provided by another information content provider."

While newspaper publishers of online news sites do not directly qualify as ISPs, courts interpreting Section 230 are widening the definition of internet service provider to include others who provide interactive services on the Internet. But ISPs and others are required to act in good faith to claim the protections of Section 230.

In the Digital Millennium Copyright Act, Congress gave ISPs similar protections for the redistribution of infringing content. The DMCA limits liability as long as the provider lacks "the requisite knowledge of the infringing activity," and upon receiving notice of a possible infringement "must expeditiously take down or block access to the material." Again, providers are obliged to show good faith.

UCITA also addresses liability for electronic content. Specifically, Section 404 of UCITA eliminates an implied warranty-in essence eliminating liability-for inaccuracies within "published informational content," which is defined broadly as "informational content prepared for or made available to recipients generally, or to a class of recipients, in substantially the same form."

Drafters of UCITA saw "published informational content" as news: "This is the information we read, listen to, enjoy and communicate.

It is the content of digital newsletters, multimedia encyclopedias, and online databases. This is the material of the First Amendment. It is published and made available generally, in contrast to the type of information that a consultant or lawyer provides for its specific client." Thus, UCITA seeks to eliminate the liability of online news providers for inaccuracies and errors on their sites and inaccuracies and errors in links to other published material.

On the surface, legislation that limits liability for republication and inaccurate content appears to support an open marketplace, both for the exchange of speech and commerce. But such legislation, because its interpretation is still evolving and not clear whom it covers (beyond traditional ISPs) and what constitutes good faith, may unwittingly contribute to the growth of user agreements.

User agreements become the tool by which these issues (and others not addressed by legislation) are clarified. But problems may arise when a user is unable to negotiate the terms of an agreement that expands limitations on liability or the scope of the law.

His choice is either to accept these terms or look to read his news or engage in news forums elsewhere. As private actors, online news publishers are within their rights to limit their liability and the activities and speech of readers on their sites by using private contracts. But when such terms are overreaching and unnegotiated, fundamental First Amendment values may be at stake, even in the absence of state action. Thus, this study evaluates the extent to which those values may be threatened by examining online news user agreements, their terms, and the implications for readers of online news.

Research Questions and Method

This study analysed the online news user agreements of the Top 50 daily circulation U.S. newspapers according to the 2000 Editor & Publisher Yearbook. The sample included Monday through Friday newspapers that also have online news Web sites. The Top 50 circulation newspapers were selected because they are assumed to be among the top investors in producing online news products and represent the majority of newspaper owners in the United States. Financially viable and successful, these newspapers will be at the forefront of developing terms of use policies for their online news readers.

The online user agreements of the Top 50 newspapers were studied during 25 and 26 March 2001. Each user agreement was entered into an N-Vivo database and was coded for:

- User acceptance terms,
- Copyright restrictions,
- Rules regarding acceptable language on the site and limitations of liability.

Each of these subjects was common to all the agreements, although the actual wording and extent of the provisions varied.

These categories were chosen to address the following research questions:

- Are news user agreements adhesion contracts? This question addressed the extent to which users are bound by such agreements when they read online news.
- Do the provisions of news user agreements expand

the scope of copyright law by restricting the use of material that might otherwise reside in the public domain? This question addressed the extent to which readers were restricted from reusing uncopyrightable news information found on the site.

- Is speech in interactive forums and publisher liability limited and to what extent? This question addressed the kinds of speech online publishers sought to restrict as well as the limitations of liability they claimed. It was hoped that this question might reveal the extent to which fundamental First Amendment values and standard journalistic practices were at risk.

Findings: News User Agreements as Contracts. Nearly all the user agreements in the study were found by clicking on small type found at the bottom of the home page. Half of the fifty online news user agreements stipulated that use of the site was an acceptance to the terms. Only the Wall Street Journal Online required users to click "I agree" to the terms of use. The Denver Post's acceptance provision was representative of the other agreements: "By using this site, you signify your agreement to all terms, conditions, and notices contained or referenced herein ('Terms and Conditions of Use'). If you do not agree to these Terms and Conditions of Use, please do not use this site."

Twenty-nine of the fifty user agreements in the study restricted an online news user's choice of forum for litigation. The Arizona Republic's forum restriction was characteristic of most other sites: This Agreement is entered into in the State of Arizona and shall be governed by and construed in accordance with the laws of the State of Arizona, exclusive of its choice of law rules. As a party to this Agreement, you agree to submit to the exclusive jurisdiction of the state and federal courts sitting in the County of Maricopa in the State of Arizona, and waive any jurisdictional, venue, or inconvenient forum objections to such courts.

Additionally, thirty of the agreements specified that the terms of use could be changed at any time without notice to the user. The Miami Herald's terms were similar to many of these provisions: "You agree that we may modify the terms of this Agreement (or discontinue this site) in our sole discretion, without advance notice, and that your right to access this site is conditioned on an ongoing basis with your compliance with the then-current version of these Terms and Conditions. You should therefore visit this page frequently."

These findings indicate some departure from the traditional view of contract law in which there is an offer, acceptance, consideration, and mutual agreement. Indeed, with these provisions, the agreements look more like contracts of adhesion, contracts that "you didn't bargain over, but which were presented as a take-it-or-leave-it offer." For half the readers of online news in this study, use of the site constituted an agreement to the terms of the user agreement.

In practical terms, this finding may be and often is an acceptable risk for online readers, much as the act of parking in a parking garage indicates a driver's agreement to the risk posed by rules of parking in that particular garage. But the nature and importance of "condition-less" news in a free society is easily more important than "condition-less" parking. Online news user agreements make access to news a condition of conduct that is fundamentally different from walking down the driveway or to the local newsstand to pick up a newspaper. It imposes on the reader a series of limitations that he is obliged to accept or else look elsewhere for his news, a restraint that arguably impinges on an uninhibited and robust marketplace of ideas.

Online Reader Restrictions on Use of Site Material: The study also revealed that online news providers were particularly concerned about protecting their copyright. Forty user agreements contained copyright notification and restrictions on redistribution and retransmission of content. Typical of these provisions were the New York Times' requirements:

You may not modify, publish, transmit, participate in the transfer or sale of, reproduce, create new works from, distribute, perform, display, or in any way exploit, any of the Content or the Service (including software) in whole or in part. You may download or copy the Content and other downloadable items displayed on the Service for personal use only, provided that you maintain all copyright and all other notices contained therein. Copying or storing of any Content for other than personal use is expressly prohibited without prior written permission from The New York Times Rights and Permissions Department, or the copyright holder identified in the copyright notice contained in the Content.

In sixteen sites, online news providers either overstated copyright law's ability to protect the reuse of material on their sites or simply created a new property right by virtue of the agreement. These agreements claimed copyright in the "text" of the site; prohibited use or "exploitation" of "any" or "all" content; or simply prohibited the "creation of new works" from material on the site. Copyright protects original expression, not "any" or "all" elements of expression, and the "creation of new works" is exactly what copyright law was designed to protect. One agreement went as far as claiming a right to public domain material: "The entire contents of the Web site, including public domain Content, are protected as a collaborative work under the U.S. copyright laws (emphasis added)." While online news publishers were within the scope of copyright by asserting derivative rights, these agreements reflected an attempt to expand those derivative rights or create new rights in public domain material.

Other restricted uses included: database construction (twenty sites); reverse engineering, a process by which the original components or source code of a programme are identified (twenty-four sites); deep linking, a link or links to pages deep within a news organization's site (thirteen sites); and framing, in which users place their ads or other content around another site's content (nine sites). Database construction may or may not violate copyright, depending on whether the content taken by the user is sufficiently original to be copyrightable. Facts, often a large component of databases, are not sufficiently original to be copyrightable and may be freely used in the construction of databases.

Certain aspects of reverse engineering-the process by which a user copies or downloads the source code of a programme or Internet site-have been ruled a fair use by courts.

Restrictions on deep linking (thirteen sites) attempt to prohibit other sites from linking to pages deep within a news organization's site, bypassing its home page. Framing restrictions (nine sites) prohibit users from placing their ads or other content around the provider's content, thereby "framing" the provider's copyrighted material. Both practices are controversial and have only recently been brought before the courts. Not surprisingly, both practices are prohibited by the Washington Post, which in 1997 sued Total News, a Web site that took news content from the Post by framing it.

Another provision in the agreements claimed copyright ownership of any material posted by users. In the study, twenty-three online news sites claimed ownership to material posted or e-mailed by users. In some agreements, publishers claimed ownership of submitted material, but refused to take responsibility for the content. Some agreements also claimed a right of publicity based on the use of such content, giving online news publishers a right to use the contributor's name for any submitted material, for nearly any purpose. This apparent contradiction between claiming a right to a user's name and/or ideas but limiting liability for the content was found in the Los Angeles Times user agreement, which first stated: "You assume full responsibility for the content of all messages posted by you or through your Account." But the next paragraph stated:

You grant TI (Tribune Interactive), its affiliates and related entities, including Latimes.com, a royalty free, perpetual, irrevocable, non-exclusive right and license to use, copy, modify, display, archive, store, distribute, reproduce and create derivative works from all information you provide to us, in any form, media, software or technology of any kind now existing or in the future.... You also grant TI and its affiliates and related entities the right to use your name and any other information about you that you provide in connection with its use and with the reproduction or distribution of such material, and also grant TI the right to use any material, information, ideas, concepts, know-how or techniques contained in any communication you sent to us for any purpose whatsoever, including but not limited to developing, manufacturing and marketing products using such information.

The study also revealed that online news publishers are telling users how they will cooperate with investigating authorities looking to prosecute infringers. At least ten online agreements contain provisions that explained how users may or may not be notified in such cases. Furthermore, twenty-three sites in the study stipulated that the online publisher has the right to remove or block potentially infringing content.

While these findings lend support to the notion that online publishers may be overly restricting the reuse of information, the study indicated some recognition for the public domain and notions of fair use. As the only subscription service and the only clickwrap agreement of the fifty sites studied, the Wall Street Journal Online appeared to accept the importance of some copying and redistribution, but cautioned against wide electronic redistribution:

You may, on an occasional and irregular basis, disseminate an insubstantial portion of content from WSJIE, for a noncommercial purpose, without charge, and transmitted in non-electronic form, to a limited number of individuals, provided you include all copyright and other proprietary rights notices with such portion of the content in the same form in which the notices appear in WSJIE... You may not post any content from WSJIE to newsgroups, mail lists or electronic bulletin boards, without the prior written consent of Dow Jones. To request consent for other matters, please contact Dow Jones Customer Service.

Furthermore, twenty-eight sites had provisions that allowed users to make one copy for "personal, non-commercial use." One site went as far as allowing users the right to make ten copies of "part or all of its contents" for personal, non-commercial use. While at first this would seem to embrace the reuse of some site material, the subsequent restrictions on redistribution and some of the more expansive provisions outlined here generally indicated otherwise. Furthermore, restrictions on redistribution of online news content essentially abolished copyright's doctrine of "first sale," in which the buyer of a copyrighted work is permitted to share, sell, or give his tangible copy of the work to another. Under these user agreements, sharing a copy of online news with a friend or co-worker violated the terms of access to news.

Limitations on Liability and Speech: Thirty agreements in the study expressed limitations on liability. These limitations focused on two primary concerns: limiting liability for the inaccuracy and reliability of the site's content and limiting liability for material posted by users in interactive forums.

A sampling of the provisions in these user agreements revealed:

- Twenty-seven sites limited or eliminated liability for errors or inaccuracies in site content.
- Twenty-one sites limited or eliminated liability for the transmission of viruses; for any damages caused by the site to user computers, businesses, etc.; or for errors and inaccuracies in third party content, such as news from syndicates.
- Eight sites limited or eliminated liability for delays in service.

While the provisions suggested a legitimate interest in protecting publishers from frivolous lawsuits, particularly on the basis of links to third-party content, the language of some provisions appeared to contradict time-honored traditions of fair, accurate, and timely news reporting. For example, from the Chicago Sun-Times: "By using this Web Site, you assume the risk that the information on this Web Site may be incomplete, inaccurate, out of date, or may not meet your needs and requirements." And from the Daily News, a provision that seemed to redefine the concept of news: "The Daily News assumes no responsibility for any errors or omissions in these materials. The Daily News makes no commitment to update the information contained herein."

As for restrictions on speech in interactive news forums, twenty— seven agreements contained varying restrictions on "libelous," "defamatory," "obscene," "harassing," or "hateful" speech in interactive news forums.

Bans on various forms of commercial speech, including spam, solicitation, and advertising, were also common. While some forms of expression mentioned in the agreements were indeed unprotected by the First Amendment-obscene language, for instance-other forms of restricted expression appeared to reflect attempts by online publishers to promote polite behaviour among participants in news chat rooms. Agreements commonly prohibited the use of language that was "inaccurate," "disparaging," "indecent," "abusive," or "objectionable." Much of this language was left undefined.

The New York Times user agreement contained some of the longest and most specific terms of conduct for behaviour and speech in its online forums:

Be courteous. You agree that you will not threaten or verbally abuse other Subscribers, use defamatory language, or deliberately disrupt discussions with repetitive messages, meaningless messages or "spam."

Use respectful language. Like any community, the Forums flourish only when our Subscribers feel welcome and safe. You agree not to use language that abuses or discriminates on the basis of race, religion, nationality, gender, sexual preference, age, region, disability, etc. Hate speech of any kind is grounds for immediate and permanent suspension of access to all or part of the Service.

Debate, but don't attack. In a community full of opinions and preferences, people always disagree. NYTD encourages active discussions and welcomes heated debate in our Forums. But personal attacks are a direct violation of this Agreement and are grounds for immediate and permanent suspension to all or part of the Service.

The user agreements of the Boston Globe and New York Post curiously required users to "strictly limit yourself to discussions about the subject matter for which the Forums are intended." The Star-Tribune agreement prohibited "false" material on its service. As private actors with interactive services, these online news publishers are allowed to set the terms for use and access to their services.

Agreements that limit online liability and speech may simply reflect standard business practice and make smart business sense.

But some of these provisions clearly neglect key First Amendment values and standard journalistic practices that the traditional press has sought long and hard to protect: the right to an uninhibited, robust, and wide-open forum for debate; tolerance for vehement and sometimes caustic viewpoints; and room for the kind of error that is inevitable in free debate (followed by a demonstration of accountability when errors are made).

The lack of state action should not end our inquiry into how online news publishers are defining their obligations to these values and to their readers in this new medium. The evidence here supports the argument that some online news publishers are not including these key First Amendment values and journalistic practices in their user agreements. They seek to limit speech online and limit their responsibility for content. Again, such stated limitations may be well within their rights as private actors,but the force and substance of these agreements-in their highly legalistic form— allot more freedom to online news publishers than to their readers and don't serve to strengthen ties to readers that the Internet makes possible.

Summary and Conclusions

Online distribution changes the conditions under which news consumers may be informed about their world. Where previously readers bought their news, now they must access it-and in the process, agree to the provisions spelled out in user agreements. In some cases, they must either accept those provisions or look for their news elsewhere. Furthermore, this study revealed that some provisions attempted to expand ownership of information that might otherwise flow freely in the public domain. It also demonstrated that some agreements expanded notions of copyright law. Finally, it revealed efforts by publishers to limit speech in online news forums and limit liability for unlawful and objectionable content. While these latter provisions may be well within the rights of online news publishers, the content and effect of such agreements raise serious questions about fundamental First Amendment and journalistic values for online publishers.

Although limited by an examination of fifty online news user agreements, the results of this study suggest that user agreements can protect a publisher's rights and show evidence of his desire to control what can, at times, be a rather lawless Internet. But by defining their relationship with readers in legal form, publishers risk distancing themselves from readers rather than creating new ties-and revenue-the Internet was supposed to promise.

For readers, agreeing to the terms of an overbroad user agreement may seem an insignificant or safe risk. But the cumulative effect of promoting terms of access to news may create new risks for a healthy marketplace of ideas and a vibrant, free-flowing public domain from which new works, including news stories, are created. Restrictive terms of access shrink the availability of public domain information, the lifeblood of journalism and of all new creative and informational works. While it is still early in the history of online news, publishers would be wise to reread their user agreements with the intent to promote the values they have long preached.

Chapter 7

First Amendment Freedoms Meet Private Property Claims

As we enter the twenty-first century, a conflict between fundamental rights that has been in many ways long suppressed is coming increasingly, indeed insistently, to the fore. First Amendment free speech and press rights, and related interests in newsgathering and the free dissemination of information, are colliding head-on with a variety of property claims.

Although there has always been some tension between property ownership and free speech, a number of developments suggest that the intersection of property rights and free expression will be an increasingly important feature of the First Amendment landscape. Decisions currently being made by legislatures and courts may well have a profound influence on the future course of free speech and the free flow of information.

To those of us interested in free expression, property rights hardly have the same cachet as First Amendment freedoms. Yet, as legal scholar Justin Hughes has pointed out, property rights are almost certainly more fundamental to our legal system than are conceptions of freedom of thought and expression.

Hughes noted that "ideas about property have played a central role in shaping the American legal order. For every Pilgrim who came to the New World in search of religious freedom, there was at least one colonist who came on the promise of a royal land grant or one slave compelled to come as someone else's property." Property rights thus have a central place in the legal universe and often tend to trump competing claims. Because various property doctrines developed both earlier than, and largely in isolation from, legal concepts of free speech, the intersections between legal principles from the two areas are often confusing.

Property claims that potentially conflict with free speech interests are legion. They include copyright, trademark, the right of publicity, newsgathering torts, and a host of other possible claims. As intellectual property scholar Diane Leenheer Zimmerman, writing nearly a decade ago, noted: "The truth is that, despite large areas of peaceful coexistence between the values protected by the Speech and Press clauses and those defended by property doctrines, conflict between the two is serious.

What seems to have happened in the course of this conflict is that an everexpanding array of new or reconstructed property theories is cannibalizing speech values at the margin. In large part, this has occurred not because speech claims are inherently weaker than property claims, but because courts fail to think critically about the justifications for, functions of, and limitations on property rules in the sensitive area of speech." If anything, the conflict between speech and property rights has intensified in the years since Professor Zimmerman wrote those words.

This chapter will examine a few "hot spots" in the ongoing struggle between property claims and concerns with free expression and the free dissemination of ideas and information.

No claim is made that this brief survey is encyclopedic. Rather, the attempt is to touch on a few key intersections that highlight the larger theme under discussion. In the interest of an accessible discussion, I have in some spots omitted a few legal niceties, for which I hope my fellow legal scholars will forgive me. The chapter first touches on "real" property claims that affect free speech, and then moves on to a brief discussion of (intangible) intellectual property claims that have similar implications.

It is important to note the sort of claims this chapter is not making. I am not urging, with Proudhon, that property is theft. The claims herein are rather arguments about the balance between property rights and speech rights, between ownership and that which is held in common. Ownership is important, but property rights should not be wielded in a way that seriously undercuts the vital social interest in free expression and the free flow of information.

FIRST AMENDMENT RIGHTS AND "REAL PROPERTY"

SPEECH ON PRIVATE PROPERTY

One of the fundamental conflicts between the freedom of speech and property is the ability of speakers to use private property to deliver their messages. This is a claim toward which the U.S. Supreme Court has in recent years been unsympathetic, although the Court has left the states some leeway.

In one of the first cases in which the Supreme Court encountered the issue of free speech on private property, Marsh v Alabama, it appeared the Court was eager to make some accommodation between First Amendment rights and those of property owners.

In Marsh, decided in 1946, a Jehovah's Witness sought to proselytize in the business district of a "company town" that, although acting as a municipality for its residents, was entirely situated on private property. One crucial issue in the case was whether there was "state action," that is, whether government was acting to prevent speech-a prerequisite to any First Amendment speech claim.

The Court upheld the speaker's right to distribute literature by finding that the private town, by performing a "public function," created the necessary state action. "Ownership," the Court noted, "does not always mean absolute dominion." Because the property's owners had opened it to public use, they were not thereafter completely free to limit the expression of ideas. The Court expanded the

Marsh holding in 1968 in Amalgamated Food Employees Union Local 590 v Logan Valley Plaza, Inc.

In this case, the Court, noting the similarity between a shopping centre and the privately owned business district in Marsh, held that a union had a First Amendment right to picket a store in a private shopping centre. The Logan Valley Court pointed out that public streets, parks, and sidewalks had long been considered public fora for speech and that the private shopping centre was closely analogous to such fora. Once again, the mere existence of private property was not necessarily a bar to expressive activities under the First Amendment.

In several opinions over the next few years, however, the Court moved away from allowing speech rights on private property.' In 1976, in Hudgens v NLRB, involving a labour union protest within a private shopping centre, the Court explicitly overruled the Logan Valley decision. The Court rejected the constitutional equivalency of the shopping centre and the company town in Marsh.

The Court's majority rested its analysis primarily on the state action issue, eventually concluding that the First Amendment simply had no application to the union protest because it was not on public property, hence the government had not acted in preventing the speech. It is worth noting, however, that the Court has ruled that individual states, under their own state constitutions, can provide access for speakers to private property that is greater than that offered under the First Amendment.

Thus, with the exception of some important cases involving access to the broadcast airwaves, the Supreme Court has largely rejected free speech rights in connection with private property. The Court's rationale, as noted above, was not so much that private property rights "trump" free speech rights, but that constitutional free speech guarantees simply do not operate in the absence of state action, which the Court found lacking in private property disputes.

This is an important distinction, because in the absence of state action, speech claims simply lack the legal standing to gain even a glimmer of recognition in the realm of property law.

NEWSGATHERING ON PRIVATE PROPERTY

While the absence of any federal constitutional right to speak on private property has been clearly established, recent attention has focused on the ability of private property holders to win large damage awards from journalists for venturing onto their property-not to speak, but to gather information for later speech-related activities. A number of important recent cases have challenged the rights of journalists to gather news on private property.

These newsgathering cases have largely sprung, ironically enough, from the success press defendants have had over recent decades immunizing themselves against such publication-oriented claims as libel, false light invasion of privacy, and infliction of emotional distress.

As plaintiffs experienced increasing difficulty in winning awards for the content of what journalists wrote or broadcast, astute plaintiff's lawyers began to focus on the means by which the information was gathered, including any newsgathering that may have taken place on private property. Thus claims for trespass or the "intrusion" branch of privacy law became more common, even though many plaintiffs were, in all likelihood, really seeking damages for the publication of the information.

A classic illustration of this phenomenon is the Food Lion case. In Food Lion, Inc. v Capital Cities/ABC, Inc., a jury awarded more than $5 million dollars in punitive damages for trespass, fraud, and breach of fiduciary duty after ABC producers armed with hidden cameras obtained access to in-store "deli" areas by obtaining employment with the supermarket chain. The award was later reduced significantly. Food Lion did not make a libel claim, which would have been subject to significant First Amendment barriers. The Food Lion court was careful to point out that reputational damages, such as those recoverable with a libel claim, were unavailable, but still allowed the jury to award punitive damages.

A better-reasoned federal appeals decision, Desnick v American Broadcasting Co., rejected a variety of claims, including a trespass claim, against persons posing as patients at an ophthalmology clinic suspected of performing unnecessary surgery.

The pseudo-patients, who were sent by ABC, used hidden cameras to gather information. Noted federal appellate judge Richard Posner held that the clinic's trespass claim was without merit because the law frequently recognizes consent obtained by misrepresentation as a valid defence against trespass.

For example, the court noted, the law rejects trespass claims in cases of visits to restaurants by restaurant critics, browsing by shoppers who cannot afford the merchandise, and dinner guests "who never would have been invited had the host known their true character." By concluding that the pseudo-patients had not truly interfered with the possession of the property, Judge Posner seemed to recognize the true aim of the clinic to use a property claim simply to punish ABC for its broadcast.

The Desnick case notwithstanding, an increasing number of lawsuits are successfully using property-based claims to attempt to recover for harms caused by publication or broadcast of the information.

The key point is that property law is seemingly being used as a legal subterfuge to inhibit freedom of speech, since many plaintiffs have little or no genuine damages from the invasion of their possessory interest that trespass law protects, but instead are seeking a "neutral" cause of action that can punish the press in some way for the content of the subsequent news report.

ELECTRONIC TRESPASS ON THE INTERNET

Private property doctrines are being extended metaphorically from the physical world to the digital environment of the Internet in ways that may significantly limit the free flow of information. A number of courts have accepted the notion that trespass law applies to the unconsented transfer of electronic signals to a company's computer system, including unsolicited e-mail. In one of the most widely publicized cases, a federal district court in May 2000 issued an injunction preventing an on-line business called Bidder's Edge from using a software robot to "crawl" through Internet auctioneer eBay's computerized listings. Bidder's Edge is an "auction aggregation site" that allows users to search for a given item on numerous Web-based auctions simultaneously.

The court based the injunction on a trespass claim springing from the electronic signals Bidder's Edge sent to eBay's computer system. Although eBay did not argue that its computer systems had been damaged or that it had suffered any financial loss, it did claim that the loss of bandwidth resulting from Bidder's Edge's robotic activity was an appropriation of property eBay could have used for other purposes.

In the wake of the district court's injunction, twenty-eight Internet law professors filed a "friend of the court" brief urging that the injunction be reversed. The law professors argued that electronic commerce holds out the possibility of improved social welfare because of increased competition and because consumers can comparison shop with relative ease on the Internet. The eBay injunction, however, threatens those benefits by allowing online merchants to bar the use of tools that facilitate comparison shopping, such as Bidder's Edge's software robots.

Moreover, the law professors argued, the injunction raises the possibility that individual web sites could use trespass law to block search engines and even simple linking to their sites, effectively eviscerating the openness and the free exchange of information that is the very foundation of the Internet. As one commentator has argued, the Internet is "a public accommodation that is accessible to all users. While servers are private property, a server's voluntary inclusion on the Internet is conditional on affording general access to the public."

Fortunately, other courts have affirmed this general

openness of the Internet. For instance, a California federal district court denied an injunction sought by Ticketmaster Corp., the well-known ticket broker, in August 2000. Ticketmaster claimed trespass, along with a host of other legal theories, against Tickets.com, a competitor that sent customer through "deep links" to the interior of Ticketmaster's web site to purchase tickets for entertainment and athletic events. Although the Ticketmaster court claimed to be "impressed by the original and resourceful thinking" of the judge in the eBay case, the court denied the injunction due to an inadequate showing of harm to Ticketmaster. Still, the court left open the possibility that the trespass theory might have merit given different facts.

As the law professors' brief suggests, allowing trespass claims to succeed on the basis of information gathering on the Internet poses a significant threat to the medium. The trespass approach creates the possibility of a once-open Internet enclosed through trespass doctrines, allowing web site operators unprecedented control over the terms of entry. The great social and economic advantages of the Internet could be significantly undermined through the metaphorical barbed-wire fence of trespass law.

As economics professor James Brock told Fortune magazine: "In many ways the beauty of the new economy is that it perfected the functioning of markets by expanding the information available to people. The question is, Should eBay-or any other company-be able to refuse to be part of the loop?"

INTELLECTUAL PROPERTY AND FREE SPEECH

EXPANDING COPYRIGHT AND RELATED RIGHTS

Not only are doctrines derived from real property law creating new and potentially serious impediments to freedom of speech, but intellectual property law is doing so as well. Intellectual property protections are often conceived as consisting of patents, copyrights, trademarks, trade secrets, and, in some taxonomies, rights of publicity. Copyright protection is a special form of intellectual property that derives from the Constitution, which authorizes Congress to enact both copyright and patent statutes "to promote the Progress and Science and useful Arts by securing for limited Times to Authors and Inventors the exclusive Right to their respective Writings and Discoveries." Copyright law was thus conceived from the outset in U.S. law as less a means to secure some "natural right" for creators than as a utilitarian scheme that creates public benefits (more creative works, more knowledge) through limited monopolies.

One of the continuing controversies within copyright law is how to create the right mix of incentives to encourage creation of new works while still allowing maximum use and dissemination of that same material by others for the public good. Among other doctrines, the idea of fair use has been seen as an important mechanism to achieve this goal.

Fair use allows for the unconsented dissemination of at least portions of copyrighted works for such purposes as criticism, news reporting, and scholarship. Other devices that seek to ameliorate the monopoly aspects of copyright law include the first sale doctrine, which allows a purchaser of a copy of a copyrighted work to dispose of that copy however the purchaser wishes, including selling, lending, or giving away the copy, and the limited term of copyright, which guarantees that after the copyright on the work expires, the work will return to the public domain where it is available for use by all.

Scholars have long recognized potential conflicts between copyright law and the First Amendment right of free speech. To the extent copyright creates monopolies in certain expressive material, other speakers are thereby precluded from using that material in their own expression.

In a series of articles published in the 1970s, a trio of copyright scholars explored the tension between copyright and free speech. Leading copyright scholar Melville Nimmer, while recognizing the potential conflict, argued that the idea-expression dichotomy generally provided a sufficient means of sorting out the competing interests at stake. The idea-expression dichotomy holds that copyright protects only the expression of an author-his or her unique presentation of a more general idea or aesthetic-while leaving the ideas in the public domain and thus free for use.

Nonetheless, Nimmer noted circumstances in which copyright doctrine and First Amendment interests could not be squared, and urged independent judicial use of the First Amendment in those cases. Both Paul Goldstein and Robert Denicola suggested, among other things, interpreting the fair use provision in light of First Amendment interests in a vibrant public domain.

The Supreme Court of the United States has claimed that copyright doctrine itself already adequately accounts for First Amendment interests. In Harper & Row v Nation Enterprises, the Court stated that First Amendment interests are "already embodied in the Copyright Act's distinction between copyrightable expression and uncopyrightable facts and ideas, and the latitude for scholarship and comment traditionally afforded by fair use."

Despite the popular attention to Napster, MP3.com, and other challengers to intellectual property rights holders, the digital future seems to hold, if anything, even greater and more precise control by rights holders over their creations. Through both technological and contractual devices, rights holders are striving to create maximum control over their works, often much greater in degree than that allowed by the "default" copyright regime of the federal Copyright Act. On the technological side, "trusted systems" are being developed that will allow copyright holders to prevent unauthorized uses of material, even after it is in the hands of consumers.

Consumers will not so much be "buying" the work as obtaining a limited license that is subject to continual technological monitoring by a digital gatekeeper. As trusted system developer Mark Stefik explains:

Suppose that you have a digital work stored on a trusted system, and you do not have the right to copy the work. Then, if you asked the trusted system to make a copy, it simply will not do it. Instead, it will give you an error message. If you do have a right to copy and, for example, exercising the right requires paying a fee and certification that you are [of a given age], then the trusted system would first make sure that the conditions are satisfied. Only then would it make the copy.

Not only would such systems provide for the increased propertization of works, but recently enacted federal law provides sanctions for those who would seek to circumvent trusted systems, encryption, or similar devices. The Digital Millennium Copyright Act of 1998 outlaws the circumvention of technical protection mechanisms that inhibit access to copyrighted works, as well as devices designed to help in such circumvention.

Moreover, there is no fair use under the DMCA. Although the Librarian of Congress has exempted very limited noninfringing activities from the Act, on its face the DMCA provides the legal enforcement for a regime of perfect control by copyright owners. Perfect control is, of course, highly problematic from the standpoint of the First Amendment and the free flow of information.

Aside from technological "fencing" of content, various contractual strategies also create the possibility of a much-enhanced control of intellectual property. Cases such as ProCD, Inc. v Zeidenberg stand for the proposition that information providers can create "shrinkwrap" licenses (contracts that consumers agree to simply by opening the package) that extend protection of works far beyond what copyright law alone would protect. (In the digital environment, consumers are often asked to consent to similar "click on" or "clickwrap" contracts.) In ProCD, the issue was whether Matthew Zeidenberg could use material from a compilation of telephone directories in ways that violated the terms of the shrinkwrap license.

This material, which very well might not have been protected under the federal Copyright Act, was subject to control by ProCD, a federal appeals court held, because of the contract on the box. Even though by no stretch of the imagination does a consumer truly assent to such contracts, the court found that because of the presumed "voluntariness" of the exchange, ProCD could legally extend its control of the information far beyond what the "default" law-the Copyright Act-would allow.

A lower court had refused to enforce the contract, claiming that such contracts "would alter the 'delicate balance' of copyright law" and "allow parties to avoid the copyright law by contracting around it." Theoretically, such contracts could eliminate defenses such as fair use, extend the term of protection indefinitely, protect underlying ideas, and even protect exclusive rights in information that is presently uncopyrightable, such as simple facts.

The question of control of facts brings up another means by which expanding property doctrines, at least potentially, may encroach upon material that was previously considered part of the public domain and thus free for all to use. Under current copyright law, as noted above, facts are not copyrightable and are freely available to all. In an important 1991 U.S. Supreme Court decision, Feist Publications, Inc. v Rural Telephone Service Co., Inc., the Court held that the "white pages" of a phone directory constituted mere facts that were not arranged with sufficient originality to justify copyright protection.

Even though the telephone company that published the white pages had put effort into assembling the phone book, that alone did not mean that copyright protection was warranted. Because U.S. copyright law was intended as an incentive to promote original creations, mere compilations of facts without sufficient originality in selection or arrangement did not qualify.

The Feist case illustrates the important point that facts are-and should be-available as building blocks for future knowledge and creations and should not be monopolized by the first individual who happens to assemble them. Since Feist, a number of database publishers have pushed Congress for the adoption of so-called sui generis protection of compilations of facts.

Sui generis protection, which already exists in Europe,

would create a statutory monopoly outside of copyright law and have potentially ominous effects on the free use and dissemination of factual information by scientific, educational, and other users. Depending on the version considered in Congress, these sui generis statutes could create monopolies of at least fifteen years, and potentially much longer, on the use of all or a substantial part of information or data that was created as a result of a substantial investment if the use would harm the market for the database.

Under such a regime, anyone who wished to use the facts or data subject to protection would have to pay whatever price the market would bear. As one critique of sui generis protection put it:

The technological convergence that creates promising new markets for information goods also opens new opportunities for scientific and educational uses of data and information. However, a powerful movement to commodify data and information previously treated as a public good-that is, as an inexhaustible, indivisible, and ubiquitous component of the public domain-could limit the ability of the scientific, technical, and educational communities to capitalize on such opportunities.

Sui generis protection thus threatens to constrict the public domain by limiting access to facts and information previously available for dissemination and use by all.

Although sui generis protection would exist separately from copyright law, copyright law itself has numerous doctrines that arguably overprotect the property interest of the copyright holder at the expense of free expression interests. One deeply disturbing distinction between copyright protection and other realms of free speech law concerns the ease of attaining injunctive relief.

In standard First Amendment jurisprudence, injunctions against speech, known as prior restraints, are anathema. In the seminal case of Near v Minnesota, the Supreme Court in 1931 struck down a Minnesota law that allowed injunctions against the publication of newspapers in certain circumstances. The Supreme Court's decision established an extremely high constitutional bar for future prior restraints, and later cases have affirmed the judicial reluctance to enjoin speech in all but the most extreme circumstances. That stringent constitutional standard goes out the window, however, as legal scholars Mark A.

Lemley and Eugene Volokh point out, when the case involves alleged copyright infringement. As Lemley and Volokh note: "In copyright cases... preliminary injunctions are granted pretty much as a matter of course, even when the defendant engaged in creative adaptation, not just literal copying." Lemley and Volokh point out that simply asserting that copyright law protects a "property" interest is inadequate to explain the disparity. Libel law, for example, could be characterized as protecting a property interest in reputation, and yet libelous speech can almost never be restrained via a preliminary injunction.

As Lemley and Volokh argue: "Congress can't get around the First Amendment merely by characterizing otherwise protected speech as treading on a property interest... "This key point in the prior restraint argument is one that could be widely applied to property claims in general-the invocation of the word "property" is not an incantation that magically dispels free speech rights. Indeed, in the copyright context, prior restraints are aimed at the content of the speech, and content-driven restrictions are particularly disfavored under the First Amendment.

A final point that merits a brief mention is the continuing expansion of copyright terms, which impoverishes the public domain by lengthening the period of protection under the Copyright Act. In 1998, Congress passed the Sonny Bono Copyright Term Extension Act, which added twenty years to most copyrights. This creates the specter of what legal scholar Peter Jaszi has called "perpetual copyright on the installment plan."

Not only does such a retroactive extension, supported by Time Warner, Disney, and others, prevent important cultural products from entering the public domain, but it is potentially unconstitutional. A group of plaintiffs, represented by cyberlaw scholar Lawrence Lessig, has argued in the courts, so far unsuccessfully, that retroactive extensions violate the First Amendment and the Copyright Clause of the U. S. Constitution. The Copyright Clause states that copyright law should promote "the progress of science and the useful arts," yet retroactive extensions cannot achieve that goal because the authors are usually long dead and thus the extension provides no incentive for additional creation. The public domain from which all creative works arise is thus impoverished for the benefit of a few large corporate "content providers."

RIGHTS OF PUBLICITY AND RELATED CLAIMS

Another form of intellectual property that of late seems to be muscling its way into previously protected territory under the First Amendment is the right of publicity. The right of publicity, which exists in both common-law and statutory forms, is a right particularly valuable to celebrities that protects the use of one's name, likeness, or other aspects of one's persona, particularly in advertising or promotional contexts. Initially connected with the law of privacy, publicity rights have in the last fifty years or so taken on an explicitly "proprietary" character (hence their frequent association with other intellectual property rights), including the notion that the right can be "assigned" or transferred to others.

A number of commentators have recognized the expanding nature of these rights, including legal scholar Mark Lemley, who noted that "one need not use an actual person's name, likeness, or voice to run afoul of the right of publicity—Vanna White, Bette Midler, and Tom Waits are apparently entitled to prevent anyone (or anything) from looking or sounding too much like them."

Publicity rights, which can vary depending on state law, have long been limited by a broad "newsworthiness" or "public interest" defenses. These defenses, sometimes based explicitly on the First Amendment, have been particularly successful for news organizations in arguing that portrayals of celebrities are legitimate, newsworthy dissemination of ideas, even if the news operation in question thereby earns a profit. A few recent cases, however, suggest that publicity rights are being pushed beyond their traditional zone of protecting against commercial uses.

In Hoffman v Capital Cities/ABC, Inc., a California federal district court in 1999 ruled that Los Angeles Magazine infringed actor Dustin Hoffman's right of publicity (among other claims) by publishing a digitally altered photo of the actor in a designer dress and heels. The original photograph was of Hoffman in a different dress as he appeared in the 1982 motion picture Tootsie.

The altered photograph appeared in a Los Angeles Magazine article titled "Grand Illusions," in which photographs of past and present movie stars were digitally altered to clothe the stars in current fashions. The Hoffman photograph was accompanied by the text: "Dustin Hoffman isn't a drag in a butter-colored silk gown by Richard Tyler and Ralph Lauren heels." Even though the photograph appeared in the editorial pages of the magazine, the court ruled the use a "commercial" one and rejected a First Amendment defence.

The court concluded that the article "provided no commentary on fashion trends and no coordinated or unified view of current fashions. The article contained no statement that any particular style of clothes is in vogue, that any particular colour is becoming popular, or that any type of fabric is attracting the attention of designers."

Moreover, the court held, the use of Hoffman's likeness was "unnecessary." The court also found that, despite numerous disclaimers, as well as the title of the article ("Grand Illusions"), the magazine's First Amendment defence failed because the computer-altered photograph was knowingly false.

The Hoffman case was a disturbing one for many in the press, who believed that valid editorial uses of the names or likenesses of celebrities were protected under the First Amendment. Although the court suggested the photograph was an advertisement in disguise, many observers were concerned that the case entered dangerous new territory for a right-of-publicity claim, particularly with the judge's observations about the "proper" elements of a fashion story.

Another cause for concern came with a case brought by golf prodigy Tiger Woods' agent against the publisher of an art print titled "The Masters of Augusta" that included Woods' likeness. Woods contended the work, which was sold as a "limited edition print," infringed his right of publicity. The judge, fortunately more attuned to First Amendment concerns than the Hoffman judge, rejected Woods' right of publicity claim, ruling that the use of Woods' likeness in an art work was not commercial in the sense of merely proposing a commercial transaction and thus was protected by the First Amendment.

The court noted that the print was "an artistic creation seeking to express a message. The fact that it is sold is irrelevant to the determination of whether it receives First Amendment protection." Although the First Amendment argument prevailed in the district court, the case is on appeal at this writing and has generated friend-of-the-court briefs by a number of organizations concerned about its implications, including the Society of Professional Journalists and the Reporters Committee for Freedom of the Press.

Although the preceding cases are only trial court decisions, and only the Hoffman case actually resulted in a verdict with serious First Amendment implications, it is nonetheless clear that right of publicity claims (as well as related Lanham Act, unfair competition, and trademark suits) are a pressing concern for First Amendment advocates. Unquestionably, celebrities should be able to protect their personae from commercial exploitation to some degree, but when they seek to withdraw their images from valid news, public affairs, or artistic uses, they are cutting into the public domain that must be available to ensure free expression on matters of culture, whether high or low.

Private Property and a Vibrant Public Sphere: The troubling collisions between property claims and free speech interests discussed briefly above do not admit to any uniform remedy.

In the case of real property claims that seek to inhibit newsgathering, it is important that courts avoid formalistic analyses and recognize that property claims are often deployed simply to squelch or punish otherwise protected speech.

Trespass claims on the Internet also required careful, nuanced handling to avoid significant inhibitions on an open network. The apparent expansion of intellectual property rights has even more far-reaching implications, with at least part of the cure found in a clearer recognition by courts that First Amendment rights should not stop at the shoreline of intellectual property law. The potential privatizing of the public domain should be cause for great concern.

The larger point is that, despite their differences, the issues discussed above illustrate an unfortunate tendency of property owners to use their ownership rights to limit free expression and the free flow of information. How can this tendency be combated? One way is through a frank recognition that property claims are not absolute. The use of the word "property" cannot serve as a legal object of worship that simply stops all thought. In the intellectual property area, it is also important to recognize, following a number of important commentators, that a vibrant public domain is the raw material from which all important ideas and creations arise, and that the notion of the romantic author, creating ex nihilo, is simply a myth.

As Jessica Litman points out: "The very act of authorship in any medium is more akin to translation and recombination than it is to creating Aphrodite from the foam of the sea. Composers recombine sounds they have heard before... novelists draw their plots from lives and other plots within their experience.

This is not parasitism; it is the essence of authorship. And, in the absence of a vigorous public domain, much of it would be illegal." Thus, to the extent the law fences off larger and larger portions of our intellectual and artistic commons, scholarly, artistic, and cultural discourse will suffer.

Moreover, the public domain, as Litman notes, includes

not just those works whose copyrights have expired, but those aspects of currently copyrighted works that are not protected by the statute, including facts, ideas, and portions of copyrighted works that are used fairly. To the extent that technological and contractual devices, along with new sui generis protections, seek to render the copyright scheme irrelevant, the recognition of a First Amendment interest in a vibrant public domain is even more critical.

At the end of the day, private property claims must not be permitted to overwhelm First Amendment values. While various statutory and constitutional remedies may be called for within each of these substantive areas, it may also be worthwhile to recognize the broader themes that are being played out. A vibrant public sphere requires that ownership claims sometimes give way to First Amendment interests, to what Justice Benjamin Cardozo once called "the matrix, the indispensable condition, of nearly every other form of freedom."

Chapter 8

Good Intentions, Questionable Practice

Reformers see journalists following their own stars, distancing themselves in egregious ways from their audiences, and from society, and failing to serve First Amendment purposes. Some proposals redefine constitutional protections to favour audiences. Others would reconstitute journalism itself within the Constitution's protective fold. All encourage journalists and their corporate owners to abandon self-destructive policies, challenge their newsroom orthodoxies, and formulate coverage policies that bring citizens into informed participation in the democratic system.

Christians et al. redefined the role of the individual in society, rejected the individualism created by the Bill of Rights, and elevated community needs over individual needs. Journalists, who derive protected individualistic status from the Constitution, were invited to consider community above other concerns, consciously shaping the community: "A revitalized citizenship shaped by community norms becomes the press's aim—not merely readers and audiences provided with data, but morally literate persons".

The goal of the press, in their view is "not a luminous cranium [of the information function], but surefootedness... not merely correct doctrine, but proper action". Public and civic journalism advocates call for journalists to return to "dialogical inquiry between press and public" and the "exercise of a stewardship of free expression".

Changes, however should assure a cure that does not

ultimately become worse for participatory democracy than the illness.

Consequences of immediate communitarian attractions are widely visible in the world. Nearly 80% of the world's population live in rule-bound traditional cultures that change little from generation to generation. These cultures appear to be victims of communtarians of a millennium past. Yet, today's drive toward this collectivity ignores history.

News media are in deep trouble. Despite best efforts the past two decades, audience losses threaten the existence of traditional news media.

One dramatic indicator of the slippery slope newspapers find themselves on: In March 1995 only 45% of Americans said they had read a daily newspaper the previous day, down from 58% in February 1994, and 71% in 1965. Should declines continue, newspapers could find themselves verging on the extinct by the year 2000.

Over-the-air television, particularly news, is also suffering a remorseless audience decline. Households that watch news from any source (network, magazines, local) dropped from 74% in 1994 to 64% in 1995 to 58% in 1996.

These losses may not all be attributable to journalistic misdeeds, but it is possible that journalists, by their actions, are not making themselves competitive in the drive to attract audiences needed to inform public consent.

Thus, both the journalism establishment and its communitarian critics may be on a destructive path in their scramble for solutions.

Many media problems are the product of the very developments at least one of the critics seek. Christians et al.'s arguments for a community-based press may be pressing a change from one deplorable communitarianism for another collective behaviour.

Much of current media woe may be traced to classic symptoms of a communitarian syndrome. The difference is a matter of emphasis.

A fearful media has become highly communitarian (*selective* as distinguished from the more inclusive Christians et al. communitarianism). Even so, any communitarianism is resistant to changes that might reinvigorate the media and bring them closer to publics they are expected to serve. Such resistance is frustrating to solution-minded onlookers, even to the reformers. This entrenchment, however, offers an instructive lesson in long-term consequences for those who advocate a more extensive brand of cooperative community.

Christians et al. described a system in which significant parties unite to act for broad community benefit. In fact, communitarianism is now widespread in narrower settings of profession, religion, or ideology.

Remedies for media ills may lie with individualists whose selfish excesses are the target of communitarian campaigners. Individualism is the alternative to the idyllic communitarianism.

Individualists are the only hope for pluralism communitarians devalue and assume present in "shared value"s deliberations: "The real enemy is an empty, shallow, unfed pluralism that neglects or trivializes serious political issues and matters of moral substance".

That unfed pluralism, historically endemic in small town newspapers, is rapidly spreading to desperate television news in all markets and to midsized metropolitan dailies where circulation loss is most dramatic.

In these areas, the media have already become convulsively communitarian in desperate efforts to survive the combination of public disaffection and exploding media forms. These are predictable and observable consequences of both communitarianism's mesmerizing attraction and its predictable results. Communitarianism, for all its virtues, historically can be relied upon to seduce the insecure.

Selective communitarianism of current American media, observable in shallow political coverage, is in part media reaction to audience drain.

This communitarianism has produced cloned products indistinguishable among competitors. Media orthodoxy, using the simplest, visible example, dictates to television stations that story importance is determined by audience-attracting visual footage. This practice squanders valuable newscast minutes on insignificant stories with available visuals: crashed small planes, house fires, bullet holes from drive-by shootings, and so forth.

Christians et al. used examples of the communitarian orthodoxy to illustrate the destructive individualism that grips journalists. One was a Florida judge's divorce story with accusations of spouse beating and child molestation (though one-sided and ambiguous, and for which no criminal charges were filed):

> A news story would invariably give a slant that could devastate the judge's career and embarrass his daughter at school. Obvious private solutions are being tried. Yet the editor knows against every measure of community decorum that he must run the story. To withhold publication would deny the courage of independent journalism.... When the story appears, the troubled family is humiliated publicly.

Christians et al., interpreted the editor's decision as a selfish "professional integrity" act of individualism when it may equally be interpreted as an act of an editor in the thrall of professional dogma, knowing this is "what journalists do." Visceral dependence on newsroom, professional dogma may be more prevalent in journalism than the individualistic decision making attributed to the Florida editor. It merely may be that the editor was more closely tied to his professional community than to his residential community. Examples of community journalism find editors so tuned to their communities (particularly leadership groups) that communities have unrealistically virtuous images of their leadership.

Societies, subgroups, and individuals inevitably grasp at communitarian discipline as an answer to the troublesome unpredictability of crises, or even the inconveniences of life.

Durable, living examples of this practice on a broader scale are found in more than 75% of the world's population (80% by the year 2000), on all continents, composed of peoples who centuries ago organized into freeze-frame, cooperative, change-resistant, high consensus-low controversy cultures that endure today much as they were those hundreds of years ago. Today's media are responding to intense competition by installing audience-oriented policies ("Tell people what they want to hear.") and requiring policy-oriented orthodoxy in coverage ("Don't make them angry," and "Don't take risks."). These characteristics of much present-day journalism are important elements in the durability of traditional societies.

The Flaw of Maintaining the Community: A fundamental flaw in communitarian cultures is their obstinate resistance to change and an almost unreasoning compulsion to shape the system to facilitate community maintenance or survival.

In the American context, media have become compulsive profit-seekers, abandoning original roles of providing pluralistic information.

A liberal democracy was born from the commitment to individualismthe inclination and ability of individuals to retain rights to self-determination in the face of community pressures.

It is those rights of self-determination that breed creativity and risk-taking to meet the challenges of competition and shrinking audiences.

Who can doubt that collective, cooperative efforts are desirable, even critically necessary, for short-term social good? Enlistment and organization of individuals and organizations (even media organizations) into unified groups is vitally necessary for much achievement.

But as media "cooperation" with community and audience rises as a highly seductive, but ultimately mandatory, alternative to unruly individualists, it is imperative that the inevitable consequences of unconditional membership be explored.

Media desperation is creating unconditional membership in professional communities. A "we will do whatever you want if you will read/listen" attitude gallops through society.

Such a communitarian drive blinds media to their function of stimulating participation in the decision making processes, both locally and nationally. Instead, they provide what they think is wanted and the result is, at best, trivia. At worst, it is pandering. This communitarianism is far more responsible for social problems than is individualism.

A defence of individualism, the riskiest of alternatives, must start with the dangerous structural tendencies of communitarian societies and the inevitable information philosophies they produce; disastrous end results of the communitarian path critics would have the media travel.

The communitarian threat is greater because shifts to communitarianism, unlike those toward individualism, tend to be irreversible, or reversible only at great social cost. Communitarianism at its most effective is intolerant of individualism and controlling of information. Individualism, on the other hand, must tolerate both communitarian and pluralistic information.

It is not that communitarian effort is undesirable, or that individuals should not commit themselves to cooperative behaviour based on shared values. However, problems result when the individual is so submerged by communitarian structures that the ability to make her own decisions, or to survive outside the collective community is lost. Many editors and journalists today appear to find themselves captivated by a professional community desperately circling its wagons to cope with competitive forces. This apparently reduces or eliminates the possibility that media can shake the demands and venture on their own into the substantive, principled journalism of Rosen and Lambeth.

There are notable exceptions, even in the television industry. KVUE of Austin, Texas "decided to steer away from the age-old news motto 'if it bleeds, it leads' and adopt a new set of standards for each crime piece it ran". The thoughtful approach produced "best ever" ratings the following month.

The community of shared values turns sinister in an entrenching process that immunizes those values to change, reducing the probabilities the community will remain dynamic and progressive.

Riesman suggested that sense of community is socialized into individuals; his outer-directed person who needs to look to others for decisions. Market researchers find two-thirds of

Americans outer-directed, incipient communitarians needing confirmation of correctness from others. Such is the nature of a community with shared values and goals; a community in which the individualist with differing views is dangerous just for not reinforcing the values of the community.

Despite the attraction and undoubted short-term benefits of cooperation, problems soon begin, feeding a generalization that consensus groups (communities)—by the nature of their evolutionary structure—morally bankrupt themselves. Evolution from dynamic to static society (as occurred with today's traditional societies) is a particularly virulent corruption, despite the attraction and apparent comfort in such societies, but there are two specific corruptions in a dynamic culture.

TWO POINTS OF CORRUPTION

Journalism is vulnerable to the two demands of community. The first is necessary, but deplorable on principle, because of inherent individual dependency in an increasingly complex society.

It lies in the loss of individuality and autonomy community membership requires. Every group requires as a membership fee some sacrifice of autonomy, ranging from adapting to a small group of friends (learning their minimum standards for continued association) to virtually total abandonment of individual rights entailed in entering the military in wartime. Dedicated individualists may join groups from self-interest, yielding some individualism but departing once their goals are achieved. Communitarians tend to find homes in groups, and yield identity in their search for clues about how to behave. Media units yielding autonomy become part of the tyranny of the majority, or at least of the community power structure.

Submission to the collective distances the communitarian from the individual, shaping the treatment of information and its distribution, and leading to power concentration for the collective good. A journalist who yields to community loses the ability to assure pluralism for the community.

The second point of corruption, inevitably, is crossed when the group becomes more important than the reason it was established. It is this second threshold that is most important from a moral perspective.

Two sets of conflicting principles are specifically affected by sense of community. First, Loyalty to a community is the inevitable price of acceptance, the membership fee creating sharp conflicts with fidelity to Truth. Second, attitudes toward information shift from the need for a broad range of information (Pluralism) to a reliance on information necessary to maintain community values and fortify the status quo (Reinforcement). Other conflicts are inevitable, but these two have a particular relevance for journalists and their constituents.

LOYALTY VS. TRUTH

Sooner or later in formation and maintenance of a community, group importance transcends the value of distributing accurate information both internally to members of the group, and externally about the community or group. Indeed, the very demand for communitarian journalism is a call for selective information appropriate for community well-being. Criticism of the Florida editor's story about the judge's domestic problems was, at root, a call for community tranquility in preference to the stresses of an open-information community.

Once the successful group establishes itself, optimizing membership, and wins its niche as a recognized social institution with power to pursue its original goals, emphases change. It is an obvious evolutionary process. Drives change from trying to achieve socially beneficial ends to maintaining hard-earned position in the social structure. Priorities subtly reverse.

Once success is achieved through pooling the power of shared values, the community (by now directed by a power elite, including journalists) inevitably turns to valuing itself and its perpetuation above its individuals and surrounding communities. This, of course, is at odds with the needs of a dynamic society in a liberal democracy committed to truth and accuracy. It probably is at odds with the community envisioned by Christians et al. Such a society in the end can only rely on the moral sense of journalists and other maverick individuals to pressure the community, reducing probabilities of disproportionate power accumulation.

Group loyalty, achieved through the reinforcing ability of a compliant media, increases the power of the group, and centralizes power in leadership. Groups intent on self-perpetuation find no shortage of adherents.

As Hoffer said, "the chief passion of the frustrated is 'to belong,' and there cannot be too much cementing and binding to satisfy this passion". Riesman recognized the need to belong soon overrides the need to achieve and the organization soon exists for its own sense of community, though it may profess to seek goal achievement. Presentation of a united front, and confidence that belonging is a primary goal of many members, invests great power in a professional leadership, even in voluntary organizations, that has a vested interest in perpetuating itself.

An ideal community in a liberal democracy is one that forms on an ad hoc basis, fills its function, and disperses without need for perpetuation; or whose leadership is, perhaps, voluntary and amateur, without vested interest in maintaining power.

Alternative newspapers of the 1960s and 1970s, for example, formed to protest government policies. Once demands for such protest died (the end of the VietNam War, primarily), many alternative publications faded (the *Los Angeles Free Press* comes to mind).

Others moved closer to establishment values in seeking stable readership in order to establish advertising rates (*Rolling Stone* magazine and the *Bay Guardian* of San Francisco are far milder of tone than they were 25 years ago) and perpetuate themselves through an arguable form of corruption. Thoughtful editors do their more contributive work when they make common cause with community leaders for limited projects for the common good.

The manager who replaces the idealogue in the successful community demands loyalty and establishes structures to maintain the group. Hence, members who relinquished substantial individual autonomy for an altruistic purpose ultimately find themselves lending little but their numbers to the perpetuation of the group, having been locked out of the administration by an efficient bureaucratic structure dedicated to, first, strengthening the organization and, second, advancing the cause, a reversal in priorities.

Even an editor who lends herself to the community in these ways loses the power of self-determination and becomes a slave to community maintenance; a cheerleader.

The need to perpetuate the organization reorders priorities to require that Loyalty transcend Truth as a virtue. While the individualistic editor has the possibility of exhibiting a commitment to Truth—no guarantees, of course—the goals of a community inevitably blind her to the value of truth if it endangers community. Protesters are banished or otherwise punished. Journalism history is littered with accounts of small town editors run afoul of community power.

Community tranquility prevailed for the small-town Utah editor who kept from her community for two years the knowledge that the mayor and the town's hospital administrator, in a sexual relationship, were plundering the hospital's soft drink machines to finance trysts. Community leaders successfully discouraged the disclosures.

The ideal community, of course, sees little need for power struggles for it is established to achieve certain goals and disbands when those goals are achieved. Such a community is likely to be composed of individuals who have a larger vision of life than the immediate achievement of short-ranged goals. They may see such achievement as a stepping stone toward the rest of the life's endeavors. The communitarian, on the other hand, is most likely to see participation as the overridng activity that gives life meaning.

When group maintenance (loyalty) overpowers commitment to Truth, a terrible subversion occurs. This end is inevitable when the communitarian dominates generations of members. Such communitarian selfishness is rampant today: Public reaction of the law enforcement community to the Rodney King beating case was based less on truth and justice than on the effect public debate and disclosure would have on the professional group's ability to make its own rules in filling what it sees as its public role.

Loyalty, while a relative virtue, is destructive when it conflicts with more absolute virtues such as Liberty.

PLURALISM VS. REINFORCEMENT

Communities and individualists require differing information systems. An individualist needs high volume, high quality information to function in a competitive society, while the community requires maintenance and enhancement. Continuous group reinforcement is a central device for creating individual self-esteem important to community. The individualist generally does not control the channels through which information flows, thus has an interest in having those channels open to virtually every message as the only practical way of assuring at least the possibility of adequate information to inform individual decisions.

The individualist opts for an informationalist system with its general assumption that audience members, or consumers, have rational abilities to make decisions with some hope they will be informed decisions. The informationalist journalist accepts the responsibility to distribute pluralistic information about causes she abhors. Implicit in this is acceptance of the likelihood that views change as one adds more information to her knowledge base.

Truth, of course, is of highest priority in this system, for information retains its validity only so long as there is a perception of routine breadth and fidelity. Perception must be that the system is adequate to warn one of items needing attention, and the warnings substantially accurate. Such a system allows a maximum of autonomy in individual decision making. The editor's obligation is clear for the individualist.

The purposive community, on the other hand, requires a much different internal system. A communitarian editor, trading moral autonomy for group membership, necessarily becomes a cheerleader, or reinforcer.

Such a stance assumes (for either selfish or altruistic reasons) the community view of the world is correct and should neither be challenged nor subject to change. A reinforcer sees group loyalty as a primary virtue (almost an absolute) and is typically concerned about maintaining the status quo, suspicious of information that might threaten that state. Further, there is approval of questionable, or even false, utterances that reinforce the status quo.

TODAY'S WELL-MEANING COMMUNITARIAN FLAW

Today's communitarians envision societies in which participants with shared values discuss rationally and decide in the community interest. However, the very information systems installed by those with shared values will ultimately fail to inform the discussions. Decisions by these groups will be flawed by ignorance, products of, first, the narrowness of shared values, and second, information restrictions.

Another scenario describes a community of passive individuals seeking self-esteem through the reinforcement system led by a shared values elite. Nevertheless, those decisions, will not be of community, but of a questionably informed elite, with questionable goals, imposed on the community.

Inherent in communitarian arguments is that cooperative behaviour entails open discussion in a community of shared values. This must certainly be a fallacy, for the very nature of a group structure, with shared values, and membership incentives will inevitably—as restrictions on dissonant information increase—tend toward the views of strong leaders. A pluralistic, problem-solving dialogue in a communitarian setting is difficult to picture. More likely, a discussion based on shared values will work its way toward a predictable conclusion. Hence, creativity and risk are lost.

Group norm behaviour, "seeing the system itself as more basic than the rights of individual members", almost naturally controls those who do not see legal and moral transgresssions as of "different kinds", but, when they think of comparative virtues at all, lump loyalty with truth, a choice from among equals. Loyalty is a strong favourite, traditionally, to win such a battle in the community. In the 1990 Utah congressional election, for example, last minute disclosures about a candidate's moral character placed an "assured" election in jeopardy.

A major city mayor, the state governor, and two U.S. senators appeared on television two days before the election, praising the character of the questionable candidate. They gave no indication of ambivalence about the candidate and offered whole-hearted support. Three were elected officials from the candidate's party. The nonpartisan mayor later received an appointment to the State Tax Commission.

This action, typical of communitarian behaviour and a demonstration of communitarian value ordering, is deplorable to a community placing Truth high on its list of virtues. Under the circumstances, could there have been an open discussion among the four men before they made their commercial? Even a pretense of a discussion would predictably revolve around the party's (a group) best interest; not those of either the candidate or the public. In short, the group was willing to prop up a morally questionable candidate rather than endanger party unity.

Cheerleading is a socially pervasive self-preservative state of mind for audiences, sources, supervisors, practitioners, all of us, that springs from the control effort explored above. This is thoughtless and short sighted, resulting in social stagnation and an information vacuum. One who seriously questions the morality of elevating community tranquility to the superior position over truth will find the answer in the traditional societies of the world. Problem solving progress must stop because unity is the higher value.

ABOUT THE INDIVIDUALIST

The individualist marching to her own drummer is often not a comfortable person with whom to associate. However, some comparisons of best and worst in individualistic moral development are important to the communitarian perspective.

Only through individualism is moral autonomy, and therefore moral development, possible. A communitarian adapts to the communty's moral stance. As leaders become captives of the group, and the group, in turn, is captivated by its leaders, the group's values dominate, reinforcing the assertion that moral corruption of those values is inevitable. Conformity is valued over moral autonomy. If the group is "moral" the loyal individual will be moral. When the group corrupts the member goes with the group.

When moral development of the individualist fails, on the other hand, she becomes dangerous, for group values that restrain members are not effective. As a litmus test, the degree to which selfishness rampages in a society may well be an indication of the moral development of its individuals, and the state of its communities in fostering and encouraging individual moral development. A communitarian community, by its very nature, shuns the individual moral development that leads to moral reasoning, anathema in a cooperative community.

That is, nothing restraints the selfishness of the individual, nor does a corrupt, self-serving group contribute to a healthy moral climate.

Consider briefly the example of 75% of the world's people currently living—happily until options are presented—in the traditionalistic, conservative societies formed hundreds of years ago with "shared values conferences." Those conferences, we conjecture, sought the idyllic, low stress, cooperative society of minimal conflict and high predictability, a society in which members naturally cooperate for the common good. The results are easily observable today, vast cultures which froze themselves in time by rejecting controversy and change and deifying consensus and agreement. Information systems in those societies reinforce the correctness of the conventions. Pluralistic systems become alien intrusions to be rejected or converted.

At the same time, the selfish individualist of a stunted

moral development environment is not likely to contribute to the social good, because "There is very little to be said in favour of an individualism which takes its orientation from a conception of the individual as essentially 'the proprietor of his own person, for which he owes nothing to society'".

Ideally, the morally developed individual accepts a broad communitarian responsibility and looks at effects of her behaviour on society at large. Such behaviour is, at root, individualistic/moral in nature because groups inevitably lure the individual from the absolute moral virtues toward the self-perpetuating, or group maintenance behaviour that favors the smaller, immediate group at the expense of society at large:

In Rawls's view, the morality of principles is the final and highest stage in the individual's moral development. For the morality of principles does not depend upon our relationship with our parents. Nor does it depend upon ties of friendship and mutual trust. It depends upon allegiance to the principles of right.

Prime example of a communitarian, collective society in embryo is a new marriage, the beginning of a new family unit. With 47% of these units currently disintegrating within a few years, the suggestion must be that selfish individualism is alive and strong. Among solutions to this problem are a communitarian-oriented uncritical acceptance by marital partners of values that reject divorce as a option, thus forcing some incompatibles to cohabit for life (one of them, perhaps, to be brutally abused), or for principled individualism to recognize the need for early self-sacrifice by both partners for the later benefits offered by a strongly supportive, cohesive family unit.

Society is better served by avoiding shortterm attractions of collectivism and self-serving individualism, as painful and as taxing-of-patience as it may be. Such a society should place a high priority on the development of moral reasoning and the application of principles in the lives of its citizens—education, rather than conditioning.

As for group unity as prerequisite to achievement of

worthy goals, the group's ultimate purposes are best served when the group has some principled individualists lending their creativity to the process but reserving the right to, with principled judgment and knowledge, withdraw when the group loses sight of the "end rather than means" attitudes toward its compliant members inherent in communitarian appeals. The possibility of resource defection constantly confronting group leaders, and continually threatening group existence, has a sobering effect on power centers, reducing their willingness to exploit members for sake of group continuance.

Moral sensitivity is necessary for the individualist. A communitarian is largely regulated by the discipline of the group while an individualist is largely a free agent; therefore, moral sensitivity is imperative in an individualistic society. On a pessimistic note, it is well to consider a society's loss of faith in the moral judgment of its individuals compels it to seek communitarian solutions because individualism is too dangerous to survive. Society will evolve to fit conditions described earlier, rule-bound, predictable, and convenient; all questions answered, no new ones needed; all behaviour prescribed, few examination of existing rules required or allowed.

Chapter 9

Web to Gather News

Like other users at information-oriented businesses, news media uses of online technologies such as the World Wide Web and Internet have grown rapidly. At least one media critic has boldly labeled the Internet as the future for journalism.

- Another scholar argued that the roles and nature of work of journalists are changing with the introduction of new online technologies.
- Most professional news organizations had some form of Web or Internet presence at the beginning of this decade. While some news organizations use their sites for promotion, community relations or electronic commerce, many news organizations use the sites as extensions of their traditional news missions.
- Use of the Web as a newsgathering resource has also grown rapidly since public awareness and commercial use—including that by news organizations—of the Internet and Web began rapid expansion.
- New media—in the form of the Internet and the Web—have had a revolutionary impact on journalism.
- It is changing the role the journalist has served as an intermediary. It offers a broad range of new technologies with which to deliver messages and is creating its own form of journalism. The current technologies of new media make newsgathering and production more efficient, faster and cost-effective.

These technologies also enhance producer creativity and encourage new approaches to old tasks.

- Internet, the latest generation of network computing, is thought to have an even more significant impact on news reporting and content delivery.
- Most newspapers today use the Internet and Web in some manner to distribute news and other types of information. Approximately 4,900 online newspapers have been created throughout the world and about 3,600 of those are in the U.S.
- The content of online newspapers is maturing. Instead of their original duty of carrying the print edition content, many of these publications have developed their own personalities through original content and purpose.
- These publications give attention to accuracy as well as speed in reporting information.
- The newspapers' sites have generated considerable traffic.
- Online journalism has been characterized as having three dimensions—interactivity, personalization and convergence.
- With newsroom use of the Web and the Internet approaching 100 per cent penetration, it is important to fully understand how the Internet and the Web are used in news media newsrooms.
- The purpose of this study was to analyse Web usage through the study of daily newspaper journalists. The study focused on how news organizations used the Web to locate information, types of sites that were used, perceptions abcut the strengths and weaknesses of information found, Web-based technologies most often used and perceived advantages and disadvantages.

Theoretical Perspective

Theoretical perspectives and communication models integrating the use of interactive technologies are slow to emerge in journalism and mass communication literature. The newness of interactive networked information media must be viewed as a contributing factor.

- Diffusion theory and the uses and gratifications approach are the dominant theoretical paradigms for research focusing on new media.
- Some studies have viewed use of the Internet and the Web in the diffusion of innovation theory context, discussing the spread of use of the new technology in news organizations and in the general public.
- Because of its fluidity and rapid integration into many business and other work environments, few other models or theoretical contexts exist for study of the use of the Web. While diffusion research, the study of the introduction and spread of new technological innovations, has value in understanding the flow of information or new innovation through a system such as newsgathering, it does have limitations. Like information flow theory, diffusion theory is source, not end-user, dominated.
- Other theoretical perspectives are also problematic in their application to use of interactive online media. Uses and gratifications research, which studies the motivations for media exposure, how media are used and the rewards derived from that use, focuses on the receiver or user of a medium and his or her purposes for using it. Such a framework offers an approach or model at best and is not very theoretical.
- As Severin and Tankard observed, research literature does not reveal a deep foundation of uses and gratifications research aimed at understanding new technologies and active audiences. "Researchers have only begun to study the ways that cable television and other new media offering expanded user choices relate to the user's pursuit of uses and gratifications," they wrote.
- The literature on uses and gratifications of new technologies such as cellular telephones, computers,

networked computers and other interactive media is evolving.

- Application of the Web and Internet in news organizations remains widely under-studied and weak in theory, but a first generation of literature about Internet and Web use in general
- As well as Internet and Web use by journalists
- Has appeared. It remains, however, a goal of such scholarship to identify a suitable explanatory framework for analysis and study.

The Web as an Information Resource: Newsrooms are making a serious commitment to the use of computers and computer training in gathering news.

- Daily newspapers are using the Internet and Web to search for, and gather, information.
- Hundreds of Web search tools have been developed and have become available. In 2001 there were several hundred major search engines in use and that number was growing.
- Ross and Middleberg found that print and broadcast journalists most often used the Yahoo! search index and their favourite search engines were AltaVista and Netscape Search.
- Yahoo! and AltaVista were clearly dominant, another study found, suggesting that journalists like to use both the index approach and the key word search strategy in their online research.
- Web users are often frustrated by the sheer volume and complexity of finding authoritative information. The common reaction is to give up and claim there is nothing on the Internet about the subject.
- Advanced search options are usually indicated by a hypertext link to a different page at the search site. Advanced options offer tools employing Boolean logic to combine user-defined key words. Other approaches of advanced searches include setting inclusive or exclusive dates, searching by domain names or categories using quantitative search

parameters. Some search engines and indices permit truncated searches that produce results similar to search terms and proximity searches that find terms adjacent to search terms.

- Not all search indices and engines are the same, of course. They often vary in the basic software they employ to search at the basic and advanced levels.
- Selection of a search tool has a significant impact in locating information.
- Paul and Williams listed selection of resources, site stability, currency, usability, searchability, listing and usage fees and link descriptions as indicators of quality search sites.
- The requirement of fees by some Web search sites has become a restrictive factor. With a growing number of sites that charge fees, individuals have greater access to information that was previously not on the Web or was very hard to find.
- Because search engines differ in the size of their databases, procedures used to develop the database, frequency that the databases are updated, search options, speed of response and even basic user interface, users must be aware that search outcomes vary widely.
- Successful searchers employ a variety of strategies.
- Bates attributed the accomplishments of experienced professional searchers to their curiosity, use of an iterative or repetitive process, personal expertise and knowledge, analytical abilities, background discussions with clients and a sense of when to end the search.
- Journalists may have difficulty, like other persons using the Web, in separating high quality information from that which is less valuable. This is due, one study found, to Web designers who seek to disguise information quality, to inadequate training of journalists using the Web, and in the verification processes involving online content. This maybe

significant because the study concluded that the Web would eventually become a substitute for other sources of information.

- In one analysis of online newsgathering problems, the leading concerns expressed by newspaper journalists were verification of information, unreliable information, badly sourced information, and lack of Web site credibility. Technical problems, such as download time or finding site addresses, were not perceived to be as severe.

A wide range of new Web technologies has made gathering and delivering information challenging for even experienced online users. Interactivity through various features of Web sites is one of the most distinguishing characteristics of online journalism. Journalists can interact with readers and sources using electronic mail, video and audio conferencing, instant messaging, chat rooms and similar features.

Despite the new technologies available to enhance interactivity with audiences, critics have argued that newspapers are not using these new technologies to their full potential. Daily newspapers have not made necessary changes in the way they collect and distribute news. Some have said that newspapers are following the old model of presenting news every 24 hours instead providing continuous updates and that they are just creating "shovelware"—the term used to describe the process of taking the content of a print edition and reproducing it on a Web site.

Experts have also argued that newspapers are not taking advantage of special features of the Web such as its interactivity, hypertext and multimedia. Dibean and Garrison found that most online newspapers have adopted Web technology innovations such as links to related information and consumer services such as searchable classified advertising. Emphasis seemed to be on electronic commerce, they concluded, perhaps at the expense of news content delivery.

On the other hand, journalists were not using other

Internet-related technologies as frequently as they used the Web. Evidence indicates that electronic mail has been commonly employed for communicating with sources and for gathering information.

But other potential information retrieval resources on the Internet, such as file transfer protocol, telnet, "push" Web technology, audio and video-based conferencing, telephony and other multimedia features were used much less or very little.

Journalists using the Web have expressed concern for the quality of sites when gathering information. One German study found that journalists sought well-structured sites with more information on content than graphics and sites that adequately attribute information. Journalists perceive success in using the Web when they find information they seek, especially when it has been a challenge to locate. They seek background information and what they consider to be "difficult-to-find" information using online resources.

Journalists also believe extension of government coverage and success in finding sources were positive aspects of online research. Other studies of what makes useful Web content for journalists underline the value of local information. The most often perceived failure of online newsgathering determined in a recent story was that journalists did not take advantage of the potential of online research. A related complaint, lack of online access, was also cited. Lack of training and slow learning of online tools was found to be additional causes of online research frustration for journalists.

The literature leads to the following research questions:

*RQ*1: How do journalists find information on the World Wide Web? What search tools are in use? How are they used?

*RQ*2: What type of content Web sites are most often used for gathering information for news stories?

*RQ*3: What characteristics of Web sites used for gathering information are perceived by journalists to be strongest? Weakest?

*RQ*4: What Web-based technologies do journalists use for gathering information?

RQ5: What are the perceived successes and failures of use of the Web as a newsgathering tool?

METHODS

Self-administered questionnaires were mailed to a census of daily newspapers with 20,000 or greater Sunday circulation in January-March 1997, January-March 1998, and January-March 1999.

Because literature related to this project was found in industry or trade publications but was quite limited in journals, questionnaire items were developed from interviews with journalists and from group discussions at national conferences about investigative reporting, computer-assisted reporting and news research in addition to available literature. While most of the questions used each year were the same, some questions were added of deleted from individual instruments as changes in availability of tools or use of computers required.

The unit of analysis was the newspaper. Questionnaires were mailed with postage-paid return envelopes to the computer-assisted reporting supervisor, the managing editor, or the executive editor. When sent to a general editor, the letter asked recipients to forward the questionnaire to individuals most qualified to respond. This resulted in a respondent group of specialists that included investigative reporters, computer-assisted reporting specialists, news librarians, news researchers and editors.

Respondents were asked to reply on behalf of the entire newsroom, indicating their perceptions of newsroom use. While a longitudinal design was used and consistency in individuals responding at a particular newspaper each year was sought, the same individual did not always respond because of turnover and changing responsibilities. Population sizes were 510 newspapers in 1997 and 504 newspapers in both 1998 and 1999. In each census, two follow-up mailings were used to enhance response. Response rates were n = 226 or 44.3 per cent in 1997; n = 185 or 36.7 per cent in 1998 and n = 176 or 34.9 per cent in 1999.

FINDINGS

Respondents to the three surveys were demographically diverse and provided circulation, respondent newsroom role and regional representativeness of the population studied. They represented a range of newspapers, from small to very large, within the defined population. Individual respondents were computer-assisted reporting specialists or supervisors, news researchers or editors-newsroom managers.

Most respondents described themselves as editors but another large group consisted of computer-assisted reporting supervisors. Some respondents, especially those at smaller dailies, held multiple roles. The mean and median newspaper circulation each year was consistent. Respondents were also geographically balanced.

*RQ*1: How do journalists find information on the World Wide Web? What search tools are in use? How are they used?

Data indicate clear patterns of World Wide Web use by journalists. In 1998 and 1999 journalists preferred to use Yahoo! (62.2 per cent and 68.2 per cent) and AltaVista (65.9 per cent and 61.4 per cent) as their primary search resources. Other major search tools, such as Excite (22.7 per cent and 26.7 per cent), Netscape (18.4 per cent and 22.7 per cent), HotBot (18.4 per cent and 22.2 per cent) and InfoSeek (24.3 per cent and 20.5 per cent), were not as widely used and suggested limits to the range of search tools used.

Respondents reported that they selected the search tool according to the type of search the site conducts, familiarity with the site, and the type of information that was needed. Advanced search options, offered on almost all major search sites, were used by nearly three-quarters of respondents—but only about one in six "always" used the option. About three in five "sometimes" used such options.

*RQ*2: What types of content Web sites are most often used for gathering information for news stories ?

State and federal government sites dominated the categories of most-often used sites. Over the three-year period, state sites were most often used, but there was considerable dependence on data from the federal government's Bureau of Census Web site (17.2 per cent, 24.4 per cent and 10.2 per cent) or the Securities and Exchange Commission's EDGAR site. State and local government sites included state, county and city public records sites, school system sites and elections sites. Newspaper sites, particularly those with searchable archives, were also in wide use by respondents. Furthermore, search sites were also often named as "favourite" sites. These included Yahoo!, AltaVista and Switchboard.

*RQ*3: What characteristics of Web sites used for gathering information are perceived by journalists to be strongest? Weakest?

Journalists evaluated Web sites and the information on the sites in much the same way they assessed other, more traditional, information such as faxes, mailed documents, or information obtained from personal interviews. "Strong" Web sites in both 1998 and 1999 were those provided by reputable sources and those offering valid and accurate information.

Web site functions, such as searchability and design that affords easy access to information, were also valued. "Weak" sites in both surveys had inaccurate information, bad or outdated links, lack of attribution and useless content. Identified problems included lack of verification, unreliable information and lack of contact information or sourcing. Journalists were less concerned about truthfulness and lack of speed in finding a site URL.

*RQ*4: What Web-based technologies do journalists use for gathering information?

Journalists did not take full advantage of technologies available for communication using the Internet. The main resources used were electronic mail (90.3 per cent in 1998 and 86.9 per cent in 1999) and file transfer protocol (51.4 per cent and 52.8 per cent), but other tools that could have been used were not.

This is particularly true of other interactive tools such as bulletin boards (28.1 per cent and 26.7 per cent), audio streaming (8.1 per cent and 6.8 per cent), push technology (6.5 per cent and 5.7 per cent) and video and audio conferencing (3.7 per cent and 5.1 per cent).

RQ5: What are the perceived successes and failures of use of the Web as a newsgathering tool?

Despite lack of use of some interactive technology innovations on the Internet, data presented show that journalists believed the use of online resources have benefited their newsgathering. Online resources added depth and context, extended government coverage, assisted in locating sources and built background for news coverage. Even the reported "failures" showed a positive view of the Web as an information resource. Journalists most frequently lamented about not taking greater advantage of online resources that were available. They also noted lack of access to the Web, the need for more expertise and training and the inability to find information.

The literature has shown that the World Wide Web and Internet have become dominant newsgathering tools in a short period of time. While this study provides some additional evidence for understanding the uses of the Web and Internet by journalists, that understanding is limited when considering the social or psychological gratifications, if any, which are obtained by users.

For the most part, scholars still do not understand the impact of these changes on newsgathering and news distribution. This study placed primary focus on uses of the Web. It would seem to be particularly valuable to study the social, professional and psychological gratifications that are derived from the uses found in this study. This may be the next step and part of a research agenda for further investigation of Web use in news media newsrooms.

There is need for a strong theoretical perspective in which to frame this avenue of research. "[T]he uses and gratifications approach may have a chance to come into its own as we move into the information age and media users are confronted with more and more choices," wrote Severin and Tankard. With the evidence found in this study, their suggestion has considerable merit.

Among private and public information resources that are online, there are no rivals to the Web. Because of this widespread use, it is essential to study how these resources have become part of the news reporting process. Strengths and weaknesses of the Web and Internet may become characteristic of the reporting itself. Data depicting how journalists use the Web suggest certain innovation adoption tendencies. Perhaps the most interesting finding is that information search habits are still evolving. The search strategies used by respondents to these surveys described a wide range of personal approaches.

This suggests considerable experimentation and trial-and-error approaches during learning. The limited use of certain search tools also generates questions about the effect such practices have on news content. Not only are these approaches and strategies important to understand among professionals, there are implications for individuals who teach journalism students or offer continuous education and training to working professionals. There is a basic need to learn more about the online research process and how it impacts news content.

Use of government sites as leading sources of information underscores that news organizations were using the new technologies in old ways—simply to use existing credible sources of information faster and, perhaps, in a more comprehensive manner.

There is little evidence offered here that these new technologies have brought new sources or perspectives of information used in news reporting, but more inquiry is needed in this area of online research as well.

Respondents indicated concern for traditional quality issues in newsgathering. When using interactive technologies for news reporting, respondents expressed concern for many of the same problems that might have been presented long before creation of the Web.

While concern for reputation, accuracy, validity and other traditional characteristics of information sources are critical to a journalist's success, they have little to do with the interactive technology of the Web. Only when the respondents addressed such factors as download time, site organization, finding URLs, access to downloadable data and searchability did they venture into the world of the technology and its performance characteristics. This is another item for an online news and online research agenda.

Since there are implications for use of the Web and Internet, it is necessary to look at content of these online resources in more detail than achieved by this study. Analysis of the differences of search procedures and content specialization by leading search tools certainly can have impact on reporting. There is a need, similarly, to evaluate the content of local, state and federal government Web sites. These sites are, in many cases, quite new. Assessments of the quality of information contained by the sites should study accuracy, thoroughness and currency of information, for example. Furthermore, study of how this content is integrated into news coverage will be helpful to understanding the entire process.

Some of the evidence in this study points to possible gratifications of the use of online research tools. Measures of successes and failures of use of online resources may be seen as indicators of professional satisfactions. They may not be the best measures, but it seems that use for these respondents brings with it better journalism in the form of more depth and context, deeper government coverage, improved sourcing and additional background. These gratifications are achieved at some expense, such as frustration with limited online resources, user abilities, search inefficiencies and search speed. This clearly needs further investigation with the specific goal of further understanding the gratifications—or the lack of them—involved.

The findings, although representing 1997 to 1999, have theoretical relevance despite the timeframe used. The data presented in this analysis will provide a baseline or benchmark for additional Web uses research. It would be quite useful, for example, to conduct similar national surveys of Web use in newsrooms at, perhaps, three-or five-year intervals to determine long-range uses and effects patterns in the next decade. It is also necessary to look more closely at reasons why journalists do not use advanced technologies for information gathering and communication on the Web. Is it a form of technophobia?

- Or is it a lack of gratification or satisfaction with results? Or something else? Why have journalists not become users of interactive, multi-media tools such as conferencing? Further study is necessary, especially looking at training and computer literacy issues. Finally, this study has provided only descriptive analysis of the perceived advantages and disadvantages of use of Web-based information gathering. As Jones noted, the Internet is "an engine for social change, one that has modified work habits, education, social relations generally, and, maybe most important, our hopes and dreams.
- "Scholars must take steps toward better understanding its impact on journalism.

Chapter 10

The Newspaper's Responsibility

Every reporter or editor who has ever been responsible for the education beat has received "the Call." On the other end of the telephone line is a principal, teacher, or parent. The caller is responsible for public relations at a local school and wants your paper to cover this year's sponsored walk, canned-food drive, or reading marathon. "You write so many negative stories about schools," she begins. "Don't you think it's time you printed something good?"

The Call can take many forms. Sometimes it is from the local superintendent trying to get positive press on a pet project. Sometimes it is from the governor's spokesperson looking for coverage of the latest state education initiative. Teachers, union leaders, college professors, and, of course, professional public relations people make the Call, too. They all deliver the same argument when they phone a newspaper office looking for a story promoting their cause or product: Isn't it time someone wrote something positive about schools?

Exasperated education writers share war stories about the Call whenever they get together at seminars and press events. "Why," they ask one another, "don't people understand that our job is to cover schools, not to make them look good?" They recite all the positive stories they have written about outstanding teachers, curriculum programs that work, and successful students at the same time as they have probed the more difficult issues of dismal test scores, curriculum battles, school violence, and crowded classrooms. "Is it our fault," they ask, "that people only remember the negative stories?"

Just what is the responsibility of newspapers for shaping

public perceptions of education? As a line editor supervising education coverage for a large regional newspaper, I ask myself that question frequently. I have become aware that the public views schools in a harsher light than do either my reporters or I. Parents constantly fret about school violence, even though crime statistics show relatively few serious incidents in most schools. Readers worry that children across the board are no longer learning to read or do arithmetic, even though schools in our region generally score well above state and national averages on achievement tests. Families are considering private schools even in wealthy districts that send most of their public school graduates on to four-year colleges. What is going on here?

Research on the media's impact on public perceptions of the schools is sparse, and what there is mostly dates back to the past decade, before newspapers caught up with the national preoccupation with education. Furthermore, who can separate the influence of newspapers, magazines, television, radio, and even newsgroups on the World Wide Web? To what degree are perceptions also shaped by personal experiences and what people hear from their children, friends, and neighbors? We working journalists are left with little more than our own hypotheses, most of which - naturally - reflect favorably on our efforts and intentions.

In any case, there is no question that schools face significant challenges. In such well-documented cases as the school governance reforms in Chicago, inner-city districts appear to be fighting a losing battle against poverty, neglect, and neighborhood violence, despite the heroic efforts of some dedicated educators. Students in poor neighborhoods rarely receive as good an education as those in affluent communities. Is that the fault of the media? Only the top students take enough math and science to prepare them for the technological age.

And universities report a steady increase in entering students who need remedial classes in basic subjects before they can tackle college work.

As journalists, my team of reporters and I try to raise

public awareness of such problems as a first step toward solving them. Education has become one of the most visible beats at the Mercury News, and the work of those who cover education is often on page 1. Still, in examining the critical issues facing schools, are the media somehow creating the impression that there is nothing worth saving anywhere?

Jim Ritchie, the outspoken superintendent of the respected Moreland elementary school district in suburban San Jose, argued that the Mercury News and newspapers in general play a strong role in forming public perceptions of schools, both good and bad. In his community, he said, "I haven't seen any other entity that has the ability to change public perceptions for the short term. If it appears there and it appears in a strident and dramatic fashion, it will have an immediate effect on public opinion."

The power of specific stories fades over time as parents and readers move on to other issues, in Ritchie's experience, but the impression of critical stories remains strong in the common memory. "I definitely think the image of the public schools reflected in the media is much more negative than it is positive," he said. He pointed to the steady stream of stories about critical reports on education as well as articles about business leaders and politicians who lambaste the schools' inadequacies. In his view, those stories, lumping all schools together in broad, general terms, do little to illuminate the vast differences between schools and even classes within a school. "That constant drumbeat - I really think it's created the impression that public schools do not reflect quality," he said.

Newspapers, indeed, are in the business of news. And ever since 1983, when a blue-ribbon panel warned in A Nation at Risk of a "rising tide of mediocrity" in America's schools, there has been a flood of impressive reports cataloguing education's ills. The country has learned from the National Assessment of Educational Progress how little its children know about history, geography, reading, and math - although their degree of knowledge is probably not significantly different from that of previous generations. Numerous studies, including the Third International Mathematics and Science Study, have found that students in the United States do not stack up as well on academic achievement tests as Americans would like them to do against their counterparts around the world. (U.S. eighth-graders scored below average in math, an area in which their lessons are not as advanced as in the top-scoring countries, and above average in science, an area in which the U.S. curriculum is more focused.) The National Commission on Teaching and America's Future said that many of the nation's teachers are inadequately prepared.

There have been so many reports and studies from this or that commission and think tank that the stories rarely get on the front page anymore. Still, they add fuel to the public debate over the future of schools and cannot be ignored by any responsible reporter or broadcaster.

In The Manufactured Crisis, David Berliner and Bruce Biddle argue that the media have reported the international comparisons, in particular, unfairly and created the impression that America's schools are failing. They contend that journalists have neglected to ask critical questions about the groups tested and the subject matter covered, while ignoring comparative studies in which American students have done well. They insist that schools in the United States, on average, are doing as well as or better than ever, although they concede that there is still much room for improvement.

While the media seem quite willing to report bad news about our schools, they are much less willing to report news about the strengths of American education. One wonders, Why? Is it possible that bad news about education is thought to be more newsworthy? Or have reporters by now been so brainwashed by the critics that they cannot believe good news? Are too many of the reporters' employers friends of powerful people who wish the public schools no good? I find it hard to swallow such hints of a media conspiracy, and I object to inclinations to paint both print and broadcast reporters in the same light.

I suspect, as well, that such criticisms arise from dissatisfaction with the work of the national press rather than with that of the nation's 1,500 daily newspapers, from which most readers get their news.

There may be some truth, though, in the contention that journalists have not done a good job of analyzing the comparative studies. Few reporters are comfortable with statistics - we joke among ourselves that, if we had been good at math, we could have ended up in lucrative jobs instead of in journalism. Also, speed is essential in daily reporting, and we do far too much of our analysis on the fly. We do not come back to a topic for deeper consideration nearly often enough. Compounding the problem, newspapers rarely provide enough space in which to analyse the nuances of a huge study. So, at even the best papers, complex stories on all topics become oversimplified more frequently than reporters would like.

All of this said, education itself has shortcomings that it would be irresponsible for the media to ignore. The national anxiety about education appears justified from many perspectives. As we approach the millennium, parents, business leaders, and politicians alike question whether schools on the whole are producing citizens adequately prepared for the Information Age.

Even educators who are proud of what teachers and students are doing in their classrooms would most probably agree that schools need to reach higher to prepare more students for jobs that require such academic skills as advanced math. Economists maintain that students can no longer expect to graduate from high school with minimal skills and move right into well-paying factory jobs that allow them to join the middle class. It is not enough, others suggest, to prepare only our top students for college. For many jobs, the new standard is becoming at least two years of college.

THE PUBLIC CARES

Education places near the top of the public agenda in most polls, right behind crime and the economy. Even in notoriously tax-stingy California, education is one of the few items on which voters often say they are willing to spend more money. When Policy Analysis for California Education conducted its 1996 poll on public views of education, 38% of the respondents named "improving the quality of public schools" as the most important issue facing the state. In the same poll, 66% said that it was important to increase funding for schools.

Education took on even more significance in a 1996 Mercury News poll, which found that 88% of the people were concerned with the quality of public schools in their community - a notable departure from national polls, in which people have consistently defended their own schools. With that level of public interest, newspapers should not only report the debate but help inform it with stories that explore the issue from all perspectives.

Those who still believe in public education as a social good propose shifting more resources into the schools, setting high academic standards, and helping all students reach them. In his 1997 State of the Union address, President Clinton set forth a 10-point plan "to ensure that all Americans have the best education in the world." In addition to setting national standards and drafting examinations tied to those standards, Clinton called for expanding Head Start, creating 3,000 charter schools, spending $5 billion on school construction, and establishing college scholarships.

On the other hand, some advocates of choice propose subjecting public schools to market forces by giving students vouchers to attend private schools if they wish. They argue that public schools would have to shape up and compete for students or find themselves out of business for want of customers.

In the midst of the debate, David Mathews, president of the Kettering Foundation, warns that the public's connection to its schools is waning. He says that his research has found what other studies have reported: whereas Americans believe that the country needs public schools, they are torn between a sense of duty to support these schools and a responsibility to do what is best for children. "They are ambivalent and agonize over the dilemma. And, however reluctantly, many are deciding that public schools aren't best for their children or anyone else's."

Critics and many educators blame the media for public perceptions that schools are failing because of a combination of growing social problems, declining discipline, and falling standards. Yet, Mathews writes, "The people we talked to based their conclusions on personal experience or the experience of family members and close friends." So discouraged were most of the parents in focus groups conducted for the Kettering Foundation that even those who spoke relatively positively about their public schools said they would send their children to private school if they could receive a "check" to pay for the tuition.

It must be noted, though, that voters have consistently rejected voucher proposals that would give parents such checks.

There is no denying that the public has mixed feelings about schools. One of the best indicators is the annual Phi Delta Kappa/Gallup poll.

In 1996, for example, 66% of public school parents gave the school their oldest child attends an A or a B - a figure that gives educators great comfort. At the same time, only 21% of respondents gave the nation's schools an A or a B. Compare that to the 48% who gave top grades to public schools in 1974. Although 54% of the people who responded to the poll in 1996 opposed vouchers that would give families public money to send their children to private schools, most clearly felt that private schools were better: 63% gave private schools an A or a B.

It is hard to tell where the poll respondents obtained the information for that assessment. Most newspapers print very little about private schools, whose business is not conducted in a public forum with taxpayers' dollars.

In most cases, private school students do not take the same tests as public school students, so it is tough to compare them on objective criteria. Perhaps it is their word-of-mouth reputation as bastions of discipline, decorum, and traditional curricula - and not portrayals in the media - that makes private schools so popular with a public committed to discipline and basic skills.

This is not the first era of hand-wringing over American education. Stanford University education professors David Tyack and Larry Cuban have pointed out that the country has been fretting about its schools for more than a century. In Tinkering Toward Utopia, they note that the U.S. has worried most about the effectiveness of schooling at times of crisis, when national leaders obsess about the country's struggle for survival in a competitive world. In the 1890s, the Germans were the source of that anxiety; in the 1950s, the Soviets; in the 1980s, the Japanese. Tyack and Cuban write:

Commentators in the media, muckrakers, leaders in business and unions, government officials, legislators, social reformers, activists in women's associations, foundation officials, leaders of protest movements, and policy makers in education all starkly expose problems and confidently propose educational solutions. Then they pressure legislatures, school boards and public school administrators to adopt their reforms.

What has been different in the latest wave of education debates is the public's current disenchantment with all institutions, from city councils to the Congress. At the same time, college graduation rates are up, and many parents, educated as well as or better than their children's teachers, now appear to be quite comfortable criticizing what goes on in the classroom. For the most part, parents do not buy the education establishment's arguments. They call for a greater emphasis on the basics and turn up their noses at most of the reform proposals from researchers and educators.

The conflicts that arise out of such disagreements are the grist of journalism. It is our job to write about the issues without taking a side. When the media do it right, they help readers and viewers understand what is at stake and explain the arguments. The media must take care, however, not to get caught up in the enthusiasm that educators have for the latest fad or in the ideology of the critics. That role belongs to the editorial writers and the commentators. Although it seems difficult for most readers to distinguish between the editorial pages and the news sections, good newspapers keep them separated by the journalistic equivalent of a fire wall. Editorial writers tell readers what they should think. Reporters give them the information to make up their own minds.

Negativity is in the Eye of the Reader

So what should newspapers be writing about in this time of ferment in education? Robert Frahm, a prize-winning education reporter with the Hartford Courant in Connecticut, says that newspapers have an obligation to help their readers understand what's really going on in schools.

That means going into classrooms to show readers how teachers and students try to cope with difficult issues of learning, often against overwhelming odds. It also means holding the people in charge of the schools responsible for education in the community. "We get some complaints from school officials that we are too negative," says Frahm, former president of the Education Writers Association. "I don't believe that's true. I believe that if you were to count our stories and rate them as positive or negative, there would be more positives."

One of the most serious variables, reporters understand, is who is passing judgment on their work. If a story raises critical issues about schools that may lead to the improvement of education for children, most reporters would consider it a positive piece.

In 1996, Frahm and fellow Courant reporter Rick Green did just that when they wrote a revealing study of the Hartford schools' management after its partnership collapsed with the for-profit corporation then known as Education Alternatives, Inc. Their stories, running over four days, chronicled the district's deep problems, ranging from serious financial mismanagement to chronic disputes between the union and the administration that reverberated in the city's classrooms.

As a result of that series, the Connecticut Department of

Education announced that it would conduct a comprehensive review of the system. Six months later, the state education commissioner called for sweeping changes in management, curriculum, enrollment policies, and union contracts. At last, it appeared, someone was going to make a concerted effort to fix the problems that had crippled the inner-city school system for years. Many Hartford readers might well view those events as a positive outcome.

Rarely do reporters get to see such a direct link between their work and a shift in public policy. Frahm took great pride in articles in the series that went beyond the facts and figures of the investigation to look at teachers' struggles to make the system work for their students. For instance, the articles cited a kindergarten teacher whose 22 students - all children of unmarried mothers - live in some of the city's poorest neighborhoods and arrive at school often not even knowing their colors or the alphabet. This was a reality that few Courant readers would recognize. The newspaper's subscribers more often live in the affluent suburbs surrounding Hartford than in the inner city. That is why the story must be told.

Educators, however, frequently appear to misunderstand the reporter's role as the public's eyes and ears. "We are conscious of not ignoring things that are going on in school that are good, but we also believe we can't ignore what is bad," Frahm says. "We feel if we were just to create a rosy picture of the schools, it would be a lie."

Although the Hartford stories were exemplary, such journalism is no longer an anomaly in America's newspapers. The Philadelphia Inquirer catalogued the failings of the city schools in such indisputable detail that in 1994 a new superintendent used the series to launch substantial reform. In Denver in 1995, the Rocky Mountain News so graphically outlined conflicts between research and teaching in Colorado universities that the schools ended up giving more attention to undergraduate instruction. Newspapers from Alaska to Kentucky have explored issues ranging from the inequities of special education to the intricacies of school reform. More and more, ambitious reporters go beyond school board meetings to try to explain why schools are working or not working.

Steve Barkin is familiar with this trend. A journalism professor at the University of Maryland, Barkin has judged the National Awards for Education Reporting since 1985. He has read countless education stories over the years. The newspaper stories Barkin reads for the contest - admittedly some of the best work in the field - increasingly delve into the reality of what goes on in classrooms. There are still the traditional stories about test scores, budget battles, school board politics, and superintendent searches. But there are also many stories that try to explain how schools go about their true work - teaching children. "When I was reading about education 20 years ago, I was reading about test scores," Barkin says, "and I'm still reading about test scores, but the mix is a little richer than it used to be. I think you learn a lot more of what's going on in newspapers."

Even George Kaplan, who has censured newspapers for putting too many inexperienced young reporters on the schools beat and then covering education only superficially via school board meetings, modified his tone in a 1997 interview. Although still fairly critical of the national newspapers for inadequately treating trends in education reform, he cited improvement among all papers. "In general, I think the smaller communities are getting a fairly objective picture. They don't care about national trends," Kaplan said. "For the name papers, the reporting is mixed. But overall I think the reporting is good."

Jay Rosen, a New York University professor and an advocate of public journalism, questions the quality of education reporting. He contends that newspapers are still not giving their readers what they need in order to make informed decisions about education policy and that reporters spend too much time writing about the school board and not enough time writing about schools. "I think the major failing of newspaper coverage of education is the failing of most public institution coverage," Rosen says. "It's institution driven, it's conflict driven and tends only rarely to be concerned with the resolution of issues or problem solving." Rosen wants reporters to get away from their dependence on school trustee meetings for day-to-day education coverage.

As an example of a better approach to education coverage, Rosen points to the 40,000-circulation Sun in Bremerton, Washington. Editor Mike Phillips became frustrated when the Sun education reporter wrote numerous stories about the local school superintendent's salary. Instead, he suggested, the reporter should ask parents what was on their minds and then write about that. The answer that came back was "homework," and the Sun responded by looking into why so many Bremerton students didn't bring home homework. A new approach to schools coverage was born. Phillips says: "What happens in a school board meeting has little to do with the rearing of children, the education of children, most of the time.

A lot of people recognize the problem with that pattern, but they're not very successful in changing it, simply because it's easier." I would argue that many larger papers have all but abandoned school board-related coverage except in the most dramatic cases, such as the very public conflict between Mayor Rudolph Giuliani of New York and former chancellor Ramon Cortines. In an illustration of the new style of education coverage, the Miami Herald in 1996 devoted three months to producing a four-day series that answered Dade County parents' most pressing questions about their public schools.

Mercury News reporters rarely attend board meetings. But in countless other newspapers - particularly smaller publications for which reporters are required to churn out several stories a day - such institutional coverage remains the staple of education reporting. What some critics say about newspapers is true: not all education stories are extensively researched pieces about both the positive and the negative aspects of an issue. By necessity, such thorough articles are only a small portion of what we print over time.

Even if local education reporters fill their articles with

context to help readers understand what is really going on, countless stories from other reporters and wire services do not. When Bob Dole attacked teacher unions in the course of his Presidential campaign, it made headlines, but there was very little critical analysis of his charges from the political reporters covering the speech.

When SAT scores go up or down by a single point, it is news, even though the change is insignificant statistically. And papers still run the Associated Press-produced charts ranking the states by SAT scores, even though the College Board notes that only a small proportion of high school students usually those aiming for elite colleges take the test in the highest-scoring states. (Average scores tend to decline when more students take the test.) As a nation, we love benchmarks even if they are flawed. Readers demand them, and newspapers deliver them - usually with caveats that are routinely ignored.

Yet newspapers arguably remain the most complete and objective general source of information on education for the public, producing as true a picture of schools as is possible in limited space and time. Look at the case of the move by the school board in Oakland, California, to recognize as a separate language the dialect of African American students. Within hours of the school board vote, Ebonics - a term taken from ebony and phonics - was topic number one on radio talk shows across the country. Newspapers from Phoenix to London ran stories about the board's action. Within days, Jesse Jackson and Maya Angelou were denouncing the school board's action and Secretary of Education Richard Riley was announcing that there would be no federal funding for bilingual classes in Ebonics.

Through it all, newspapers did a far better job than did broadcast media of reporting just what the board did and what it meant. The school board's resolution referred to "genetically based" African language systems and argued that "recognizing the English language acquisition and improvement skills of African American students is as fundamental as is application of bilingual education principles for others whose primary languages are other than English." It also ordered the superintendent to "immediately devise and implement the best possible academic programme for imparting instruction to African American students in their primary language" and talked of "maintaining the legitimacy and richness" of Black English. The language of the school board was incendiary, and the intent was obvious: at least some people in the district were hoping to get bilingual funding to help raise the dismal achievement levels of African American students.

Newspapers reported those facts and followed up as the school board subtly revised its position to focus solely on improving achievement by acknowledging and working with the dialect that black children brought into the classroom. Trustees insisted that they had never intended Ebonics to be taught as a separate language in Oakland schools.

Print reporters covered every twist and turn as trustees won Jesse Jackson over to their side and then finally backed off some of the more controversial wording of their resolution. But reporters also took a hard look at the problems that black children face in classrooms across the country when they are expected to speak a language markedly different from their own.

The Mercury News and other California newspapers went into Oakland classrooms to describe just how the district was already using Ebonics to help students master standard English. The Washington Post ran a front-page story on the search for a solution to the national problem of low academic performance by many poor black students. It quoted linguists as saying that the use of Black English as a bridge to standard English might be effective in the classrooms, then explored the views of skeptics.

"I think newspapers handled it a lot more responsibly than the school board acknowledged," says Michael Bazeley, then education reporter for the Oakland Tribune. "Television did a horrible job, in my opinion. On day 6 or 7 they were saying kids were going to be taught Black English in the classroom." Rush Limbaugh had a field day. So did editorial writers and columnists from Los Angeles to New York and beyond. As late as February, a Newsweek columnist expounded on the topic, and Garry Trudeau lampooned Ebonics in a Sunday Doonesbury strip. Yet readers of the news columns got a fairly clear understanding of one of the most controversial education stories of the year.

Explaining the News

That is how it should be. Newspaper articles should help readers understand their world better. The huge, controversial stories are exhilarating. Reporters love it when the world hangs on their words. But they also write smaller, yet still important, stories that they hope will illuminate pressing issues. Often those articles are good news by almost anyone's standards.

Early in 1997, the Mercury News ran a front-page story about a district that consistently performed well against all odds. The report showed how San Jose's Evergreen elementary district, with a large proportion of impoverished students who speak little or no English, had managed to raise test scores and win national recognition for its schools. Evergreen's secret, reporter Maya Suryaraman revealed, was its teachers.

The district emphasized teacher training and curriculum planning and gave teachers a strong role in making decisions that affect their classrooms. As a result, many teachers took a more professional role in diagnosing and solving their students' learning problems. But the story, focused as it was on solutions, received only slight notice from readers. The public seems to have a better memory for the negative story.

As a case in point, Jodi Berls, education reporter for the Austin American-Statesman in Texas, likes to tell the tale of two big projects that her paper produced in 1996. One was on the local district's efforts to get parent volunteers into the schools. The other was on lunchtime violence in schools. "Both packages got front-page play, with extensive space inside; both had lots of photos and some graphics; both involved numerous campus visits and myriad phone calls; both took about a month to put together," she says. "The cafeteria violence story got a lot of response - parents, teachers, and students called afterward to tell us they liked it, offer us tips and ideas related to it, et cetera. The volunteering story... went down a black hole except for one guy who referred to it in a board meeting in a snide comment suggesting that I'm in the school district's pocket."

Even as they are berated for their work, most reporters realise that public opinion often seems to have a life of its own, with little relation to journalistic enterprise. Conventional wisdom quite frequently rules, in spite of evidence to the contrary.

To see how newspapers can fail to sway public opinion, consider the series that the Mercury News produced in 1996 looking at the otherwise unquestioned push for more computers in the schools. The newspaper performed its own computer analysis in concert with a University of California researcher, working with data from a national technology data collection firm. When they were finished, the reporters concluded that there was no hard evidence that California schools with large investments in technology performed any better academically than comparable schools without similar equipment - except in low-income neighborhoods.

Evidently, few readers bought the idea. Letters ran heavily in favour of a bigger investment in school technology in all schools. Local superintendents called for a meeting with the publisher and executive editor to complain that the Mercury News was anti-education. And the paper, located in the heart of Silicon Valley, continued to run story after story about high-tech executives trashing the schools for not doing enough with computers, as well as articles on politicians urging greater expenditures on technology. Even though the newspaper included a paragraph in most of those stories about our reporters' findings, it was clear that most people still believed that computers are the answer to schools' academic shortcomings.

Such experiences are frustrating, but journalists are accustomed to them. So most journalists decide that they just have to do their best to keep their minds open, their eyes peeled for good stories, and their judgment unclouded by ideology. Journalists try to keep up with research and the broad range of emerging thought in the field. They look for issues and trends that may make a difference in their readers' lives as well as interesting features that illuminate what's going on in schools. In the end, journalists cannot allow themselves to be swayed by consideration of whether a story will be good for the public image of schools. Their job is to tell the truth and help readers understand the challenges that society is facing. And the truth is often unpleasant.

Chapter 11

Analysis of Narrative Risk Disclosures

This study examines whether companies report risk-relevant information to protective investors. While corporate risk communication is importantant for the well-functioning of capital markets, our current understanding of risk reporting practices is limited. The sample consists of Dutch companies raising capital on the Amsterdam Stock Exchange in the late 1990s. In this setting, companies had much discretion in writing the risk section of the prospectus.

After a detailed content analysis of the risk sections, the author demonstrates that a measure of risk extracted from these texts successfully predicts the volatility of companies' future stock prices, the sensitivity of future stock prices to market-wide fluctuations, as well as severe decline in future stock prices. Overall, these results support the view that prospectuses of Dutch companies provide adequate information about material investment risks. Our history of substantial net losses may continue indefinitely and make it difficult to fund our operations.

This excerpt comes from the so-called "risk factor" section in the initial public offering prospectus of VersaTel Telecom International. It provides an example of warnings (risk factors) that corporate managers communicate to buyers of shares in companies going public. Offering prospectuses are legal documents, describing an enterprise to prospective investors. The risk factor sections in these documents are intended to provide investors with a clear and concise summary of the material risks to an investment in the issuers' securities. As such, these sections have the potential to alter investors' risk judgments and promote sound investment decisions. Because there is little empirical evidence on the information content of the risk factor sections, the aim of this chapter is to explore if these texts actually contain risk-relevant information for investors.

For this purpose, I use a sample of 90 prospectuses of Dutch companies and perform a detailed content analysis of the textual information in the risk factor sections. Next, I examine to what extent an aggregate risk measure extracted from the information in the texts successfully predicts future volatility of stock prices, the sensitivity of stock prices to marketwide fluctuations, as well as large declines in future stock prices.

To facilitate linking the study to the communication practices of corporate managers and their advisors, I assume a financial communication perspective in this chapter. Foremost, studying current risk disclosure practices can make clear to financial communication practitioners if risk reporting in prospectuses can be viewed as an area of best practice for corporate risk communication.

The latter has been suggested by professional bodies like the Institute of Chartered Accountants in England and Wales (ICAEW), who see great merit in better risk reporting. Based on an exploratory study of a small number of prospectuses and annual reports of U.K. companies, the ICAEW put forward that companies provide limited risk information in annual reports but make more extensive risk disclosures in prospectuses. Following up on this research, this study more formally tests the claim that risk disclosure in prospectuses provides risk-relevant information to investors.

While this chapter views risk disclosure in prospectuses through a financial communication lens (focusing on shareholder relations and shareholders' concerns about investment risk), two issues need to be stressed before proceeding. First, corporate communication is part of larger organizational systems. Other business functions traditionally involved with financial communication include finance and accounting. Beside corporate communication research, I therefore draw on research in these disciplinary areas to study risk disclosure practices in prospectuses.

Second, the broader topic of risk communication that this chapter deals with clearly links to other subfunctions of corporate communication, including media relations, employee relations, community relations, and crisis communication. Within the field of public relations research, for example, many studies have focused on employees' and communities' concerns about health, safety, and environmental risks. Palenchar and Heath provide a concise summary of this growing branch of risk communication research, in which the stakes for participants in the communication process are evidently high.

MOTIVATION AND PRIOR RESEARCH

Studying risk disclosure is important because corporate transparency about risk is vital for the well-functioning of capital markets. To achieve and maintain an accurate valuation of a company's stock, confident and well-informed investors are necessary. Lacking adequate disclosure, managers have superior information to outside investors, who may not fully understand the underlying risks and rewards of a firm's business. By providing investors with information about the risk associated with pursuing the company's strategic goals, managers can increase transparency and eliminate disparities between what investors understand and expect and what management can deliver.

This disclosure enables investors to make more accurate corrections for risk when they value their investments, thereby preventing stock prices from becoming unhinged from intrinsic business value (i.e., prevent them from becoming critically higher than they would be if the market had the information that is available to managers). According to Fuller and Jensen, "Trying to mask the uncertainty that is inherent in every business is like pushing on a balloon; smoothing out today's bumps means they will only pop up somewhere else tomorrow, often with catastrophic results". Consequently, being clear about the risks and uncertainties involved can prevent severe damage to the reputation and long-term health of a company that may otherwise result from overvalued corporate equity.

Recognizing the potential benefits of risk disclosure to investors and the long-run health and reputation of a company, an important question becomes whether managers are forthright about the underlying risks in their firms' business. On the one hand, they may understand the benefits of risk disclosure and realise that markets will penalize companies that provide inadequate information relative to their peers. As a result, an increasing number of managers may perceive that risk disclosure is a competitive advantage in attracting capital. Furthermore, managers may fear litigation and reputation costs if they do not provide sufficient risk information to investors.

On the other hand, being candid about risk can cause the stock price to fall to a more sustainable level in the short run. Short-sighted managers may not recognize that the associated pain of this is slight compared to that arising from colluding in myth-telling. Additionally, disclosure is not a costless undertaking. First, creating and distributing timely and accurate risk information consumes valuable management time. Second, managers may perceive that there is a cost imposed on the firm by competitors who exploit the information to the detriment of the disclosing firm. Third, there is the possibility of litigation in connection with a disclosure. Finally, companies may be afraid to set a disclosure precedent they cannot stick to.

PRIOR RESEARCH

Corporate reporting has generated broad interest from business communication researchers. Whereas some studies have investigated graphical presentations of financial information and photographs, many studies have examined narrative portions of annual reports, mostly the president's letter to shareholders and management's discussion and analysis. The focus in these studies varies considerably and includes analyses of readability, positive and negative words and negative messages, thematic differences, linguistic structures, rhetorical elements and symbolic meaning, verbal tone, and genre. Focusing on different aspects, several researchers have investigated if past or current performance of a company is reflected in the texts of corporate reports. Contributing to this literature, I investigate to what extent texts of corporate reports reflect future outcomes.

Several findings in prior business communication research are relevant for this study. First, managers seem predominantly optimistic in their writing, seeking to create a positive perception of themselves and their companies. Arguably, a bias toward the positive (the so-called "Pollyanna effect") may hinder managers in providing effective warning signals. Essentially, providing investors with information about risk demands explicit attention for the downside. Second, Crombie and Samujh present a case of an executive who did focus on problems in his letter to shareholders.

The problems discussed were, however, relatively minor and seemingly intended to distract attention from more serious issues, thereby likely causing longer term credibility problems. This case recalls the assertion that what is omitted is as significant as what is included in a narrative. In the context of risk lector disclosure, texts that describe every minor risk (without considering the likelihood and potential impact) can obscure major risks. Third, Kohut and Segars find a predominant emphasis on the past and conclude that executives feel more confident discussing a certain past than an uncertain future in their letter to shareholders. This can further hinder providing risk-relevant information.

In the field of accounting, prior risk disclosure research has almost exclusively focused on quantified risk disclosure in financial statements and on specific categories of risk, especially market risk, thereby overlooking narratives and possible interrelationships among many types of risk that are present in an organization's environment. Notable exceptions of studies in accounting and finance that have examined the relation between risk-related information extracted from narratives and future outcomes are Abrahamson and Amir and, more recently, Li.

The results of both studies suggest that risk-related information in text can be used to assess future firm performance. Abrahamson and Amir measure the information contained in the president's letter to shareholders in annual reports by counting the relative number of words with a negative connotation used in a negative context. In this way, they locus on linguistic style (how it is being said) rather than linguistic content (what is being said).

Assuming that words convey information independent of their semantic context, Li measures emphasis on market risk in annual reports by counting the frequency of words related to risk and uncertainty. Li argues that in a general setting such as annual reports, a context-specific measure of risk is difficult to establish at this stage. A limitation of both studies is that only very few words could actually be classified as expressing negativity or risk (0.4% and 0.04%, respectively). Taking a different approach, this chapter extracts the content of risk-related information in texts of risk sections relative to the particular context of their use.

For standard setters, the burst of the Internet and telecom bubble and the unanticipated subsequent collapse of large companies with a false image of being low risk and highly predictable (e.g., Enron) created an urgency to reconsider the set of requirements for disclosure of relevant and understandable forward-looking information about risk. As a result, narrative risk factor disclosure is nowadays increasingly required in periodic reports (both annual and quarterly) by law or formal codes of best practice in corporate governance worldwide.

In prospectuses, regulators have long since required firms to provide, under the caption "risk factors," a concise and logically organized discussion of the most significant factors that make an offering speculative or risky. This requirement offers the opportunity to examine whether these documents actually contain risk-relevant information.

A potential problem when regulating risk factor disclosure is that much of the risk information is industry- and company specific and that the most relevant information changes constantly, as a result of rapid economic and technological changes. As put aptly by Hutton (2004), "Relevant information does not lend itself to standardization". Recognizing this problem, most standard setters allow firms a large degree of discretion in drafting risk sections.

The narratives must explain in simple language how certain risk factors affect the company but should exclude risk factors that could apply to any company. Furthermore, it is up to preparers of risk sections to decide which risk factors are significant and should therefore be discussed. Consequently, some have argued that risk sections do not contain reliable information, because the rules are "subjective, open-ended and ambiguous, which allows firms to report almost anything (or nothing) without violating the requirements". Others have also questioned the qualitative nature of the information provided in risk sections.

Quantification of risk disclosure, in contrast, is viewed as beneficial "because it improves the credibility of the disclosures and makes them ex-post verifiable". Hodder, Koonce, and McAnally maintain that narrative risk disclosures do not compensate for the lack of quantitative risk information because "even if companies do disclose this information, it is very difficult, if not impossible, for individuals to use this qualitative information to generate their own quantitative risk assessments".

Concerns about the narrative nature of risk factor disclosure may be unwarranted, though. Prior research shows that textual information can help investors better predict future firm performance. Vanstraelen, Zarzeski, Marilyn, and Robb further document that a higher level of forward-looking non-financial disclosure in annual reports is associated with lower dispersion and higher accuracy in financial analysts' earnings forecasts.

While current risk disclosure rules indeed depend on managers' willingness to actively disclose the right information, risk sections in prospectuses might contain reliable information for two related reasons. First, due to the high information asymmetry when raising capital from outside investors, market participants and regulators insist on the disclosure of material information in prospectuses, especially when it concerns an initial public offering. Second, the information contained in a prospectus is the joint product of several parties.

Underwriters (usually investment banks) function as intermediaries between the company and investors and coordinate drafting of the prospectus. Other parties involved in preparing the prospectus are auditors and lawyers. While auditors provide assurance to the issuers' financial statements, lawyers advise on the disclosures required in the narrative sections, including the risk section (Draho, 2004). The heightened litigation and reputation risk for all parties involved leads to intense scrutiny, more so than for annual reports.

Research Question

The lack of empirical evidence on the informative nature of narrative risk disclosures motivates me to explore the following research question: Do the texts of risk factor sections in prospectuses contain risk-relevant information for investors?

To address this research question, I followed a two-stage approach. First, I extracted a reliable aggregate measure of risk disclosure from the texts. Second, I examined whether this measure was associated with a number of outcomes in the period after publication of the prospectus:

- Future total return risk (volatility of the stock price);
- Future systematic risk (sensitivity of stock price to market-wide fluctuations);
- The likelihood of severe declines in stock price.
- Finding a significantly positive association between the risk disclosure measure obtained from the texts and the above-mentioned outcomes would demonstrate that companies that turn out relatively

risky ex-post are generally disclosing more risk ex-ante. Alternatively, finding a significantly negative association would show that companies that turn out relatively risky ex-post are generally disclosing less risk ex-ante. While the former would support the claim that managers are actively providing risk-relevant information in risk sections (i.e., the texts represent what they purport to represent), the latter would indicate that managers are actively withholding risk information.

RESEARCH DESIGN

The data that I used in this study were obtained from 90 prospectuses of Dutch firms that issued securities on the Amsterdam Stock Exchange in the period from 1997 to 2000.

- More specifically, the sample includes 49 (54%) initial public offerings (IPOs) of common stock, 31 (34%) seasoned offerings of common stock and/or convertible bonds, and 10 (11%) stock offerings relating to a merger or demerger.

The information required in a prospectus is set out in the listing and issuing rules of the Amsterdam Stock Exchange. While the regulations require a risk assessment to be included in the prospectus, they provide no further guidance on the nature, degree, and form.

- This lack of guidance allows companies and other parties involved in writing the risk sections a large degree of freedom in expressing their judgment. The cover of the prospectus typically refers to the risk section as "certain factors that should be carefully considered by prospective investors."

The stock market data required for this study (i.e., monthly stock price data and value-weighted index data) were retrieved from the financial database "DATASTREAM."

Institutional Setting

While the Dutch capital market is well-developed, the institutional environment in the Netherlands has some unique characteristics that likely affect the quantity and quality of corporate disclosure in general.

- First, Dutch companies make extensive use of anti-takeover mechanisms, thereby reducing the threat that management is replaced by a raider. In corporate control models, this threat disciplines managers.

Consequently, Dutch managers likely lace lower pressure from the capital market to publicly account for their performance via corporate reports. Second, like in some other Continental European countries, Dutch firms have a two-tier board structure.

To the extent that this results in better monitoring of management's performance by independent boards, there could be less need for monitoring by outside shareholders and, consequently, less incentives for management to publicly disclose information. Third, management or large shareholders often hold large parts, or even the majority, of outstanding shares.

Large shareholders are often thought to have better access to operational information (i.e., lower information asymmetry) and have higher incentives to monitor management's performance. Managerial ownership better aligns the interests of management and shareholders.

Economic theory predicts that both the alignment of interests and better monitoring by large shareholders reduce potential problems between management and shareholders, thereby reducing the need for public reporting.

Consequently, the overall institutional environment in the Netherlands seems to make it less evident in advance that management discloses relevant information to outside investors. From an international perspective, the Dutch environment is therefore an interesting setting to study disclosure practices.

The time period in which this study is conducted is also interesting, because public equity markets in the late 1990s seemed willing to invest in high-risk companies that never made profits and might never do so. Although the new prospects looked very promising, with the benefit of hindsight the risks of investing in these companies were not clear at the time.

This situation makes it particularly relevant to examine whether the risk sections in prospectuses actually reflected the material risks.

Extracting an Aggregate Measure of Risk (RDS)

In previous research on IPOs, the number of risk factors described in the risk section of the prospectus is a common proxy for ex-ante risk. A simple count of these risk factors combines them into one single measure that is comparable to a summated scale.

- An advantage of this approach is that it does not focus on one particular risk, that is, isolating specific risks to the exclusion of other possibly interrelated risk factors.

However, a disadvantage of adding up (different) risk factors is that unidimensionality and internal consistency of the risk factors are assumed but cannot be tested for. Unidimensionality and internal consistency are essential requirements for a composite measure and imply that the composite measure should consist of risk factors that load highly on one single dimension and are strongly associated with each other, representing a single concept. For a multifaceted concept like risk, however, unidimensionality and internal consistency are not realistic assumptions when simply counting the number of risk factors disclosed in the risk sections of the prospectuses.

Instead of a mere count of the number of risk factors, the alternative approach taken in this study is to investigate the attributes of the risks described.

A discovery-oriented procedure known as content assessment was applied first. The purpose of this procedure was to take an open-ended look at the risk sections across prospectuses to make a preliminary identification of the kinds of risk that are described. Next, a content analysis was undertaken to systematically evaluate the content of the risk sections.

The content analysis involved three broad stages:

- Development of an appropriate coding scheme that lists the expected risk factors that are disclosed in the risk sections;
- Coding of the texts of the risk sections;
- Reduction of data into composite measures of risk disclosure. Each stage is discussed below in more detail.

CODING SCHEME

In the first stage, a wide range of literature on risk and risk management was used to develop an appropriate coding scheme that lists broad content categories and different risk factors related to these categories. Each risk factor of the coding scheme is described by a number of words or phrases that detail the meaning of the risk factor. Typical examples of risk factors per category are provided in the Results section.

CODING PROCEDURE

In the second stage, 1 matched the words and phrases in the texts of the risk sections with the coding scheme and identified for each text whether or not the risk factor was mentioned. A pretest was performed on a subset of the sample, providing further understanding of the textual disclosures. As a result, several risk factors of the coding scheme were refined and others were added. Using the improved coding scheme, the coding process was applied to the full sample.

An advantage of this manual approach over a computer-aided content analysis is that humans can better judge the meaning of words and phrases within a context. A disadvantage is that a manual approach is less cost-effective and flexible. In addition, human raters can make mistakes and are prone to researcher bias. To assure the reliability of the coding process, two trained, independent raters coded the texts. Percentage agreement for the risk factors ranged from 83% to 100%. Perreault and Leigh's interjudge reliability index ranged from.82 to 1.00, where.80 (and.70 in exploratory research) is considered a lower limit. All coding discrepancies were resolved by jointly reexamining the texts and determining an appropriate identification.

DATA REDUCTION

The third stage of the content analysis concerned a statistical reduction of the collected data (48 dichotomous variables for each firm in the sample, each variable representing a different risk factor) into a smaller set of new, composite dimensions or component scores with a minimum loss of information.

While the nature and character of the original data are retained, a smaller set of composite measures enables subsequent multivariate empirical analyses.

The technique that was used for this purpose is principal components analysis by alternating least squares optimal scaling (PRINCIPALS). Compared to standard principal components analysis, which assumes linear relationships between numeric variables, PRINCIPALS allows variables to be scaled at the nominal or ordinal level. In addition, the method substantially increases the number of variables that can be included in the analysis, given a certain sample size. PRINCIPALS is used as an exploratory technique that does not set any a priori constraints on the estimation of components or the number of dimensions to be extracted. Theoretical support or prior research that justifies a confirmatory approach is currently lacking. Hence, an exploratory approach is considered most useful as a data reduction method.

The data reduction procedure resulted in three component scores that were named Risk Disclosure Score 1, 2, and 3.

The following section provides detailed results on these component scores. Because RDS1 explains about twice as much variance of the risk factors as RDS2 and RDS3 and represents far more risk factors than RDS2 and RDS3, the main analyses focus on RDS1. Supplementary analyses considered RDS2 and RDS3.

TOTAL RETURN RISK, AND SYSTEMATIC RISK

Total return risk (TRR) is commonly defined as the standard deviation of stock returns. Systematic risk (BETA) is defined as the covariance of stock returns and returns on the market portfolio, divided by the variance of returns on the market portfolio. A value-weighted index of all stocks listed on the Amsterdam Stock Exchange is used to calculate the returns on the market portfolio.

SEVERE DECLINES IN STOCK PRICE (FAIL)

Riskier firms can be expected to have a higher probability of extreme negative outcomes, particularly if managers typically associate risk with negative outcomes. For a sample of IPO firms, Hensler, Rutherford, and Springer find that a simple count of the number of risk factors listed in the offering prospectus is significantly related to the failure to survive in the aftermarket, which is defined as delisting from the trading exchange for negative reasons, for example, a stock price below the acceptable level (so-called "penny stocks"). Listing and issuing rules of the Amsterdam Stock Exchange, however, do not require delisting of firms in case their stock price falls below five Euro or even one Euro.

CONTROL VARIABLES

To control for firm size, I added the variable SIZE, which is defined as the natural logarithm of the market value of the firm in million Euro one month after publication of the prospectus.

To control for industry effects, I added an indictor variable IND that is equal to one if the firm operates in a high-risk industry (information technology, biotechnology, or telecommunication), and zero otherwise. In the models estimated for the full sample, I also controlled for the type of offering by adding an indicator variable 1PO that is equal to one for IPO firms, and zero otherwise.

RESULTS

This section addresses five areas: content analysis of risk

sections, predicting TRR and BETA, predicting FAIL, supplementary analysis, and robustness checks.

CONTENT ANALYSIS OF RISK SECTIONS

The content analysis reveals that management mostly assigned the label "risk" to factors, either external or internal to the firm, that could adversely impact future firm performance. In this sense, risk actually referred to sources of downside risk. In no single risk section did management refer to risk as being associated with the probability of high performance. These findings confirm March and Shapira's observations of high-level executives' risk perceptions.

In accordance with Miller's integrated risk framework, I broadly classified the sources of risk as related to the following:

- The macro environment;
- The industry environment;
- The internal environment of the firm;
- Other

Apart from describing sources of risk, management's discussion of risk frequently resembles investors' conceptualization of risk as surveyed by Baird and Thomas and Olsen. For this reason, I discerned four additional categories:

- Loss or probability of loss; for example, "We have a history of losses and expect to continue to incur losses in the foreseeable future," "The share price may decrease due to future sale of shares," "Shares purchased in this offering will be diluted immediately because the initial offering price is substantially higher than the book value per share."
- Variance; for example, "Our share price may be volatile," "Our operating results may be subject to significant fluctuations."
- Lack of information; for example, "Limited relevance of historic activities and financial performance," "Our forward-looking statements may not be accurate," "Lack of operating history."

- Lack of control: for example, "Anti-takeover provisions may prevent a beneficial change of control," "Control by principal shareholder."

The four most frequently reported risk factors, in order of frequency of reporting, were the following:

- General economic conditions (78%); for example, "Sensitivity of results to economic developments," "Fluctuations in the general economy."
- Competition (74%); for example, "We operate in a highly competitive industry."
- Regulation and legislation (69%): for example, "The company's ability to commercialize its products depends upon its compliance with government regulations," "Unexpected changes in regulatory requirements could adversely affect our business."
- Acquisitions, alliances, and joint-ventures (69%); for example, "Costs and difficulties of acquiring and integrating businesses could impede future growth," "No assurance can be given that desired acquisitions and alliances will be available."

Aggregating the reported risk factors per category, the most frequently disclosed risk factors appeared to be related to the industry environment and the internal environment of the firm (both 29%), followed by the macro environment (22%) and the other categories (20% in total).

As expected, the risk disclosures were not unidimensional. I extracted three dimensions that together accounted for 48% of the variance of the risk factors. The eigenvalues were used to decide how many dimensions should be used in the analysis. Using a plot of the eigenvalues (so-called "'scree test"), all dimensions were retained with eigenvalues in the sharp descent part of the plot before the eigenvalues started to level off. Component loadings exceeding.40 are considered important; if the component loadings are.50 or greater, they are considered practically significant. The squared loading reflects the amount of a risk factor's total variance that is accounted for by the component score.

Higher component loadings represent a higher correlation of the risk factor and the component score. As can be seen, the component loadings were scattered across the eight categories.

Dimension 1 had the highest eigenvalue (11.82) and accounted for 25% of the variance of the risk factors. The component score of Dimension 1 was simply named Risk Disclosure Score 1 (RDS1). Conceptually, RDS1 represents the degree to which each firm in the sample reported on the group of risk factors that had high loadings on Dimension 1. Thus, the more disclosure of risk factors with high loadings on Dimension 1, the higher RDS1.

Management's warning for future volatility of the share price had the highest component loading on Dimension 1 (.76), followed by the possibility of dilution of the share price (.72), a history of losses and the expectation to continue to incur losses (.69), and dependence on strategic partners (.60). Twelve other frequently reported risk factors have loadings between.50 and.60. Cronbach's coefficient alpha assessed the internal consistency of RDS1, and its value of.91 was well above the generally agreed lower limit of.70 (Robinson, Shaver, & Wrightsman, 1991). Hence, RDS1 was a statistically reliable composite measure.

Dimensions 2 and 3 accounted for 13% and 11% of the variance of the risk factors, and the component scores were RDS2 and RDS3, respectively. Conceptually, RDS2 and RDS3 represent the degree to which each firm in the sample reported on the group of risk factors that had high loadings on Dimensions 2 and 3.

Management's warning about their ability to manage growth had the highest component loading on Dimension 2 (.66), followed by absence of a prior public market (.63). Only two other risk factors had loadings between.50 and.60 on Dimension 2.

The most frequently reported risk factor, general economic conditions, loaded highly on Dimension 3 (.74). Only one other risk factor had a loading between.50 and.60 on Dimension 3. Cronbach's coefficient alphas of RDS2 and

RDS3 were adequate, suggesting that RDS2 and RDS3 were also statistically reliable composite measures.

Although PRINCIPALS reduced the widely diverse risk disclosures into three unidimensional and statistically reliable composite measures of risk disclosure (which was the main purpose of the data reduction procedure), it is unclear what caused the different dimensions in the risk disclosures. Because RDS1 explained about twice as much variance as RDS2 and RDS3 and represented far more risk factors (16 component loadings above.50 compared to 4 and 2 for RDS1 and RDS2, respectively), the main empirical analyses focused on RDS1. Supplementary analyses considered RDS2 and RDS3.

Due to the statistical procedure that was used to construct the variable, RDS1 had a mean of zero and standard deviation of one. Additional tests showed that the difference in RDS1 for seasoned offerings and unseasoned offerings was significant, indicating that management makes more extensive risk disclosures in the case of an initial public offering. In addition, firms in a high-risk industry had significantly higher RDS1.

The total number of observations N decreased in the period after the offering due to delisting of firms that merged or were taken over. FAIL1 (+30) shows that 30 months after publication of the prospectus, eight firms in the sample (10%) had a stock price that was lower than one Euro.

Panel A presents the correlations among the independent variables in the models tested. RDS1 was significantly positively correlated with SIZE, IND, IPO, TRR(–18), and BETA(-30), suggesting that RDS1 reflected, to some extent, firm size, industry type, offering type, past total return risk, and past systematic risk. Panel A further shows that IPO firms in the sample were significantly smaller and significantly more often active in a high-risk industry. As could be expected, firms in a high-risk industry had significantly higher past total return risk and significantly higher past systematic risk. Despite the relatively high correlations among the independent variables, additional tests for multi-collinearity showed no indication of any potential harmful effects in the multivariate regressions reported next.

PREDICTING TRR AND BETA

Univariate results in Panel B show that RDS1 was significantly positively correlated with TRR (+T) up to 30 months after publication of the prospectus and with BETA (+30). This finding provides initial support for the idea that companies were actively providing risk-relevant information in risk sections. Compared to the correlation coefficient for TRR (–18), the coefficient for RDS1 was higher for months 6, 12, and 18 but lower for months 24 and 30. Compared to the correlation coefficient for BETA (–30), the correlation coefficient for RDS1 was also lower. For each portfolio, I plotted TRR (+T) up to 30 months after publication of the prospectus. The high RDS1 portfolio had consistently higher TRR than the low RDS1 portfolio. The difference was on average eight percentage points and was statistically significant for all months.

Panel A presents the results of the multivariate regression analyses of Model 1 including control variables. To be able to assess the relative predictive ability of RDS1 against the control variables, I converted all variables to z scores and reported the standardized coefficients. All estimated regressions were significant, and the adjusted range from 30% to 54%. RDS1 remained significantly positively associated with TRR (+T) up to 30 months after publication of the prospectus, showing that RDS1 was successful in predicting TRR (+T) in addition to the control variables. The magnitude of the standardized coefficients further shows that RDS1 had more predictive value than SIZE and IPO, whose coefficients were not significantly different from zero. Until month 18, RDS1 also had more predictive value than IND; thereafter, the standardized coefficients for IND were higher than for RDS1.

Panel C presents the results of the multivariate regressions of Model 2. Again, standardized coefficients are reported. The estimated model was significant, and the adjusted was 46%. RDS1 was significantly positively associated with BETA (+30). Hence, RDS1 predicted future BETA in addition to the control variables. The magnitude of the standardized coefficients further indicates that RDS1 had more predictive value than SIZE and IPO (whose coefficients were not significantly different from zero) but less than IND.

Panel B presents the results of the multivariate regressions of Model 3. Again, all regressions were significant, and the adjusted ranged from 62% to 79%. RDS1 was significantly positively associated with TRR (+T) up to 30 months after publication of the prospectus. The standardized coefficients of TRR (–18) were not significantly different from zero, indicating that RDS1 had more predictive value than past TRR.

The findings further show that RDS1 had more predictive value than SIZE (whose coefficients were not significantly different from zero) but less than IND (whose coefficients were significantly positive and, except for month 6, higher than the coefficients of RDS1).

Panel D presents the results of the multivariate regressions of Model 4. The model was significant, and the adjusted was 60%. Both RDS1 and BETA(–30) were significantly positively associated with BETA(+30). However, the magnitude of the standardized coefficient for BETA (–30) was lower than for RDS1, indicating that RDS1 had more predictive value than past systematic risk. RDS1 also had more predictive value than SIZE and IND, whose coefficients were not significantly different from zero.

In sum, the results show that RDS1 was successful in predicting future total return risk and future systematic risk. These results provide strong support for the idea that companies were generally providing risk-relevant information in risk sections. Furthermore, the information in the risk sections appears to be more relevant than past total return risk and past systematic risk. The latter finding provides additional support for the view that the information in risk sections reflected material risks to an investment in the issuers' securities.

PREDICTING FAIL

Overall, the results for Model 5 show that RDS1 was successful in predicting future stock price failures, especially the more extreme ones. This provides further support for the view that the information in risk sections reflected material risks to an investment.

SUPPLEMENTARY ANALYSIS

The main analyses focus exclusively on RDS1. Alternatively, I included all three component scores in Models 1 to 5 and performed all tests. For reasons of brevity, these results are not reported in tabular form. The results confirmed the associations reported for RDS1 but provided no evidence that RDS2 or RDS3 were associated with TRR(+T), BETA(+30), or FAIL(+30). While this indicates that disclosure of risk factors represented by RDS2 and RDS3 was not useful for predicting total return risk, systematic risk, and severe declines in stock price, it does not preclude that these risk factors conveyed other information relevant to investors.

From the texts analysed in this study, 67% were written in English and 33% in Dutch. Using moderated regression analysis, I further analysed whether the language in which the prospectus was written significantly affected the reported associations between RDS1 and TRR(+T), BETA(+30), and FAIL(+30). The results (not reported in tabular form) showed no systematic difference, suggesting that language did not influence the informativeness of the risk sections.

ROBUSTNESS CHECKS

When coding the texts of the risk sections, I alternatively identified for each text how often each risk factor was present (instead of whether the risk factor was present or not). The component scores that result from using the counts per risk factor were almost identical (correlation coefficients >.98 with p <.01), and the results of all empirical tests were robust to using these component scores.

Although all firms in the sample were incorporated in the Netherlands and their securities were traded on the

Amsterdam Stock Exchange, 31% of the companies in the sample had a cross-listing at a foreign stock exchange, typically in the United States (NYSE or NASDAQ) or in the United Kingdom (London Stock Exchange).

Likely, these firms faced more rigorous disclosure requirements. To mitigate potential doubts about the homogeneity of the sample resulting from different regulatory environments, I additionally included in all regressions separate indicator variables to control for a cross-listing at the NYSE, the NASDAQ, and the London Stock Exchange.

The results (not reported in tabular form) show that the inclusion of these indicators did not qualitatively change the results for the variables of interest (i.e., the reported findings were not biased due to their omission). Reported results were also robust to adding several other additional control variables in all models (not reported in tabular form), including:

- An indicator for the language in which the prospectus was written,
- Indicators for the year or quarter in which the securities were offered,
- Indicators for companies active in the manufacturing and trade sector,
- The book-to-market ratio of equity,
- Financial leverage.

To further check the robustness of the findings, the tests for the full sample were also performed for subsamples of high-risk industries and low-risk industries. The results (not reported in tabular form) show that the associations between RDS1 and TRR (+T), BETA (+30), and FAIL (+30) remained intact.

Findings were also robust to excluding any specific quarter in which the securities were offered from the sample. To check the robustness of the results of Models 2 and 4 for the calculation of BETA, I excluded the last year of security issues from the sample and calculated BETA (+42). Using BETA (+42) instead of BETA (+30) led to identical conclusions. To check the robustness of the results of Model 5 for the definition of future stock price failure, I alternatively calculated severe stock price declines of more than 50% or more than 75% over a 30-month period. These extreme negative returns are labeled FAIL50 (+30) and FAIL75 (+30), respectively.

In this chapter, I examined whether narrative risk disclosures in prospectuses generally contain risk-relevant information for prospective investors. The data that I used were obtained from a sample of 90 prospectuses of Dutch firms raising capital on the Amsterdam Stock Exchange in the late 1990s.

To obtain an aggregate measure of risk from the information in the texts, I performed a detailed content analysis of the risk sections in the prospectuses. The content analysis revealed that management mostly assigns the label "risk" to a multitude of factors, either internal or external to the firm, that can adversely impact future firm performance and can cause future operating results and stock prices to be volatile.

The results of further empirical tests showed that an aggregate measure of risk obtained by the content analysis successfully predicts the following:

- Future total return risk (volatility of future stock prices):
- Future systematic risk (sensitivity of future stock prices to market-wide fluctuations); and
- The likelihood of severe declines in stock price in the 30-month period after publication of the prospectus.

Notably, these results held when controlling for several other lectors, including firm size, type of industry, type of offering, cross-listing at a foreign exchange, and the language in which the prospectus was written.

The results further showed that when it comes to predicting future risk, the information extracted from the texts is more successful than market information on past risk. I conclude from these findings that prospectuses of Dutch firms in general clearly contain risk-relevant information for prospective investors.

LIMITATIONS

The findings should be interpreted with some limitations in mind relating to the statistical reduction of the data, which was required to obtain an aggregate measure of risk. First, due to the exploratory nature of the technique, it is unclear what caused the different dimensions in the data. This fact makes it difficult to put a label on the component scores. Second, several risk factors identified in the texts did not load significantly on any of the three dimensions resulting from the data reduction.

Basically, this implies that these risk factors could not be measured reliably in this study. Consequently, I can draw no conclusions about the potential relevance of these risk factors. Third, while the findings suggest that the risk factors represented by RDS2 and RDS3 were not helpful for predicting future total return risk, systematic risk, and large declines in stock price, it is unclear whether they are useless to investors or contain relevant information about other future outcomes that are not examined in this study. Due to these limitations, I believe the findings provide a conservative assessment of the information content of risk sections.

More generally, a limitation of the study is that it exclusively focuses on what the risk sections contain. Further research is needed to gain a better understanding of how risks are disclosed and why. Concerning the latter question, in a related study on the economic incentives for voluntary reporting on internal risk management and control systems, Deumes and Knechel (in press) show that Dutch-listed companies disclose less information when they face fewer information and agency problems, as proxied for by the degree of ownership concentration, managerial ownership, and financial leverage. Future research could investigate if these factors also influence the quantity and quality of risk disclosure.

IMPLICATIONS

For corporate communication researchers, a potential implication of this study is that it requires rethinking the role of corporate communication. Seemingly grounded in uncertainty reduction theory, Kohut and Segars posit that a major goal of communicators is to reduce the audience's uncertainty through language and information. According to Brashers, this traditional and more narrow conceptualization of communication in uncertainty reduction has long dominated communication research. In his view, "the field's historic focus on uncertainty reduction is both a cause and symptom of underdeveloped ideas about uncertainty and methods of managing it".

In the context of corporate risk reporting, a better way to think about the role of corporate communication may be to revise constituencies' perceptions of uncertainty. For example, as soon as managers obtain inside information about new and major risks threatening the company, they may desire to communicate this to investors in order to warn them by increasing investors' perception of uncertainty. For example, managers may decide to point out to investors that details of the company's situation are more ambiguous, more complex, more unpredictable, and more probabilistic than investors may be aware of or that investors should not be overconfident about their state of knowledge because certain information is unavailable to outsiders or simply inconsistent.

By doing so, managers can make it less likely that they later suddenly fail investors' expectations of what their company can (or cannot) provide or achieve. This strategy can protect both companies' and managers' long-term reputation. At other times, managers may want to send reassuring messages in order to decrease investors' perceptions of uncertainty, for example, if a previously communicated threat ceases to exist. In a broader sense, the same principle arguably applies to corporate communication with other constituencies, such as customers, employees, and communities, on health, safety, and environmental risks, for example.

An important implication of the findings for financial communication practitioners is that risk disclosure in prospectuses can be viewed as an area of best practice when it comes to corporate risk communication. Analyzing Enron's demise, Seeger and Ulmer (2003) conclude that openness to signs of problems is a key communication-based responsibility of companies. The findings of this study suggest that maintaining prospectus standards of risk disclosure in, for example, annual and quarterly reports can help companies to fulfill this responsibility. For financial regulators, an implication of this study is that current requirements for risk factor disclosure in prospectuses seem to be effective.

In the United States, the Securities and Exchange Commission (SEC) has long required companies to disclose risk [actors in registration statements. As from December 2005, the requirement to disclose risk factors also applies to annual reports. Furthermore, companies must update the risk factor section in their quarterly reports to reflect material changes from previously disclosed risk factors. Despite these developments in practice, our understanding of the role of risk disclosure in corporate communication is limited. For example, how are the risks disclosed in terms of readability, linguistic structure, or rhetorical elements?

What is the understandability and significance of risk factor disclosure to different groups of investors and other constituencies? What is the comparability of risk factor disclosure across countries, companies, and across time? What are companies' motivations for risk factor disclosure? What explains companies' choice of the level of risk [actor disclosure? Does risk factor disclosure alter investors' perceptions of uncertainty and/or investment decisions? How does risk factor disclosure impact on companies' stock price, cost of capital, and reputation? These are important but also difficult questions to investigate. Because the questions extend beyond the boundaries of corporate communication research, some of them will be best considered in collaboration with researchers in other fields, particularly accounting and finance.

Chapter 12

Television and the Public Image

The start of the new millennium brought with it three prime-time television series featuring social workers, the latest of which to debut in the winter of 2001 was Kate Brasher. Was this a sign of greater public awareness of the essential role of social workers? Would this newest series provide a more accurate and flattering portrayal of social workers than other television shows? Unfortunately, the answer was "no" to both questions.

The power of the media to mold public images is well established. The focus here is on one source of image-making—television. Television has high impact and rapid message delivery. A study conducted by the Centre for Media and Public Affairs for the Council for Excellence in Government, for example, found that the vision of elected officials and civil servants as inept (if not corrupt), which had been promulgated and reinforced on prime-time television has undergone a metamorphosis. With new series, particularly The West Wing, government workers are now portrayed—and thus increasingly viewed by the public—as dedicated, sensitive, competent people. If only this were the case for social workers, who could use a boost in public image.

TELEVISION'S RECENT PORTRAYAL OF SOCIAL WORKERS

In the latest, but short-lived, social work entry into prime time, promotions billed the key character, Kate Brasher, as a "single mother, social worker, everyday hero." "She fights hard for the underdog... because she is one". Who was this superwoman of social work? A woman who did not complete high school. Her credentials included experience as a waitress. She landed a job simply by visiting a community centre in search of assistance with a personal problem.

There she confronted a professional staff (including an attorney and a director whose profession remains a mystery) who were rude and overbearing (albeit eventually capable of displaying humanity), and their personal issues and agenda were worn on their sleeves. Open personnel recruitment, selection, and training were simply nonexistent in this community centre. To get hired, one apparently had to walk through the door at the right time.

Kate, our social worker, however, was a dedicated mother, conscientious, and possessed other positive virtues, such as the ability to listen well and to mobilize others and advocate on the "case" and "cause" level. These characteristics were in contrast to those of Norm, her colleague on another network. The CMPA (2001) concluded that Norm represented the most negative portrayal of a civil servant to appear on television. His training was as a hockey player. His employment in social services was involuntary; it was either community service or jail for tax fraud. Although social workers walked the picket line to protest the profession's outrage about the portrayal of Norm as a social worker, we should be getting the message: Television is not kind to social workers.

NASW recognized and applauded Tyne Daly's portrayal of a social worker, Maxine Gray, on the series Judging Amy. However, the accolades ate deserved not in an absolute sense, but relative to the consistently negative images that have typified television social work characters. Whereas the character Maxine Gray is certainly a refreshing contrast to that of Norm, she is not the vision of professionalism.

First, we know nothing about her training. Does she hold a BSW or MSW? Is she licensed? Have we ever heard reference to her participation in continuing education? Her behaviour often pushes the boundaries of ethical practice. She engages in insubordination frequently. Although we can applaud the intent of such insubordination—client advocacy—the means are certainly debatable. Even Tyne Daly has acknowledged that the social work situations portrayed may be "overdramatized and some of the outcomes idealized...".

Nevertheless, one would be hard pressed to totally reject the image. Maxine Gray is committed and hard working; she takes her job seriously; she displays realistic burnout and stress; the cases with which she deals often are realistic in their intensity and complexity. However, the accolades bestowed by social workers about this portrayal seem overstated in light of the often questionable practices in which she engages.

Television conveys an anti-professional, disrespectful image of social workers. The message is "no credentials needed; anyone can do it." In reality, Kate and Norm (and perhaps even Maxine Gray, although it is less clear) represent less than 1 per cent of those classified by the U.S. Department of Labour as social workers on the basis of educational attainment at the level of"less than high school diploma." Why, then, would television programme developers focus on characters who are not representative of social workers? Possibly, the answer is that audiences are receptive to this characterization, and such portrayals are consistent with and reinforce public perceptions. There is simply more rating mileage in portraying social work as a job anyone can do.

For social workers, the positive news lies in the cancellation of both Kate Brasher (in April 2001, after only four months) and Norm (in January 2001, after a two-season run). Nevertheless, public perceptions, once formed, are less easily erased.

INFLUENCE OF TELEVISION ON PERCEPTIONS

Television has been referenced as the most powerful of all media, a not surprising revelation in light of the number of hours Americans are reported to spend in front of the screen. Thus, the images portrayed through television, particularly when repeated week after week to millions of people, tend to have a lasting influence on public perceptions.

At the same time, television mirrors existing opinions and attitudes.

Ironically, the one groundbreaking network effort to portray a more realistic view of social workers, East Side/West Side, aired for only one season. In this critically acclaimed series, the action was in the issues (child abuse, aging, discrimination, addiction), and the realism portrayed about people and about social work was not popular with viewers. What is marketable is that which is appealing; what is appealing, in turn, is generally consistent with existing sentiments or at least predilections toward certain views. Thus, who is selected by television show developers and, eventually, producers and viewers to represent heroes and villains or intelligentsia versus buffoons often reflects views about people, places, and things about which there is already some general consensus.

Television, in fact, is deluged with series that showcase professionals. ER, for example, portrays the day-to-day work of emergency room personnel, ranging from physicians to clerks. The Practice, Law and Order, Family Law, NYPD, and Third Watch illustrate the work of police, attorneys, judges, tire fighters, and EMS workers, generally in a positive light.

The portrayals of these professionals give appropriate and seemingly accurate recognition of their education and training, the challenges inherent in their work, and their commitment to and compassion about their vocations. The result, in regard to image making, is respect. But the social worker continues to be portrayed as uneducated and bumbling, if not outright laughable. The perpetuation of this view reinforces prevailing attitudes about social work and its labour force.

Substantial consequences accrue to the social work profession from these negative portrayals. How television portrays professions and professionals not only draws attention to these fields, but also affects public attitudes about them. Messages about unqualified and untrained social workers perpetuate the low status afforded the profession by reinforcing stereotypes and substantiating uninformed portrayals of who social workers are and what they do. For youths, the portrayal of social workers exemplified in the three 2001 serials may deter potential recruits into the profession. The consistency of television series—week after week, year in and out—suggests a lasting and powerful forum for image building that denigrates rather than celebrates the work of social workers.

MOVING FORWARD

The use of the media by and on behalf of social workers, the profession, and the clients served by professionals, has conveyed messages that we believe people need to hear. Perhaps it is time to adjust the targeting of our messages and begin by studying and understanding what is important to the audience. Script writers for television shows tap the public pulse, and the success of any show depends on the degree to which research about what will sell to the public is accurate. In other words, the beginning point is the audience, not the message. Messages are then adjusted to the nature of the audience and in language that the audience can comprehend.

The importance of influencing public opinion has certainly been recognized by the profession. NASW, for one, sees public education as among its major roles. For example, Professional Social Work Month activities emanating from one NASW chapter in 2001 included a public awareness campaign "to clarify who professional social workers are and what they do...". However, no matter how many people take note of a public service announcement (PSA) or hear a radio broadcast in which a social worker is interviewed about an issue, the use of media in this manner has far less impact and lasting value than do popular television shows.

The CMPA (2001) found, in its recent study, that the image of teachers in the 1990s was ranked third in terms of positive image, but dropped to 12th place in 2001 after a season's airing of the Fox series Boston Public. Although the impact of the series on public opinion cannot be isolated, the CMPA found some linkage between public views and the television show. In this series, teachers have been portrayed as making racist remarks, pulling out a gun to get students' attention, and having sex with a student. Such negative images neutralize, if not counter, the efforts of teachers' unions to use television PSAs to increase public awareness about the essential and vital role of the teacher—designed both to enhance the image of teachers and to aid in recruitment of the next generation of teachers.

INFLUENCING THE MEDIA

We need to put our networking skills to use in regard to media contacts. We know people who know people in the "industry." Those we want to reach include script writers and executive producers who control the content of popular series. The goal is to gain the ears of those with the power to form images through the medium of television. There are an infinite number and variety of social worker experiences that can forma "script line" that is compelling, dramatic, maybe even amusing, but perhaps most important—an accurate portrayal of professional practice.

The need for social workers to develop skills in working with the media has long been acknowledged. Some schools of social work include knowledge and skill development about the use of media in social welfare courses that incorporate content on advocacy. Perhaps it is time to think about offering discrete learning modules or even courses on public and media relations and to broaden our targeted public to include commercial broadcasting as well as elected and appointed policymakers. Infusing modules about popular media and the means by which to access it will help entering professionals to consider the media as a target of social action.

Continuing education provides a logical target point for specialized content on working with the media. Collaborative continuing education programs between schools of social work, journalism schools, and public relations programs might well prove beneficial to each professional group. Social workers can learn to "talk the talk" of journalists and how to cultivate and use media contacts.

Journalists, in turn, might gain knowledge about what

social workers do in ways that will augment how they seek and use background information for their story lines, whether print or broadcast. Putting aside admonishments about the deleterious effects of too much time in front of the television, the fact is that a large proportion of our population spends a whole lot of hours "tuned in" to the TV. Popular series that provide misinformation about the profession promote false images based on ignorance and affect the ability of the profession to recruit the labour force of tomorrow. The message is in the medium, and television is surely one medium that cannot be ignored.

Since the label Generation X was first used in Douglas Coupland's 1991 novel to depict the angst of the MTV generation, the label has been used by newspaper and magazine journalists, network and local TV news anchors, print and broadcast advertisers, and TV, cable, and film producers as shorthand to describe the post-baby boomer generation, those born between 1965 and 1977.

While the Generation X label may be convenient for those in the media to use, do those who read, see, or hear it understand that meaning? What are the consequences for the media if the meaning of Generation X, a label that has been used to describe 45 million young adults, is misunderstood by the audience? Would misunderstanding the label Generation X have special consequences for the newspaper industry? This chapter addresses these issues.

BACKGROUND AND USE OF THE LABEL

A 1992 New York Times article on then-presidential candidate Governor Bill Clinton's efforts to court the MTV generation's vote used a variety of labels to refer to this age group: youth vote, youngest voters, young voters, the young, young people, 19 to 30-year olds. But there was no mention of the label Generation X to describe the young adult age group. But over the past six years, the use of the label Generation X, or a variation of it, appears to have become commonplace in describing the generation born between 1965 and 1977.

A headline from a 1994 Washington Post News Service article, for example, said, Marketers tailor pitches toward 'Generation X'. Another headline for a 1996 Austin American-Statesman article, said Groups Give Voice to Generation X. This chapter listed four interest groups that had sprung up to offset the negative portrayals of Generation X in the media, including the National Association of Twentysomethings, Generation X Coalition, The 2030 Centre and Third Millennium.

As early as 1993, academic research began to use the label in conference papers and thesis reports. Books have also used the Generation X label: Generation X Goes to College by Peter Sacks, Managing Generation X by twentysomething author Bruce Tulgan, and Rob Owen's Gen X TV: The Brady Bunch to Melrose Place.

- In creating an advertising campaign for its soft drink, Pepsi Cola used a variation of the Generation X label, Generation Next to appeal to the youth market. Most recently, Time magazine prominently displayed the label in a cover story, Generation X Gets Real.
- From its 1991 debut in Coupland's fictional account of three twentysomethings, the label Generation X has conjured up negative images. Generation X has been portrayed as cynical, apathetic, disrespectful losers and slackers. But a recent Yankelovich study featured as a Time magazine cover story contradicts that negative image. The survey found today's young adult generation should be described as optimistic, savvy, confident, ambitious, determined, independent, and materialistic.
- Author of Managing Generation X Bruce Tulgan adds that the profile of Generation X is "sort of the flipslide of slacker." He described Generation X as "flexible, adaptable, comfortable with technology, independent problem-solvers who constantly monitor the world around them for feedback.
- "But regardless of whether the negative or positive attributes of the label have been emphasized by the

> media, the relevant question is: How has the label, which has become synonymous with the young adult population, been perceived? Do those who read, see, or hear the label understand its meaning and do they evaluate it positively or negatively?

Just semantics? One might ask whether the use of the term Generation X to refer to young adults is something worth worrying about. As Shakespeare suggested, would not a rose smell just as sweetly, regardless of what name we give it? Is not this just a matter of semantics?

The answer is, yes, that's precisely what it is. In fact, the group of scholars who became known as the General Semanticists offered clear guidance on this matter. Alfred Korzybski, Wendell Johnson and others in this group contributed much to our understanding of how language usage can inhibit communication.

Among the four major misuses of language the general semanticists identified was one they called "undue identification," the failure to observe distinctions among the members of a group. Undue identification has become more popularly known as categorical thinking or overgeneralization, and a particularly pernicious form of it is stereotyping, a term coined by Walter Lippmann in 1922. He said, "In the great blooming, buzzing confusion of the outer world we pick out what our culture has already defined for us, and we tend to perceive that which we have picked out in the form stereotyped for us by our culture."

Those who stereotype others often are not aware that they are doing it. Regardless of intentions, stereotyping occurs. Stereotyping is more likely to occur when communicators are unfamiliar with those about whom they are writing. In 1954, Wilbur Schramm noted that communication becomes more difficult when a communicator's "field of experience" does not overlap much with the fields of experience of those with whom he or she is trying to communicate.

The question is raised whether the term Generation X as applied to young adults operates as a stereotype. What is being communicated when this label is used? Is the audience familiar with the label? How does the age group that this label purports to describe view the label? Are members of this group familiar with the term?

Do they disproportionately consider it to have negative connotations? If answers are yes, these characteristics would suggest that the group to whom the label is being applied may consider it to be a form of stereotyping. What are the implications for those who use the term - newspapers and other mass media - if the label is perceived as a stereotype? A survey was conducted to answer these questions.

METHOD

A random sample of 489 adults 18 years or older in the Austin, Texas metropolitan area was surveyed by telephone. Phone numbers were randomly selected from the Austin area phone book and then 1 was added to the last digit of each number selected and that number was called. This method, called plus-one sampling, gives those in different prefix areas a chance of being selected in proportion to the size of the population holding that prefix and it gives unlisted numbers a chance of being selected. J.M. Lepkowski has noted that this sampling method assumes that unlisted numbers are evenly mixed among listed numbers, which may not be the case. As Paul Lavrakas and Paula Poindexter-Maxwell McCombs observed, however, it is a tradeoff worth making if one does not have the resources to field a true random-digit dialing sample, which results in a large proportion of calls to non-working numbers.

Interviews, which took place between February 20 and March 2, 1997, were conducted by students in an undergraduate class in research methods and graduate students in a seminar in survey research methods. Students in the graduate seminar also helped train interviewers and monitor interviews. The overall completion rate, calculated by dividing all completions by all eligible households, was estimated to be.67.

The survey, which took an average of 20 minutes to complete, focused on knowledge, opinions and behaviors about the mass media. Three questions were used to measure familiarity with and meaning of the label Generation X. Familiarity with the term Generation X was measured by asking: How familiar are you with the term Generation X?

Choices were:

- Very familiar,
- Somewhat familiar,
- Not familiar.

The meaning of the term Generation X was measured by asking an open-ended question with a follow-up probe: When you hear or see the term Generation X, what word or words come to your mind? Any other words?

Evaluation of the term Generation X was measured by asking: In general, would you evaluate the term Generation X as:

- Positive,
- Neutral,
- Negative.

Refusals and don't know also were coded in those cases where it was appropriate.

RESULTS

The survey respondents reflected fairly well the population from which they were sampled but they are somewhat less representative of the state and nation generally. Because Austin is the state capital, the site of the largest university in the country, a major centre of operations for the computer industry and one of the fastest growing cities in the nation, its residents tend to be slightly younger, better educated and wealthier than their counterparts throughout the state and much of the nation.

Almost one in three respondents (30 per cent) were under 30, and almost one in three (32 per cent) had some college or technical school experience. About one-third (32 per cent) had incomes below $30,000 and more than one third (35 per cent) had incomes between $30,000 and $60,000.

More than three out of four (78 per cent) described themselves as white, 11 per cent described themselves as

Hispanic or Latino(a), and 6 per cent described themselves as African-American or black. Slightly more than a third (35 per cent) labeled themselves conservatives, slightly more than a third (35 per cent) were moderates and slightly more than a quarter (26 per cent) were liberals. Slightly more than half (53 per cent) were females.

KNOWLEDGE OF THE TERM

Six years after the term Generation X was coined, nearly one out of three respondents (30.5 per cent) said they were unfamiliar with it. Of the rest, 43 per cent said they were somewhat familiar with the phrase and 27 per cent said they were very familiar with it.

Young adults were significantly more familiar with the Generation X label than were older adults. 80 per cent of adults under 30 compared to 65 per cent of adults 30 or older were familiar with the term. Further analysis showed that knowledge of the term Generation X was positively related to education, newspaper reading and TV news viewing. In other words, those who had more education, read newspapers and watched TV news were more likely to be familiar with the term Generation X. Meaning of the term

Of those who said they were familiar with the term, 33 per cent said it represented those who are youthful. Fifteen per cent said the label Generation X had something to do with age, but they didn't specify it as a term related specifically to the young. Another 15 per cent gave the label a variety of miscellaneous definitions.

Almost one in 10 said the label Generation X referred to slackers, apathetic or lazy persons. Six per cent said they considered it a stereotype or an inappropriate, misapplied, misleading label. Five per cent said it referred to a trouble-maker, those who are lawless or irresponsible. Four per cent said the term Generation X described those who are future-oriented or progressive. Other definitions of Generation X included care-free (3 per cent) confused or misdirected (3 per cent), MTV (2 per cent), selfish (2 per cent) and drug-related (1 per cent). Evaluation of the term

Of those who said they had heard of the term Generation X, very few (14 per cent) said it had a positive connotation whereas four in 10 (40 per cent) said it is a negative label. The rest (47 per cent) said they considered it a neutral phrase.

When focusing on those who said the term means something decidedly negative - slacker, lawless, dull - those who shared this sentiment had little else in common except the demographic variable, age. The relationship is modest (p=.095) but those in the youngest age groups surveyed (18-24 and 25-29) consider the term as a pejorative in greater numbers proportionally than do their elders. Forty-five per cent of those under 30 said the term Generation X is negative while only 36 per cent of those 30 or older said the label is negative.

In summary, almost one in three adults said they were unfamiliar with the term Generation X, and 40 per cent of those who were familiar with the term said it was negative. That negative evaluation increases to 45 per cent for those under 30.

The results of this study suggest that if the newspaper industry is concerned about alienating current and potential readers, it should use the Generation X label with caution when describing the 45 million young adults, born between 1965 and 1977. There are two main reasons to recommend caution. First, almost one-third of the survey participants said they were unfamiliar with the term Generation X, which means that newspapers are not communicating effectively with readers if they are using a term their readers don't understand.

Secondly, the newspaper industry, which has struggled with increasing and retaining its circulation over the past decade, continues to lose readers among young adults. In fact according to a 1997 national survey conducted by the Pew Research Centre for the People & the Press, only 39 per cent of adults under 30 read a newspaper regularly. That per cent increases as age increases. Fifty-five per cent of adults ages 30-49, 65 per cent of those 50-64 years, and 72 per cent of those 65 or older read a newspaper regularly.

These national statistics combined with the findings of this study suggest that the relationship between newspapers and young adults is precarious, indeed. The Generation X label may be convenient for reporters and copyeditors, but it may also have the unintended effect of acting as a repellent to this young cohort.

In trying to increase their young adult readership, newspapers have offered special youth-oriented sections that emphasize movies, music, and technology. In addition to being packaged with dazzling colors and flashy graphics, these special sections have been sprinkled with the terms Generation X, GenXers, and Xers. The data presented here on the Generation X label and its negative connotations, suggest that by using this strategy to appeal to the younger generation, newspapers may be reaching out for young adults with one hand and slapping them in the face, with the other.

Chapter 13

The Media in Postmodern War and Terrorism

'The battle for hearts and minds is being fought on the net', wrote Simon Rogers in the Guardian at the outbreak of the war In Kosovo on 26 March 1999. He said that there had never been a war like it before. Even though there had been articles about cyberwar In the public media, the NATO attack on Yugoslavia In 1999 may have been the first war fought also on the Internet. One of the peculiarities of modern wars since the late 1950s is that they are not declared to be wars by legitimate parliamentary bodies and often have the nature of an intervention in the internal conflicts of sovereign states. Consequently, it is difficult to define when it is a question of terrorism and when of war.

During the Cold War there was the fear that a large-scale nuclear war might break out even by accident. However, in a legal sense a war does not normally start without elaborate procedures of parliamentary or conciliar discussions, with the accompanying declarations, orders and proclamations dealing with its means, ends, modes and justifications.

In any case, even the undeclared wars are always intentional in the sense that symbolic acts which imply or lead to hostilities and war and justify them have been carried out by some government. Even the clandestine preparations for large-scale war require major preparations in the climate of opinion in which the mass media and other new sources of information like the Internet become crucial.

The 1991 Gulf War broke out on television when it

erupted on primetime evening news bulletins in the United States on Wednesday 16 January 1961. The ABC network took the viewers of its 18.30 evening programme World News Tonight to Baghdad for a telephone interview with reporter Gary Shephard. In Iraq it was just past 02.30 on a moonless night after the expiry of the United Nations' deadline for its government to withdraw from occupied Kuwait.

Within minutes the reporter said: 'Something is definitely under way here, something is definitely going on... obviously an attack is under way of some sort'. Over ten minutes later, at 23.47 GMT, British viewers who had settled down to watch ITV's recorded highlights of that evening's Rumbelow's League Cup soccer matches had the war introduced to them by sports commentator Nick Owen.

In Yugoslavia in 1999, the CNN effect was eliminated from the beginning when Yugoslavia expelled western media journalists from its territory. Yugoslavia also has capable operators for cyberwar, as Iraq did not. In recent media history, the Vietnam War was the first television war, the Gulf War in 1991 showed the power of real-time news journalism, and Kosovo in 1999 proved the strength of the Internet and cyberwar in the field of information and propaganda.

In the 1990s the western vocabulary increasingly emphasized terrorism as the threat to security. Walter Laqueur writes that current definitions of terrorism fail to capture the magnitude of the problem worldwide. In his view the terrorist operations have changed somewhat so that terrorism is not the militants' only strategy any more. He warns that terrorists can order the poor man's nuclear bomb from a catalogue and that 20 hackers with US$1 billion might shut down America: 'Chances are that of 100 attempts at terrorist super violence, 99 would fail. But the single successful one could claim many more victims, do more material damage, and unleash far greater panic than anything the world has yet experienced'.

THE MEDIA AND THE UNITED NATIONS

After the end of the Second World War (WW II) efforts

were made to rationalize the international communications system by bringing various organizations under the aegis of the UN. Their treaties and conventions were to be adjudicated by the International Court of Justice. However, the court was given no official sanctions to impose on countries against which it ruled. It had to rely on world opinion or moral authority as the basis on which the states would abide by its decisions. As a consequence, this philosophy has not produced instruments to deal with the problems of world communications. Robert Fortner concludes that 'both countries and corporate interests continued to press for, or to maintain existing, monopolies of knowledge, struggling to impose their versions of history and methods of interpretation on the world's peoples'.

But in the modern world all political, economic and military operations from preventive diplomacy to peacekeeping must take into consideration the new media environment and world public opinion. In the United Nations, world communications are a prerequisite for the work of the General Assembly and the Security Council. The media are seen to reflect the world's public opinion and it is important that the world media are as independent and free as possible to reflect people's views and opinions as well as to maintain a critical reporting of the governments.

However, since US President George Bush declared the 'new world order' at outbreak of the 1991 Gulf War, the United States and her allies, especially the UK in their attack against Iraq in 1998 and NATO in the aggression against Yugoslavia in 1999, have literally bypassed the existence of the United Nations as the only legitimate international organization for legitimizing war. Their concern has been to interfere internally for humanitarian reasons.

It is obvious that the media publicity will be increasingly important for the peace-related decisions. This is especially true of the UN-peacekeeping operations. In fact, one of the key elements in the international environment where all UN activities now take place is the international media. The increasing telecommunications capabilities result in increasingly detailed graphic, timely information being available to audiences worldwide.

A UNIDIR (United Nations Institute for Disarmament Research) research document concluded that in peace operations, national and international news media converge plays a significant role in quickly framing public debate and shaping public opinion.

It is likely that future peacekeeping operations will often be demanded and executed under the worst possible conditions. That means a situation when preventive diplomacy has failed; when impassioned calls for action submerge careful analysis in emotions and impatience; when frustration supplants caution and facts on the ground are judged primarily by the media coverage they receive. The report concludes that it is precisely for this type of environment that decisionmakers and peacekeepers should prepare themselves.

The sensitivity of these issues for the success of the UN became very clear in the media coverage of the UN operations in Somalia and former Yugoslavia. The possible mistakes of the UN are given wide publicity by the world's news media, which tend to stress action and war-related issues in a conflict rather than diplomacy, which, after all, is the strength of the UN and its true metier.

The great challenge to communication research as well as to policymaking now is to find a new approach that is forward-looking and based on enough past knowledge but free from Cold War conceptual frames. Information and communication technology present a continuity, which has a solid past but challenges many previous assumptions. The analysis of technological developments is useful in order to understand the need to treat specialized agencies and to introduce normative thinking in this field:

- It is important to look at the technological changes that have been decisive for many other changes. Currently, they are creating an entirely new learning environment for all international activities.
- How the intellectual thinking on communication and

education has developed in relation to conflicts and wars needs to be studied.

- It is important to understand that culture and communication skills are essential for the merging global information society.
- When the media turn violence and conflict into a permanent open learning environment a new challenge enters the concept of global learning. Do we really learn anything from wars and what role do the media have in this?

International communication has no precise origins but it has existed as long as there have been nations and states. As we know, as soon as groups establish their separateness, at least some members find the need to communicate with individuals in other groups. Of course, the media have developed from runners, drummers, pigeons, ships, and trains. But with the advent of the telegraph, a fundamental transformation began: as early as 1837 successful electric telegraph experiments began. The technological developments of telegraph, submarine cable, telephone, wireless and radio led to the need for international control of the technical means of communication. The objective has been to facilitate necessary international cooperation and avoid transnational interference the operations of other countries.

During the 20th century, especially between 1933 and 1969, the field of international communication became a field of increasing politicization and propaganda. Although politicization never really ended during the period after 1970, a newly complex environment emerged, the result of both the application of new communications technologies and the proliferation of new states with the breakup of Europe's colonial empires.

TOWARDS A GLOBAL KNOWLEDGE SOCIETY

In recent years fundamental changes have occurred in technology, the political world order and population growth that have had a profound impact on world economic, political and human development. The rapid developments in telecommunications microprocessors and biotechnology and the introduction of information superhighways are changing national and international economies and the world order. The development of national information infrastructures is planned; these in turn are or will be plugged into worldwide efforts to create global electronic information super-highways, which are expected to revolutionize economies as well as education and learning environments.

It has been estimated that the present decisions concerning telecommunications and electronic information highways will have a socio-economic impact similar to the building of canals, railroads and motor highways. It is believed that information highways will be the key to economic growth for national and international economies. The information infrastructure already is to the major economies of the 1990s what transport infrastructure was to the economy of the mid-20th century.

Some critical researchers point out, however, that if the future user requirements do not align with national information infrastructure-provisioning capabilities, lengthy periods of wasteful and uneconomic network underutilization will result. For instance, the mid-1980s unveiling of ISDN (Integrated Services of Digital Network) has yet to overcome initial subscriber scepticism. During the interim, resources will not have been put to their best possible use. These information superhighways have been compared to the building of interstate highways in the earlier period; certain elementary points in this comparison need to be observed. Highways function only if all roads are connected to them; in the field of information superhighways there are weak links that determine the outcome of the whole system.

In the global perspective, there is a threat that the information gap is increasing. Even in the technologically-advanced countries a great number of individual homes are without computer connections and very few home computers have modems. In fact, the first users of information superhighways will be those that have the necessary equipment. In the early stages of motor highways the first users were those who had cars and could benefit from the new infrastructure. Highways changed the whole culture, including small business and shopping centres. The shops were no longer built within walking distance of their users but near the highways. In the case of information superhighways we do not yet know how much they will serve individual citizens and how much enterprises, organizations and administration.

In the 1990s the central role of information and communication technology for social and economic development could be observed. Traditional industrial societies faced difficulties and even collapsed, particularly in cases where obsolete models of thinking had dominated management, but the number of economies that were able to utilize new communication and information resources were growing, for example in the Pacific region and also in North America.

In the light of the exponential growth of electronic communications, the role of telecommunications will grow rapidly in world affairs. Consequently, the International teleommunication Network (ITU) has to deal more and more with issues that are not technical in nature. For example, it has to define more clearly its role in relation to development. A significant move took place in 1984 when a report of the Independent Commission for Worldwide Telecommunications Development, 'The Missing Link', was published. It concluded, among other things, that 'all mankind could be brought within easy reach of a telephone by the early part of the 21st century'.

In 1994 the ITU held the first World Telecommunications Development Conference in Buenos Aires, Argentina. A Declaration on Global Telecommunication Development for the 21st Century was approved. It recognizes that telecommunications are an essential component of political, economic, social and cultural development. It is important that the document refers to the principle of 'the right of connection' between countries. The telecommunications gap between vision and reality persists, at technical and political levels, and hopes of closing it are modest. More than two-thirds of all households worldwide still have no telephone. Less that 2 per cent of World Bank lending goes to telecom projects.

MEDIA AND PEACE EDUCATION

International governmental efforts in the fields of education and communication have been carried out by the United Nations Educational, Scientific and Cultural Organization (UNESCO) and the League of Nations, which both reflected the intellectual and moral integrity of scholars of their time.

The role of international communication and the media was not perceived as central during the period of the League of Nations after WW II. The organization passed one resolution in 1925 on the collaboration of the press in the cause of peace. It referred to 'moral disarmament' which was understood to be a condition of material disarmament.

In 1936 the League approved an international convention concerning the use of broadcasting in the cause of peace. This lengthy convention came into existence after politicization and propaganda in radio and other forms of international communication in Europe. The convention, still in force today, speaks of the need to prohibit such transmissions, which are likely to damage good international understanding, but has probably had no impact on anything. Even the deliberate interference in other countries' transmissions (jamming), was started in Austria in the early 1930s.

The International Institute of Intellectual Cooperation of the League of Nations was important even though not enough was accomplished. It was a characteristic feature of the times that only 15 smaller and medium-sized states signed the 1937 Declaration Regarding the Teaching of History which none of the bigger powers accepted, albeit for different reasons: the British government did not feel entitled to interfere in the field of local educational authorities and the free expression of opinion; the United States refused to sign because the federal government had no control over education; France did not want to curb the independence of teachers and historians; while the Nazi government of Germany totally opposed the aims of the declaration."

The UNESCO Constitution was approved in 1945 after the experiences of WW II. It states that peace must be founded, if it is not to fail, upon the intellectual and moral solidarity of mankind. The means of communication between peoples should be developed and increased and these should be employed 'for the purposes of mutual understanding and a truer and more perfect knowledge of each other's lives'. The doctrine of the 'free flow of information' was assumed to be obvious prerequisite for peace. The free flow doctrine was always problematic in the light of the global economic structure and its impact on communications. Technological changes have made it even more problematic today.

The chairman of the committee that drafted the Preamble, the American poet and librarian Archibald MacLeish, was once asked if we can educate for world peace:

Of course we can educate for world peace. I would be willing, for my own part, to say that there is no possible way of getting world peace except through education. Which means education of the peoples of the world? All you can do by arrangements between governments is to remove the causes of disagreement, which may become, in time, causes of war. But peace, as we are all beginning to realise, is something a great deal more than the absence of war. Peace is positive and not negative. Peace is a way of living together, which excludes war, rather than a period without war, in which peoples try to live together.

Later history has shown us the difficulties of building truly international educational and communication systems. Much intellectual work has been carried out on the basic problems of peace. One clear finding is that the criterion of peace depends on the times and on who defines it. During the period of the League of Nations, peace research referred mostly to the causes and functions of war and necessary and sufficient conditions for abolishing it; more recently, it has been broadened to include human rights and the quality of life. Communication and education are key issues. Now education is changing into a life-long learning process where communication skills are central.

In general, communication research can be seen as part of peace education in the wider sense. While early peace research targeted the decisionmakers and diplomats, it was later discovered that in order to promote peaceful relations among nations, one had to increase the general level of awareness of what was at stake.

In principle, UNESCO is ideal for cultural, scientific and literary intellectuals to promote peace on the world stage. In the early years of UNESCO in the late 1940s, the time of Julian Huxley's involvement, the organization was still perceived as an agency uniting qualified individuals from different civilizations, representing the human mind rather than governmental spokespersons.

The UNESCO Constitution was drafted by Archibald MacLeish and the British politician Clement Attiee. The Axis governments had demonstrated the power of the media to control events; UNESCO's founders now wrote into the organization's constitution a mandate to create a communication programme that would advance the understanding of peoples.

A DIALOGUE BETWEEN CULTURES

The UN philosophy and Charter is essentially a product of European civilization, clearly intended to reinvigorate contacts among peoples and nations with its humanistic principles and aspirations. None of the countries then under colonial rule by European powers made any contribution to its formulation.

The UNESCO Constitution also reflects the spirit of the anti-fascist struggle: The great and terrible war which has now ended was a war made possible by the denial of the democratic principles of the dignity, equality and mutual respect of men, and by the propagation, in their place, through ignorance and prejudice, of the doctrine of the inequality of men and races... Believing in full and equal opportunities for education for all, in the unrestricted pursuit of objective truth and in the free exchange of ideas and knowledge, [UNESCO's founders] are agreed and determined to develop and to increase the means of communication between their peoples and to employ these means for the purpose of mutual understanding and a truer and more perfect knowledge of each other's lives.

In other words, UNESCO's mandate is to contribute to the preservation of peace and security by promoting cooperation between nations through education, science, culture and communication. In the field of information and communication the purpose is 'to promote the free flow of ideas by word and images'.

The ideologies of racial superiority have their roots deep in different civilizations and were not limited to the Italian, German or Russian societies at that time. As observed by The Economist: 'the fighters for freedom and against fascism and racism in 1939-45 were rank hypocrites, since they were themselves running dictatorial empires in which racial superiority was a strong theme'. No wonder that Mahatma Gandhi, when asked what he thought of western civilization, replied that it would be a good idea.

The scholarly views of communication at the time of the founding of UNESCO were well reflected by the report of an unofficial body, the Commission on Freedom of the Press, generally known as the Hutchins Commission, 'Peoples Speaking to Peoples'. Communication was seen to link 'all the habitable parts of the globe with abundant, cheap, significant, true information about the world from day to day, so that all men increasingly may have the opportunity to learn to know, and understand each other'.

The Commission set three objectives concerning international communication:

- To improve its physical facilities and operating mechanisms;
- The progressive removal of political barriers and the lessening of economic restrictions; and
- The improvement of the accuracy, representative

character, and quality of the words and images transmitted in international communication.

The report also noted that the 'surest antidote for ignorance and deceit is the widest possible exchange of objectively realistic information—true information, not merely more information'.

Many scholars have similarly questioned the success of a mere quantitative increase of information for international understanding.

Llewellyn White and Robert Leigh, for example, pointed out very early that there is evidence that a mere quantitative increase in the flow of words and images across national borders may replace ignorance with prejudice and distortion rather than with understanding.

In view of the 1999 war in Kosovo one might conclude with the catchphrase of the popular American writer, Francis Fukuyama, who writes of 'the end of history and the last man'. One might add, though, that the new millennium seems to have begun with the emergence of techno-barbarism. In fact, Fukuyama warned against the danger of returning to being the first men, engaged in bloody and pointless prestige battles—only this time with modern weapons.

Many scholars have addressed the issues of war, peace and the media. Quincy Wright analysed the problem in his book A Study of War. Wright observed that among the causes of war is the difficulty of making peace a more important symbol in world public opinion than particular symbols that may locally, temporarily or generally favour war. He noted that wars have always required propaganda for both their initiation and their conduct, and that the methods have long been elucidated: 'The objects of war propaganda are the unification of our side, the disunion of the enemy and the good will of neutrals'.

Wright went on to note that efforts have also been made among both 'primitive and civilized' peoples to preserve peace by propaganda. Here, the problem is more difficult than the problem of war propaganda because, to be effective, peace propaganda must gain attention simultaneously within earshot of all potential belligerents, and yet peace, in Wright's view, is intrinsically less interesting to human beings than war.

Several peace researchers have outlined the requirements for peace-oriented media at times of conflict. Johan Galtung emphasizes, among other things, the importance of giving a voice to both or all parties in the conflict, trying to make explicit the intellectual frame of reference within which conflict is to be understood, and avoiding overe-emphasis on elite nations in media reporting.

In connection with the information warfare over Kosovo in 1999 Jan Oberg raises critical issues of media coverage. He asks, for example, whether there is a larger story behind what we see on the screen. Who are the victims of what? What is a military target, and how does it differ from a civilian target?

It is always necessary to ask what are the sources of the information being disseminated by various parties to the conflict and who are the experts used in the media. The problem of violence is not necessarily problematized in the media but used to legitimize action. In some humanitarian crises like in Rwanda in the 1990s there were radio stations that openly urged people to kill. In the long run media education and critical communication skills and competencies are the only way to combat distorted information, media manipulation and war propaganda.

Strategic communication is an emerging term often applied to planned communication campaigns. Although models vary, strategic communication for both business and nonbusiness purposes almost invariably uses research to identify a problem or issue, relevant publics, and measurable goals and objectives. Research can contribute to goal identification, for example, by finding out what subjects want, establishing a baseline with which to contrast outcomes, or by illuminating trends, past performance patterns, cycles, and the like. A strategic communication plan then adopts steps, or strategies, for addressing that problem with target publics and employs a series of measurable tactics through which to implement those strategies. Strategic communication campaigns are conducted under many labels including public relations, community relations, constituent relations, crisis management, health promotion, issues management, investor relations, membership relations, outreach, public affairs, public health, public information, risk communication, strategic advertising, strategic marketing, and the like. These campaigns typically use the set of skills and approaches developed over three-quarters of a century by the field of public relations but often, especially in marketing, advertising, and health promotion, they are not called "public relations" by their sponsors.

Modern public relations campaigns are strategic in nature and most public relations practitioners and scholars see public relations as strategic communication and themselves as strategic communicators.

But there are other strategic communicators who do not see themselves as practicing public relations (interpersonal, group, and organizational communicators are often considered strategic).

As a result, the term strategic communication, which is not objectionable to public relations people, is the broader and more inclusive of the two and is an appropriate term for referring to planned, research-based persuasive and informational campaigns including those conducted as public relations campaigns. Public relations is a paradigmatic example of strategic communication and will be used that way in this chapter, the conclusions of which, it is hoped, may be applied broadly to strategic communication.

Public relations and other strategic communication campaigns can be conducted for many purposes including:

- Public diplomacy, used to persuade the people of another nation to influence their government's policies toward the sponsoring nation;
- Litigation public relations, used to influence the outcomes of jury trials;
- Public health promotions;
- Development public relations, used to build support for national development programs;

- The support of social causes such as charities, religions, the environment, or activist organizations;
- The support of particular candidates or political policies.

Such campaigns can also be used to gain acceptance for a corporation's or industry's apologies, public policy views, or products. Along with employee directed campaigns these last three examples of public relations campaigns may constitute public relations' primary contribution to business communication and are among the most common kinds of campaigns.

As divergent as the names and purposes of such campaigns are, they have as a common purpose the influencing of individuals, groups, organizations, even whole societies. A campaign intended to influence suggests a relationship, or a desired relationship, between the parties, and the ethicality of such campaigns is determined primarily by the values and relationships expressed in them, including how the target publics are treated. Indeed, the social relationships that campaigns seek to create, maintain, or change produce the core ethical issues of public relations, in particular, and strategic communication, in general.

Influence attempts of the campaign raise serious ethical questions. The more successful the campaign is at influencing others, and hence the greater its reach or impact, the more significant the ethical questions become. So, if we are moving into an era in which campaigns can reach increasingly larger audiences, or be more persuasive by reason of the media channels or strategies they employ, the ethical questions raised can be expected to become broader and more urgent.

This chapter examines ethical implications of the typical approach to public relations campaigns, and proposes a less ethically troubling alternative. First, the two basic models used to conduct campaigns are presented: monologic and dialogic. The second section of this chapter argues that in the new information age, the reach and impact of public relations campaigns can be expected to grow. But it also notes that new information technology can present increased opportunities to choose between the monologic and dialogic approaches. The third section identifies the monologic approach as the dominant model behind current public relations campaigns, and argues that the dialogic model is a more ethically sound alternative. In the final section, some of the practical objections to the dialogic model are discussed. This chapter concludes by indicating that objections to the dialogic approach are not convincing.

ETHICS OF MONOLOGICAL AND DIALOGICAL CAMPAIGNS

Public relations is often used for strategic business communication, and the ethicality of strategic communication can be analysed not so much in terms of its content as its process - the relationship it assumes or enforces between the involved parties - and the attitudes and values this reflects. It is the question of process, then, where an assessment of any communication campaigns should start. In view of Habermas's equation of ethical communication with dialogic process and the support other scholars lend to this analysis, this section identifies first monologic and then dialogic communication. These are the foundational concepts employed in this chapter.

MONOLOGIC COMMUNICATION

According to Johannesen, monological communication is: Characterized by writers such as Matson and Montagu, Howe, Gusdorf, Gibb, Shostrom, Jaspers, Meerloo, Geenagle, and Rudinow [using] much the same vocabulary as Buber to explain the nature of monologue. A person employing monologue seeks to command, coerce, manipulate, conquer, dazzle, deceive, or exploit. Other persons are viewed as "things" to be exploited solely for the communicator's self-serving purpose: they are not taken seriously as persons. Choices are narrowed and consequences are obscured. Focus is on the communicator's message, not on the audience's real needs. The core values, goals, and policies espoused by the communicator are impervious to influence exerted by receivers. Audience feedback is used only to further the communicator's purpose. An honest response from a receiver is not wanted or is precluded. Monological communicators persistently strive to impose their truth or programme on others; they have the superior attitude that they must coerce people to yield to what they believe others ought to know. Monologue lacks a spirit of mutual trust, and it displays a defensive attitude of self-justification.

As Habermas suggested, the key is process and relationships. In the case of monologic communication the process is one of seeking to instrumentalize receivers by engaging in "goal directed, feedback-oriented interventions in the world of existing states of affairs" for the purpose of achieving a relationship characterized by "power over people and view[ing] them as objects for enjoyment or as things through which to profit". As I will seek to establish later, the predominant model of public relations in use today is monological. A dialogical model may be preferable; however, and dialogic communication has several characteristics that set it apart from monologic.

DIALOGIC COMMUNICATION

In terms of process and attitude, dialogic communication is the polar opposite of monologic communication and may well be the foundation of higher standards for ethical business communication. For example, Pearson believed that "establishing and maintaining dialogical communication between a business organization and its publics is a precondition for ethical business practices". Dialogue is characterized by the relationships and attitudes the participants have toward each other in that:

Participant attitudes are viewed as an index of the ethical level of that communication. The assumption is that some attitudes (characteristic of dialogue) are more fully human, humane, and facilitative of self-fulfillment than are other attitudes (characteristic of monologue). Dialogic attitudes are held to best nurture and actualize each individual's capacities and potentials.

Pearson, for example, said that "Weaver's interpretation of Plato's Phaedrus suggests successful dialogue takes place only when speakers treat each other as ends rather than means". Indeed, "dialogue manifests itself more as a stance, orientation, or bearing in communication rather than as a specific method, technique, or format" and those using this approach attempt to generate an atmosphere characterized by authenticity, inclusion, confirmation, presentness, a spirit of mutual equality, and a supportive climate. Pearson concluded by suggesting that "ethical business practices can be analysed in terms of speech acts where ethical communication is operationalized as the opportunity among communicators [for example, practitioner or client and publics] both to engage in all types of speech acts and to move the discussion toward levels of increasing abstraction (or concreteness)".

Habermas also discussed freedom to move a discussion up or down between levels of abstraction. Examples of this would be the freedom to move to a higher level of abstraction by questioning the assumptions behind an utterance or to a more concrete level by addressing the utility of a policy or the effects on the listener of acquiescing to a request. Habermas called this kind of communication dialogue, which for him was synonymous with ethical communication.

Dialogic communication, then, would be characterized by a relationship in which both parties have genuine concern for each other, rather than merely seeking to fulfill their own needs. Many, probably most, strategic communication campaigns today define their goals only from the perspective of the sponsor so they typically seek to reduce the receivers to a vehicle for achieving those needs.

Recent advances in communication technology make such campaigns able to reach - and therefore to attempt to instrumentalize - broader audiences more efficiently than ever before. However, these same advances can facilitate dialogic relationships in many situations that have been largely monologic in the past. Therefore, before turning to a fuller analysis of the monologic nature of contemporary campaigns, some effects of the expansion of the information society need to be considered.

INCREASING IMPORTANCE IN AN INFORMATION SOCIETY

As the information age unfolds, and we become more of an information society, public relations and other strategic communication campaigns will play an ever larger role in the lives of organizations. The information society has been discussed by Beninger, Dordick, Machlup, and Machlup and Mansfield. It is characterized by a preponderance of the labour force being engaged in information work, as opposed to a minority being so engaged, which has been true since Aristotle.

Paisley defined information work as "the production, distribution, transformation, storage, retrieval, or use of information". Public relations and other strategic communication campaigns are instances of such information work and are, therefore, part of the emerging information society, both intuitively and functionally. The former because information is the primary tool of strategic communication campaigns, including public relations. The latter because this work is composed primarily of the production, distribution, transformation, storage, retrieval, and use of information. Indeed, it is hard to conceive of any endeavor that is more quintessentially information work than is strategic communication.

As we move more deeply into the information age through the Internet, cyberspace, satellites, and the like, we descend into the kind of information-centered economy and work experience that are natural for public relations and strategic communication practitioners. In fact, Bovet has suggested that:

Perhaps no field of endeavor is better suited to the new millennium than public relations. There's a 'third wave' revolution occurring in the civilized world, according to Alvin and Heidi Toffler... power and productivity in the new order are based on developing and distributing information - two of the primary activities of public relations practitioners. The development of an information society, and a concomitant information economy, brings with it a certain raising of the stakes in the communicative relationships between organizations and their publics.

Reasons for this are:

- Organizational actions can be communicated, or exposed, to audiences worldwide in a matter of hours or minutes;
- Publics come to expect large amounts of information;
- Better educated publics process information more thoroughly, or at least in greater quantities than in past eras;
- An increase in activist and consumer groups has decreased the probability that a problematic organizational action will go unnoticed.

Although assertions of a causal relationship are beyond the scope of this chapter, a significant drop in confidence in major social institutions has occurred coincidentally with the emergence of an information society. For example, in the slightly more than a quarter century between 1966 and 1994, those expressing a great deal of confidence in major companies fell from 55% to 19%.

These and other factors suggest that the need for strategic business communication will increase and that it will play an increasingly important role in establishing the ethical reputation of organizations in the next decade. Leading business executives seem to agree that public relations, at least, will be important in determining how ethical businesses and business communication will be perceived to be in the next decade.

In a 1995 study, for example, a retired Johnson & Johnson Products Vice-President for Public Relations surveyed the CEO's of ten of the largest and most influential corporations including Exxon, Ford, General Motors, Johnson & Johnson, Merrill Lynch, PepsiCo, Phillips Petroleum, Pacific Gas and Electric, Prudential, and Rockwell International. Among the findings were that "more than ever before, CEO's expect their senior management people to specifically deal with the public relations ramifications of their decisions so that potential problems are not allowed to escalate into major issues". A perceived lack of ethics is, in the final analysis, the surest way to leap from a potential problem to an actual one and this is why public relations scholars have dedicated increasing attention to ethics.

Indeed, perceived ethics may be part of the reason Edward Bernays, commonly known as the "father" of public relations, turned down many notable clients including Hitler, Franco, and Somoza. With this as a precedent, the modern generation of public relations scholars and practitioners has moved toward developing a stronger ethical foundation. This may be partially in response to the belief that perceptions of a business' ethics are largely dependent on how strategic communicators are perceived and partially in response to the realization that new information technology is assuring that increasing numbers of people will share in those perceptions more quickly than ever before.

The result is that new and greater ethical challenges, not all of which are related to technology, will confront practitioners and those who hire them. For example, a recent issue of Strategist, an official publication of the Public Relations Society of America, featured a point-counterpoint article about whether a practitioner should represent the Bosnian Serbs. At about the same time, an issue of Public Relations Tactics reported that today only 34% of public relations firms would accept tobacco companies as clients. In another example, I was the last of three public relations scholars to speak to a group of colleagues a few years ago, with no idea as to what the other two had said.

During the question and answer period the first question was, "Are all you PR people preoccupied with ethics?" The answer, increasingly, is yes, and this seems to be the case in much of strategic communication as well.

There is another dimension to the information society that is particularly relevant to a discussion of monologic and dialogic communication. This is the effect of demassification of messages. Demassification essentially involves the customization or tailoring of messages for increasingly smaller audiences and is facilitated by several new information technologies such as computer-driven on-line information systems.

These allow people to select the precise information, or mix of information, they want and avoid the cost and inefficiency of waste coverage.

One popular instance of demassification occurs when a phone user works through an automated menu of alternatives to get specialized information on topics like how to treat a sunburn or order a tax form, rather than having to watch a television programme or buy a whole book in hopes of finding a little relevant information. Because of their interactive attributes and ability to attend to small groups or individuals, demassification technologies have the potential to facilitate dialogue, but the presence of a monologic or dialogic attitude remains the primary determinant.

The emergence of an information society, and its attendant information technology, makes resolving the question of monological or dialogical communication in public relations even more urgent than in the past. The next section explains the approach to public relations most commonly used in business, the significant ethical questions associated with it, a more dialogical and negotiation-centered approach, and the ethical benefits it carries. Finally, some of the reasons why this model has not gained popularity in the business community are examined, and counter-arguments or comments are offered to strengthen the case for adopting the new model for public relations and strategic communication.

APPROACHES TO PUBLIC RELATIONS

Academics have discussed competing approaches to public relations including paradigms and four specific models. In actuality, however, practitioners tend to fall into one of two roles: technicians or managers.

A technician perspective on public relations (otherwise

known as a "hired gun" perspective) is by far the dominant model of public relations practice and teaching today.

TECHNICIAN OR MONOLOGIC APPROACH

This view sees public relations not from an ethical perspective but as a set of technical journalism-based skills to be hired out. Most important among these is the ability to write press releases well, but organizing and hosting press conferences, laying out or editing publications, taking pictures, and handling media relations are also important skills. In effect, the practitioner becomes the client's hired journalist-in-residence, or a mechanic for media relations.

The most important attribute of this approach is that practitioners and their employers assume that the practitioner should be primarily a conduit for strategies, and sometimes even tactics, that have been decided elsewhere in the organization. In doing so this approach instrumentalizes publics, and to a lesser extent practitioners, and negates both the ethical role of the practitioner and the dialogic perspective discussed below.

In a technician approach, the practitioner cedes unquestioned authority to decide major ethical issues such as message purpose, content, and targeting to someone outside themselves, in this case to corporate leaders. In doing so the public relations department usually accepts what is essentially a one-way communication role and assures that it will have little voice in deciding what is ethical for the organization to do with respect to its publics or in deciding exactly how public relations itself will be practiced.

In fact, those making the calls under this model are often organizational leaders with little or no training in communication, in communication campaigns, in persuasion, or in the media and its role in society. They often do not even have basic training in the legal or ethical aspects of public communication campaigns.

As will be seen shortly, the technician approach uses nondialogic communication. Recall that such communication frequently has the effect of instrumentalizing people, by reducing them to a site where the speaker seeks to meet his or her needs. A technician approach to public relations lends itself quite readily to such an instrumentalizing process because it focuses only on getting what the client wants. Implicit in this approach is the idea that practitioners should view publics as either a source of trouble for the client or as the possessor of something the client would like to acquire, such as money or votes.

Ethics in the technicians view is based on what Sullivan and Pearson called craft and partisan values. In this view what is labelled good public relations is a technically good product, and a good motive is loyalty to the employer. Ethical public relations, then, is simply being loyal to the client or employer's strategic interests or being good at the craft. As previously discussed, such a monologic approach to any communication, including strategic campaigns like public relations, is problematic. Thus, an alternative model is needed. One alternative approach would be dialogic in nature, featuring the practitioner's ability to facilitate a give-and-take relationship between clients and publics. This can also be called the negotiation or adaptation model of public relations.

ALTERNATIVE DIALOGIC APPROACH

In the view of Dervin, "communication cannot be conceptualized as transmission. Rather, it must be conceptualized in terms of both parties involved in creating meanings, by means of dialogue". What is called for in public relations, then, is not the primarily transmission-oriented and monologic technician model but an alternative model that features an exchange between groups and organizations. Pearson and Botan have argued that a dialogic view of public relations differs from a technician approach by being more humanistic, communication-centered, relationship-focused, and ethical.

This perspective focuses on communicative relationships rather than on technical skills. Traditional approaches to public relations relegate publics to a secondary role, making them an instrument for meeting organizational policy or marketing needs; whereas, dialogue elevates publics to the status of communication equal with the organization. This is because a negotiating relationship means that either party can take the initiative in seeking to establish a new relationship or to renegotiate an existing one, hence, public relations is equally the province of corporations, activist groups, government bodies, and employee organizations. This model is, therefore, more ethical than a monologic approach because it goes much further toward "treating each other as an ends rather than a means".

A dialogic view assumes that the ability to construct what Boulding has called mental images is a fundamental part of the human experience and that public relations practices that facilitate this process inside publics are more ethical than those that inhibit it. Consistent with the human nature and dialogic views of ethics, the dialogic approach to communication shares with the rhetorical approach the view that humans are uniquely equipped to use symbols and that it is this ability which sets humans apart from other creatures.

These writers contend that the human use of symbols to interpret our social and physical environment is a process that contributes to our humanity; therefore, communication practices that contribute to the rational use of symbols also contribute to our humanity. This view of ethics focuses on the right to free choice based on the connection between symbol use and a rational mental life which Langer described as "characteristically human and above the level of sheer animality".

A technician perspective focuses on the capacity of a message to elicit desired behaviour from publics. Although not seeking to be deceitful, to short circuit rational decision making, or to manipulate publics; the technician model has no specific interest in avoiding these behaviors. As monological communicators, they see communication partners as the means to an end. A dialogical view, on the other hand, sees communicative partners as ends in themselves. From the dialogical perspective practitioners would begin from the assumption that target publics have interpretations of the world that are as varied and valid as the client's interpretations. They would assume that the real goal is not reducing publics to the service of the client through instrumental mastery but joining with the publics in the process of negotiating new mutual understanding.

OBJECTIONS TO THE DIALOGIC MODEL

The answer seems simple. Public relations, like other communication, should be dialogic, respecting and facilitating the rights of publics to engage in informed and free decision making by exchanging persuasive and informative messages. Public relations should simply make available the information publics need, along with a forthright and honest advocacy of what the client wants. What could be simpler?

Although conceptually simple, a dialogic approach to public relations is very difficult to operationalize in the world of business, and consequently, it is rarely used. This appears to be the case for several reasons, including short-term goals, costs, and the wishes and rights of publics and mass audiences. But these impediments to dialogic public relations may not be as significant as they seem at first glance.

First, a focus on short-term goals, such as sales or product promotion, can make clients unwilling to provide information that can be used to make decisions contrary to their short term goals or to provide information that does not directly address those short term goals. If clients are convinced their interests are best served by short-term (that is, tactical) public relations it can be quite difficult for a practitioner to disagree successfully.

The fact that a long-term relationship can be much more important to the organizations future, and that building these requires a consistent practice over an extended period of time, may be overlooked when responding to the exigencies of a competitive marketplace or a crisis. Johnson & Johnson Products' classic handling of the Tylenol poisonings, however, is just one of many examples of successful and ethical public relations practices built on the clear understanding that public relations is a long term (that is, strategic) endeavor and that it is possible to build long term relationships, even in the throes of a crisis. Finally, in an information environment characterized by near instantaneous exposure of organizational errors, the whole idea of what constitutes short-term changes. Ninety days can be an eternity during a public relations crisis, so even ninety-day goals can be rendered almost meaningless if, for example, a ships captain gets drunk and spills a few million barrels of oil in a wildlife wilderness.

Second, the cost of establishing and maintaining ongoing dialogic communication with publics, in terms of both time and money, may appear to be prohibitive. This is particularly so in light of the fact that public relations is almost invariably treated in corporations as a staff, as opposed to line, function. It may be very difficult to argue for investing scarce organizational resources into what is conceived of as a support function. One source of this difficulty is perceiving public relations as merely a staff function, on a par with accounting or janitorial services.

In point of fact, public relations differ substantially from such functions. Competitive organizations exist through their relationships with the various elements of their environments, that is why the CEO's cited in the first section of this chapter expect senior executives to deal with the public relations ramifications of each of their decisions.

Marketing, purchasing, and sales are three other examples of departments that are concerned primarily with external communication but that differ from public relations in that they focus on fewer and more specific publics. Although public relations play a support role for each of these departments in dealing with their target publics, it also targets publics that marketing, purchasing, and sales typically do not. These include investors or stockholders, government bodies, news media, activist groups, employees, and the like.

Relegating public relations to a staff or support function also relegates all these crucial publics to a secondary status. If these publics are of major importance to the organization's future, public relations might best be thought of as something more than just a support function. Not quite a full line function but more than just a support function. Furthermore, in an information environment characterized in part by the demassification of messages, the opportunity to establish more cost-effective and dialogic relationships with bigger audiences is likely to present itself with more frequency.

Third, publics may not always want dialogic communication. Witness, for example, the popularity of television and other relatively nondialogic media. The assumption that dialogic communication is always "better" or more ethical than nondialogic communication comes, ultimately, out of our models and perceptions of interpersonal communication. In that context it may be reasonable to assume that people often want more dialogic communication. These same people, however, do buy a newspaper or turn on a television to find dialogue. Indeed, it is questionable whether it is ethical for practitioners to try to make publics expend the time and effort necessary to engage in dialogic communication if they do not want to do so.

No one of us could possibly engage in meaningful dialogues about all the subjects that organizations in our environment may wish us to - and we have a right not to. Too much dialogue can, under certain circumstances, be as oppressive as a complete lack of it would be. Again, the demassification aspect of much new information technology also provides increased options. With messages more specifically tailored for target publics - and those publics who are interested being free to engage in interactive communication, whereas those not interested pass it by - it may be possible to enhance dialogic opportunities while at the same time avoiding imposing on those who do not want such relationships.

Finally, public relations typically entail efforts to communicate with large and diffuse mass audiences; therefore, actually practicing dialogic communication may be very difficult, even impractical. A dialogic give-and-take is most easily achieved in a face-to-face context, although it is possible in even mass-mediated contexts. Although business communicators are not obligated to attain some ideal level of dialogue, the constraints imposed by the communication situation and the ability to demassify some messages in an information society may make it economically feasible to exercise the dialogic option.

This chapter has argued that public relations is a significant aspect of business communication. Specifically, public relations were described as planned, research-based communication campaigns covered by the umbrella term "strategic communication." It has also argued that public relations, like most strategic communication, will likely grow in importance as the information society develops. This development suggests that strategic campaigns will play an increasingly important role in how publics perceive organizations and particularly in the attributions they make about the ethics of organizations.

In this chapter, I have suggested that the monologic model currently used for most public relations campaigns is ethically problematic, and that an alternative model is necessary. I argued that a more ethically sound model for conducting public relations campaigns is one based on dialogue. Such a model has inherent ethical advantages over the monologic model, but it also has several possible business-related drawbacks. These drawbacks, however, are not significant enough to justify the continued use of a monologic model.

Chapter 14

Challenges and Chances

Many newspaper managers and editors still believe that readership research is not only overly expensive, but superfluous. Why waste time and money, they say, when research at best provides trivial evidence? Surprising! results like younger readers are more likely than older ones to accept layout innovations contribute to the general notion that research about newspaper readers results in nothing more than platitudes. And, for those who strongly oppose the trend to give the readers what they want, readership research can be dangerous - especially if knowing and uncritically accepting readers' wishes erodes the quality of journalism.

But that doesn't mean newspapers have abandoned research. Randal Beam found 50 per cent of U.S. newspapers did their own research and 85 per cent contracted with outside consultants.

In Europe, newspapers, particularly those in Sweden, are similarly involved. But simply conducting research doesn't guarantee the results will be used for relevant purposes or lead to substantive outcomes. For example, Beam's 1991 survey found most newspapers used research results to restructure the softer sections of the newspaper(like comics and entertainment) far more often than the coverage of national and international affairs.

And while newspapers continue to face decreasing circulation amidst growing competition and fragmentation in the marketplace, they don't necessarily observe their readers more regularly. Although observations like this might indicate (like comics and entertainment) far more often than the coverage of national and international affairs. And while newspapers continue to face decreasing circulation amidst growing competition and fragmentation in the marketplace, they don't necessarily observe their readers more regularly.

Although observations like this might indicate that research is held in fairly low esteem, an alternative explanation is that newspaper managers are in the process of learning about a new tool and have yet to make an all-out commitment to its use.

The rapidly changing marketplace for newspapers suggests that readership research should play a central role in securing any future industry success. We know that almost everywhere newspaper reading is shrinking or at best has remained stable. Yet time devoted to the use of virtually all other media - including books and magazines - has increased.

The general decline of the newspaper has occurred in part because a growing number of readers have discovered that it's simply not worth turning to a newspaper anymore. People either get the information they regard as important elsewhere (e.g., from local radio and television, from local weeklies, free sheets or from regional magazines) or, even worse, they don't miss the information provide by newspapers at all, even in other sources. Being well-informed about community matters, for example, has lost its importance at a time of increasing mobility, individualization, of decreasing social ties and of diminished interest in conventional politics.

Also, because newspaper reading is highly ritualized, it may also have suffered from a development that we have observed for quite a while: traditional habitual behaviors seem to lose their obligatory character - organizations, parties, churches, marriages - and, quite recently in Germany, even the sacrosanct times for shopping. But newspaper reading may not serve as a ritual for marking the time of day or for separating other activities anymore, once everyday life has become de-synchronized. It's no longer true that everyone follows the same working and leisure time rhythms.

If both the outdated appearance and function of the newspaper and principal changes in the lifestyle of its readers have made it an endangered species, then the challenge to readership research has become even greater. Readership research is no longer a luxury - something to only polish the newspaper, to make it even better than it may have been already. Increasingly, research may be necessary to keep the newspaper and its business vital in a growing diverse, competitive, even aggressive market with an ever more indifferent audience.

The marketplace may be changing, but newspapers continue to offer unique attributes and advantages. This chapter identifies challenges to newspaper research, suggests ways that readership research can help newspapers to capitalize on their strengths, and offers some ideas about its future that may improve its effectiveness and efficiency.

CHALLENGES TO RESEARCH: QUESTIONING WHAT WE KNOW

There are important challenges to readership research that must be tackled at the end of the millennium. Each requires that we question existing assumptions about newspapers and newspaper readers. The most radical challenge is whether readership research should continue to bother with the printed newspaper at all. Another challenge is to our assumptions of indisputable truths about newspapers and their readers - are we prepared to forget the truisms about what we think readers want, and address plausible alternatives instead? We are further challenged to consider the strategies that newspapers have used to compete in the changing marketplace, and whether those strategies have been effective. Newspapers could best compete in the new markets from their points of strength, but how can research help us find, capitalize on and market the functions that newspapers do best?

QUESTIONING EXISTING ASSUMPTIONS

First, many critics - and cynics - would have us assume the printed newspaper will disappear anyway, whether accompanied by research or not. If more than a quarter of the population in Western societies has access to a personal computer, isn't it time to abandon our worries about the printed newspaper and begin to focus our research and resources on a glitzy electronic newspaper, save the high distribution costs, and let the old newspaper slowly die a graceful death?

It's an easy assumption to make when hundreds of U.S. and internationally-based newspapers are on-line and more are added regularly.

Yet one of the great strengths of the printed newspaper is that its format and its principal layout have been successfully tested now for almost 400 years. It has faced and survived the challenge of many new media - journals and magazines, telegraph and telephone, cinema, radio and television. It's probable that newspapers displayed on paper or on something similar to paper (such as a large, foldable transparency connected to the newsroom on-line) [10] will persist for several decades to come.

Regardless of the delivery mechanism - paper or on-line - we should not forget what makes the newspaper so indispensable for many people. It offers a combination of guidance and surprise, a selective non-selectivity. No other medium performs this function with quite the style and grace of the newspaper, nor as completely or efficiently.

On the one hand, a newspaper provides a preselected array of information that gives readers a sense of prioritized community concerns.

It serves as a "central, shared information source and guide to help us find order and regularity in a helter-skelter world." Within this "representative resume of the relevant facts concerning the last 24 hours," however, readers still can discover new and surprising stories and events.

Their curiosity is served much better by a newspaper than by a menu or search engine on a computer screen, asking them what they want to learn about.

A data-bank approach is obviously not what most readers expect from newspapers. How many people, for instance, are really interested in printed news updated throughout the day, or in quick searches for highly specific topics? "People don't actually read newspapers," Marshall McLuhan once said. "They get into them every morning like a hot bath." They look at them instead.

They scan the headlines, read a few lines here, a paragraph there. "Reading a news story is like coming upon an accident," Kevin Barnhurst suggests. "We don't want to see it but can't stop ourselves from looking."

Good newspapers offer both their variety of information and their preselective guidance in a professional (i.e. in a trustworthy and competent) way. When it comes down to it, "the franchise is journalism, not newspapers." If this is true, however - if the major purpose of newspapers is to provide a multitude of carefully selected and written stories at a glance - then the paper product physically delivered to our mailbox or to our doorsteps every morning may indeed not be the newspaper of the future. And yet, it's unlikely to be a small computer screen, either.

Eventually, the typical combination of surprise and guidance that a newspaper has to offer requires, as an alternative to what it looks like today, either a large newspaper printed on demand at home, or the wide, flat, foldable and easily transportable TV screens of the next millennium. In sum, then, there is still a lot to do to make printed newspapers better and more attractive to the reader.

The second major challenge to newspaper research is in adjusting our reliance on truisms about newspaper readers. We all know them - the more local coverage, the better; the more pictures and the more colored graphs, the better; newspaper readers like little bits of information better than long stories; writing styles should be simple, funny, entertaining.

This is exactly what most facelifts in recent years have tried to accomplish. But are these objectives plausible in an era of increasing alternatives for local and national information; for brief, comprehensive summaries of current affairs; and for entertainment?

The indisputable propositions that have guided many

decisions fall apart when we consider that newspaper readers and newspaper editors simply don't see eye to eye when it comes to the important attributes of the newspaper. In a recent U.S. nationwide reader and editor survey, George Gladney found that aggressive, original reporting was an attribute far less important to newspaper subscribers than to newspaper editors.

The same pattern applied to strong local coverage limited to the newspaper's immediate distribution area - an entirely plausible result.

While the rationale behind ever-expanding local sections is that events that are geographically close are also interesting for readers, this truism has only partly been true - all events that are close are not interesting to all readers just because they are close.

Don't readers have to be concerned about an event to be interested in it? Geographic proximity is only one possible way to increase interest, and probably not even a good one. Do we really expect readers to find fascinating the annual convention of the local rabbit breeders, just because it takes place close by?

So far, most layout and typographical changes have been based on the taste of newspaper designers. Their language is revealing in that respect.

They declare that something looks impossible or boring. But why? Do readers really have the same opinions, and even if so, does it sell the newspaper? Gladney's reader and editor survey reveals that, once again, readers found an attractive presentation of news through use of visual tools such as typography, photography, graphics, colour, layout, design far less important than the editors did.

Yet a recent customer satisfaction study with almost 5,500 respondents in Germany showed that liking the layouts of 50 newspapers correlates strongly with the evaluation of their contents as topical and informative.

In other words: The better people evaluated the newspaper, the more attractive they found its appearance - independently of what it actually looked like. Do we have to accept that formalities do not matter as long as the contents are interesting?

STRATEGIES FOR COMPETING IN NEW MARKETS

While we've been busily focusing on changes of newspaper substance and form, our research has lacked a central concept - one might even call it a theory - which in outline could look like this: In principle, media threatened by new forms of communication have always had two choices, they either copy the more successful competitor, or they try to distinguish themselves from it the best they can.

The copying strategy accepts both television and print magazines as the most successful competitors of newspapers. Newspapers all over the world seem to imitate both. They use magazine layout; they mimic television by presenting lots of pictures and graphs and brief sound bite-type stories - the USA Today approach to saving the printed newspaper.

But let's think twice about this popular strategy. It's entirely possible that those who like television may simply watch television instead of reading a more or less well-crafted copy of it. The stereotypical response to this suspicion, of course, is that people - particularly adolescents - are used to a video approach to the world.

Newspapers, then, would be simply forced to comply with this truth by publishing newspapers as close to videos as possible. We must be careful to remember, however, that these same young people are already readers - readers of books and magazines, more than ever in history. So, one might as well ask: Why do we not tap their great reading skills instead?

This leads us to the other strategy for the survival of the printed press - doing what the newspaper can do best. In our view, this strategy so far has been somewhat neglected. What is it that newspapers can do best?

The following attributes are winners:

- The newspaper is a multi-purpose medium; it offers not only information but also entertainment and guidance - even advice - and all of it is in the hands of its readers at the same time. Newspaper readers don't have to wait for access as they would with television and radio - even at a time when 160 and more specialized TV channels may be available for some people.

- The newspaper provides an immense variety within its information, a diversity of voices and standpoints every day.
- The newspaper has space for explanation and interpretation, for everyday orientation and context.
- The newspaper offers easy access to all information, it is a simply but efficiently structured data bank that doesn't need any technical devices and computer skills. And, there's no waiting for the next screen to appear.
- The newspaper provides the aesthetic pleasure of layout and typography, and even the haptic nature of unfolding a newspaper and paging through it.
- The newspaper is mobile; it can be read almost everywhere.
- The newspaper provides a low threshold for readers to participate in public discussion. Letters or calls to the editor do not require particular professional skills or the self-consciousness that speaking up on television or radio may take.

Certainly, every one of these advantages of a newspaper can be challenged by other media - above all by magazines, by the way. But it is the mix of functions it serves every day that makes the newspaper special. Over and above their advantages, newspapers can still draw on an almost perfect image. Surveys show that they are regarded as trustworthy, credible and competent. But this image seems to create more awe and reverence among the public than the sympathy, the sense of familiarity, that is necessary for actually reading it.

HOW TO CAPITALIZE ON NEWSPAPERS' STRENGTHS

So, should research not be directed to how these

particular characteristics of newspapers may be fortified? Compared to marketing a target group magazine or a narrowly formatted radio or TV station, marketing the typical mix of purposes is probably the major challenge for newspaper readership research.

An easy way out could be to give up the mass appeal of newspapers. Should we try to make them a target group medium, a daily magazine, a medium with class appeal for instance, for loyal and affluent readers only, ready to pay higher prices for quality both in contents and appearance? In Editor & Publisher, George Garneau, for instance, suggests that newspapers cut mercilessly what he calls ego circulation - that is, copies that may contribute to better circulation figures but are sold to people that advertisers are not interested in.

Newspapers should be careful, however, not to engage in the deplorable practice of cutting back on circulation areas that, with or without research, are deemed of little value to advertisers - inner cities and rural areas with fringe distribution are already being abandoned by many U.S. newspapers under the rubric of cost efficiency.

Providing cheaper coverage that doesn't harm circulation numbers is problematic because newspapers serve more than a strictly commercial function. Many studies show that newspaper reading increases political knowledge and furthers political participation. It is much more efficient in this respect than watching television or listening to the radio. It both reaches more people and it helps them learn better.

So, we have a dilemma - the one between our responsibility for an informed audience and the need to sell newspapers. And taking a poll to see what the readers want and then giving it to them provides no easy solution. In a recent study in the German city of Dortmund, readers called newspaper articles high quality if they were complete, easy to read, well-structured and brief.

Newspaper journalists, however, ranked much higher the topic of the story, the quality of research and the objectivity of an article. With that evidence in, do we now abandon the well-researched, objective stories because readers don't ask for them explicitly? This is where the well-meaning friends of the newspaper who fear that research will diminish the quality of journalism have a point.

The American newspaper researcher Philip Meyer warns us:

- A newspaper audience is a mosaic of many small but intense interests, and if you cut back on those interests when space is short, you stand to lose more net readership than a cutback of more general material would.
- So, taking a poll to discover that numbers are low on certain features of the newspaper can backfire if those are the certain features to which particular readers are intensely attached. Lose those features and lose those readers.

LET'S ASK THE RIGHT QUESTIONS

If we still believe in newspapers as a universal medium for everybody, on what then should readership research focus? Successful newspapers with universal appeal face multiple critical dilemmas, and this makes applying research results challenging. Consider the following:

- Probably the most basic dilemma of newspapers is in finding and maintaining the counterpoise between reliability and surprise - that delicate balance between the elements that help structure the newspaper for its readers without destroying the possibility to make unexpected discoveries and to come upon interesting stories by chance alone. This dilemma leads to very practical questions for research, such as:

How long should articles be, if they are not to keep busy readers from being surprised but, on the other hand, provide enough background and context?

Do the growing number of inserts and the unbundling of the newspaper make it a bunch of magazines instead of the universal resume of the last 24 hours? How far can we go to make a newspaper more portable, probably smaller in size, without losing the surprises that two large unfolded pages provide? Whe re are the limits of a more hedonistic, less serious approach, to newspaper reading? It should be a plea sure, not a chore, to read the newspaper. Perhaps the lack of time named as a reason by so many non-readers may be due to the fact that reading a newspaper is simply not enough fun for them.

There are legitimate doubts, of course, that funny, infotainment newspapers are a good idea for the majority of readers. Certainly seriousness and competence belong to the image of the newspaper, and care must be exercised in protecting that reputation.

- How can we attract young people? Do pop music, computer games and young love as topics really do the trick? These are topics, after all, that they can find out about elsewhere and often with more competence. Some other ideas, however, are waiting to be tested:

Does newspaper reading become more attractive for adolescents if we stress its function as a rite of initiation into adulthood? Or is it exactly its grown-up image that keeps young people from turning to it? Ac cording to a 1991 U.S. experiment, young people found newspapers enjoyable if their front pages contained longer stories and more pullout quotes.

The impression of attractiveness was enhanced by more and smaller photographs and larger graphics on the front page. The use of colour and design principles like vertical or horizontal designs did not matter. The results - puzzling as they are - provide at least some indication of what could be worth looking at more thoroughly.

In the United States, it looks as if a major reason for young people to turn to newspapers is the presence of advertising geared toward them? Attractive weekend sections are another one? Eile en Lehnert suggests there might not be the monolithic youth market for newspapers but several segments of the adolescent audience that demand differently prioritized offers from newspapers.

- Newspaper reading has suffered not only among young people but also among less educated ones and those with little interest in conventional politics. So, a fourth challenge for research is a question of balance: How can we make newspapers more readable for less sophisticated readers without simplifying their contents too much for everybody else?

- Still another research question is derived from the idea of strengthening what newspapers can do best: Would public or civic journalism help the newspaper? This concept - growing in popularity in the United States - regards newspapers as a citizens' forum, a neutral place where the issues of a community can be discussed, where views can be exchanged. Civic journalism also emphasizes the digest function of newspapers - to tell readers precisely where they can find more material outside the newspaper about an issue and how good that material is.
- One last question of balance: How much does diversification of newspaper services distract from its major functions? Additional electronic offerings are beginning to spread. But is it, for instance, a good idea to provide elaborate audiotex systems where users can get the latest news, sports, stock prices, horoscopes, etc., via telephone? In other words, how much exclusive information and service can a newspaper offer to attract an audience online before it harms the printed newspaper in turn?

NOT NECESSARILY AN ARM AND A LEG

A major prejudice readership research has to deal with is its cost. Is it really expensive? Of course, the more useful it is, the less important this question becomes.

But in any case, empirical studies are costly once they involve long-term research designs, large representative surveys, or difficult data-collecting techniques: panels, copy tests, field experiments with different versions of a newspaper. But consider some cheaper and nevertheless useful alternatives:

- Important research questions can be addressed legitimately by closely listening to carefully selected readers and non-readers: In-depth interviews and focus groups are a somewhat inexpensive device. Even copy tests can obviously be conducted as tracking studies administered by the readers themselves.
- Content analyses of the newspaper and its competitors can reveal differences and commonalties in topics, pictures, language, the tone of the articles etc. - again, nothing that has to be overly expensive. This type of evidence may suffice to explain, for instance, what makes a competitor more attractive than one's own newspaper.
- A well-maintained file of subscriber data provides both useful and inexpensive information: Who are the long-term subscribers? Which types of readers are the most susceptible to canceling their subscriptions?
- Socio-demographic data of the distribution area can be bought. They are often very elaborate - lifestyle characteristics of potential readers may be segmented by postal code areas, streets and even blocks. So, these data produce a relatively intricate picture of the housing situation, income, education, household size, voting behaviour etc. They allow both micro-zoning of newspaper editions and finely tuned marketing measures both for actual and potential readers.
- Some questions can be satisfactorily answered by desk research, by using census data, for instance, or other official statistics. Even better: a data bank of evidence gathered by other newspapers - still a dream, of course, as long as newspapers do not feel the need to close the ranks. Instead, many newspapers have maintained a virtual blackout of information they have gathered from their readers. If at all accessible, research on the other newspaper

ends up years later in scholarly publications - publications that many practitioners may not read regularly.

JOINT RESEARCH EFFORTS: A PROTOTYPE

Increasingly, severe threats to the newspaper make joint research efforts inevitable. As a nice side effect, cooperation also saves money. An example of fruitful cooperation for the sake of the printed newspaper is an analysis of 350 West German newspapers. On a large scale, it deals with a very practical question that, so far, every single newspaper has tried to answer for itself and only for itself: which of all the measures taken in readership marketing have really been successful?

In a first step, the German research team systematically compared both contents and appearance of the same 350 newspapers in 1989 and in 1994. We now know about all major changes in substance and formalities, such as the structure of the paper; the amount of background and commentary, of local information, of service, of target group offers; the accessibility of its contents, its readability, the tone of its headlines (do they sound friendly, emotional, aggressive?).

But also changes in format, layout principles, colour, graphs, photos, size of articles, etc. were investigated. This part of the study already shows that West German newspapers have become lighter, fluffier, in their layout and typography; their number of pages has increased - mostly in favour of the local section. All in all, they look more serious, less tabloid. Layout and other structuring principles are observed more rigidly.

In a second step, all the other marketing measures directed at the audience were studied, such as attempts to advertise the newspaper and to work on its image, discounts and rewards for subscribing to the paper, sponsoring activities, and readership forums, among others. In a third step, all these ideas to make the newspaper more attractive were evaluated.

For this purpose, circulation and the MA data sets of 1989 and 1994 were used. With more than 50,000 respondents in West Germany, the latter provided information about the success of a specific newspaper in its distribution area.

We know now which ones among the measures that newspapers had been trying out between 1989 and 1994 were the most successful to keep or even enlarge certain groups in the audience: structured, not too crammed layouts, for instance, more variety in the daily offering (not too many inserts), a strict separation of reporting and entertainment, just to name a few. The same study has been conducted in Israel and is now underway in the United States and in Sweden.

The German study was possible only because the participating newspapers gave up some of their egocentrism. Funded by the BDZV, the German Newspaper Publishers Association, and the Stiftervereinigung der Presse, the German Press Foundation, and with the support of the Regionalpresse, the marketing organization of the German regional newspapers, we were given access to the necessary information for such an endeavor.

In France and Britain, for instance, newspapers have also joined - in SPQR and The Newspaper Society - to do research of a scale that a single enterprise could not afford alone. More cooperation between all newspapers is certainly a model for future readership research.

A FINAL CHALLENGE: PREPARING JOURNALISTS TO MAKE USE OF RESEARCH

We've listed the dilemmas - one might even say, the contradictions - in what newspapers are for their audience. These dilemmas make readership research and the application of its results particularly challenging. But let's not forget that it often is a difficult task for publishers and editors to use readership evidence appropriately - for the best of both the public and the paper itself.

Journalism scholar and frequent newspaper consultant David Weaver from Indiana University envisions a trustee editor as the ideal person who applies and uses the results of readership research. Such a trustee editor - he says - "does not sacrifice his or her editorial judgment to the readers, but he does not ignore readers' opinion either." For this purpose, journalists have to be trained in making use of readership research instead of being warned of it.z

Bibliography

Altschull J. Herbert. Agents of Power. New York: Longman, 2004.

Bagdikian Ben. The Media Monopoly. 2d ed. Boston: Beacon Press, 2001.

Barton Frank. African Assignment: The Story of IPI's Six-Year Training Program in Tropical Africa. Zurich: IPI, 2000.

Bagdikian, Ben H. 2004. The Media Monopoly. Boston: Beacon Press.

Coppa Frank J., ed. 2003. Screen and Society. Chicago: Nelson-Hall.

Dahlgren Peter, and Colin Sparks, eds. 2002. Journalism and Popular Culture. Newbury Park, Calif.: SAGE Publications.

Hallin Daniel C. 2003. We Keep America on Top of the World: Television Journalism and the Public Sphere. New York: Routledge.

Harris Julian, Kelly Letter, and Stanley Johnson. 2000. The Complete Reporter. New York: MacMillan.

Krieghbaum Hillier. 2001. Pressures on the Press. New York: Thomas Y. Crowell Co.

McCombs Maxwell, Edna Einsiedel, and David Weaver. 2002. Contemporary Public Opinion: Issues and the News. Hillsdale, N.J.: Lawrence Erlbaum Associates.

Rubin Bernard, ed. 2004. Small Voices and Great Trumpets. New York: Praeger Publishers.

Thornburg Ron. "The Liberal Arts and Sciences." In Journalism Education: Facing Up to the Challenge of Change, edited by Robert H. Giles.

Washington, DC: American Society of Newspaper Editors Committee on Education for Journalism, 2005.

Index

O

P

Q

R

S

T

U

W